Visions of Mughal India

To Paula, my toughest critic and greatest support

Visions of Mughal India

An Anthology of European Travel Writing

Edited by Michael H. Fisher

Preface by William Dalrymple

Published in 2007 by I.B.Tauris & Co Ltd
6 Salem Road, London W2 4BU
175 Fifth Avenue, New York NY 10010
www.ibtauris.com

In the United States of America and Canada distributed by Palgrave Macmillan
a division of St. Martin's Press, 175 Fifth Avenue, New York NY 10010

ISBN: 978 1 84511 354 4

A full CIP record for this book is available from the British Library
A full CIP record is available from the Library of Congress

Library of Congress Catalog Card Number: available

Printed and bound in India by Replika Press Pvt. Ltd
From camera-ready copy edited and supplied by the author

Contents

Preface

by William Dalrymple

In 1526, Zahir-ud-Din Babur, a young Turkish poet prince from Ferghana
in Central Asia, descended the Khyber Pass with a small army of hand
picked followers. Despite his fewer troops, he defeated the Delhi Sultan,
Ibrahim Lodhi, at the Battle of Panipat. He established his capital at Agra,
where he quickly began to build the first of a series of irrigated gardens.

Babur not only established the Mughal dynasty in India, he also wrote one
the most fascinating diaries ever written by a great ruler: the *Babur Nama*. In its
pages, he opens his soul with a frankness and lack of inhibition similar to
Samuel Pepys a century later, comparing the fruits and animals of India and
Afghanistan with as much inquisitiveness as he records his impressions of
falling for men or marrying women, or the differing pleasures of opium and
wine.

The Mughal dynasty's own accounts of the India they ruled include some of
the greatest masterpieces of autobiographical prose: as well as Babur's great
memoir, there is also the fabulously detailed diary-autobiography of his great-
grandson, Jahangir. Yet as Mughal rule reached its climax, it is easy to be
seduced by their own estimate of their civilisation. After all, by the accession
of Jahangir's son, Shah Jahan, the city of Lahore had grown larger even than
Constantinople, and with its two million inhabitants dwarfed both London and
Paris. From the ramparts of his Red Fort, Shah Jahan ruled an empire that
covered most of India, Pakistan and Bangladesh and great chunks of
Afghanistan. Its army was all but invincible; its palaces unparalleled; the domes
of its many mosques quite literally glittered with gold.

Like all empires at their most self-confident, the Mughals were not slow to
celebrate their own power and magnificence, and the official Mughal chronicles
such as the *Shah Jahan Nama,* like the profile miniature portraits produced by
the Mughal court, can appear somewhat one dimensional. With their long
fawning lists of gifts, processions, durbars, uniforms and fine jewels, these
authorized court productions sometimes make one feel in danger of being
suffocated under landslides of silk, diamonds and lapis lazuli.

For this reason, the dissonant witness provided by European travellers to
the great Mughal court provide a perfect counterpoint to the Mughal court's
own writings. Travel accounts like the ones collected in this book, for all their
flaws and errors and occasional fictions and tall stories, and despite the
prejudices and sometimes outright bigotry of their authors, do nevertheless

tend to provide sharper and certainly livelier pictures of the reality of Mughal India than the fawning pages of Abu'l Fazl's paean of praise to his paymaster, the Emperor Akbar, or the even more unctuous pages of the *Shah Jahan Nama.*

Instead, the travel accounts so imaginatively selected here by Michael Fisher, show the flaws in the Empire and the human reality of Mughal rule: as well as the magnificence of the court we also see the famines and shortages—what Peter Mundy calls 'a tyme of scacitie'—and the monsoon floods; the corrupt officials and the competing palace factions with their vials of 'poyson' and plots for assassinating their rivals; the seas alive with pirates and roads beset by robbers; the semi-independent noblemen who 'every day' take Cesare Federici prisoner; the quarrelling camel drivers and hostile villagers, and the incessant resistance to Mughal authority mounted by marginal tribal groups.

More enjoyably, these accounts of European travellers also demonstrate well the full narrative pleasure travel writing can give. The accounts are full of nuggets of fascination—of horses fed on peas, for example, or 'the house of the dumb' where the Emperor Akbar (like the Emperor Frederick II *Stupor Mundi* before him) brought up children with mute nurses 'to know what language they could naturally speak'. There are moments of great beauty— Father Antonio Monserrate's evocation of the Narmada 'full of fish, and its water is so clear that the fish and turtles, and even the smallest pebbles, can be counted. Its banks are covered with thick reed-beds, and with the health-giving herb marjoram'; or Friar Sebastien Manrique's description of the trees of Bengal 'full of most beautiful peacocks, of green screaming parrots, pure shy doves, simple wood-loving pigeons'.

Ruins that we can visit today such as the great Deccani fortress of Bidar spring back to life, their bazaars again buzzing with soldiers from Khorassan and horse traders from the Persian Gulf; we see again the Sultan's hunting expedition accompanied by 10,000 cavalrymen, 50,000 foot soldiers, 200 elephants, 100 monkeys and an equal number of dancers. Portuguese conquistadors and Venetian merchant adventurers once more make the hazardous journey to the great city of Vijayanagar, whose temples and palaces rise before us repopulated; the splendours of Akbar's travelling army are seen again in the plains of the Punjab, his hunting cheetahs once more let slip at their prey.

If travel writing has in general had a fairly bad press from post-colonial writers and thinkers, then European travel narratives of the colonial world have a very bad press indeed.

Following the success of Edward Said's groundbreaking 1978 work *Orientalism*, the exploration of the East—its peoples, habits, customs and past—by European travellers has become the target for what has effectively become a major scholarly assault. 'Orientalist' has been transformed from a simple descriptive label into a term of outright academic abuse, and men as diverse as the sophisticated French jeweller and aesthete Jean-Baptiste Tavernier, Cornish pilchard merchant's son Peter Mundy and the grand British judge and linguist Sir William Jones have all alike come to be seen as complicit in the project of gathering 'colonial knowledge'—and accused of being agents of colonialism, attempting to 'appropriate' Eastern learning and demonstrate the superiority of Western ways by 'imagining' the East as decayed, degenerate and 'picturesque', fit only to be colonised and 'civilised'.

Yet as Colin Thubron has pointed out in an important article in the *TLS* (30 July 1999), it is ridiculously simplistic to see all attempts at studying, observing and empathising with another culture necessarily 'as an act of domination—rather than of understanding, respect or even catharsis... If even the attempt to understand is seen as aggression or appropriation, then all human contact declines into paranoia.'

The point is strongly made. As Michael Fisher's wonderful compilation well demonstrates, travellers are individuals whose responses, motives, aims and enthusiasms vary from person to person; indeed travellers are often by their nature non-conformist, people who seek out the edge, and are often driven more by a fascination to see than by motives of power or profit—certainly the great English walker Thomas Coryate, who went on foot from Somerset to the court of Jahangir, attributed his 'exoticke wanderings' to his 'insatiable greedinesse of seeing strange countries, which exercise is indeed the Queene of all pleasures in the world'.

So any generalisation made about Jean-Baptiste Tavernier may or may not be true about his Russian horse-trading predecessor, Afanasy Nikitin, or indeed his pious successor, Friar Domingo Fernández de Navarrete. And while the buccaneering Elizabethan trader William Hawkins, an official emissary of the East India Company, was certainly out to increase his country's influence in India, the same cannot possibly be said about Niccolao Manucci, a Venetian stowaway who ran away from home aged fourteen, and who grew up to be a self-confessed con-artist and charlatan who used his 'nimbleness of wit' to set himself up as a quack doctor and exorcist. Indeed in his memoirs Manucci revelled in the audacity of his fraud:

> Not only was I famed as a doctor, but it was rumoured I had the power of expelling demons from the bodies of the possessed... Being credulous in matters of sorcery, they [the people of Delhi] began to put about that the Frank doctor not only had the power of expelling demons but had domination over them. This was enough to make many come, and among them they brought before me many women who pretended to be possessed, as is there habit when they want to leave their houses and meet with their lovers. My usual treatment was bullying, tricks, emetics, evil-smelling fumigations with filthy things. Nor did I desist until the patients were worn out, and said that now

the devil had fled. In this manner I restored many to their senses, with great increase in reputation, and still greater diversion to myself.

Then again, Manucci was himself a completely different man to the wonderfully French gourmand, aesthete and admirer of female beauty, François Bernier. Bernier was an educated and aristocratic French doctor who became much sought after as a physician by the Mughal royal family. Bernier constantly contrasts Mughal India and seventeenth century France: the Jumna River compares favourably with the Loire, he thinks; adultery is easier in Paris than it is in Delhi: 'In France it excites only merriment, but in this part of the world there are few instances where it is not followed by some tragical catastrophe.' But Indian *naan,* he regrets, can never be compared with a good Parisian *baguette,*

> Bakers are numerous, but their ovens are, unlike our own, very defective. The bread, therefore, is neither well made nor properly baked, [although] that sold in the Fort is tolerably good [yet] it can never be compared with the *Pain de Gonesse* and other delicious varieties to be met with in Paris.

On the other hand, he loved Mughal architecture:

> I have sometimes been astonished to hear the contemptuous manner in which Europeans in the Indies speak of [Mughal architecture]... I grant that [the Delhi Jama Masjid] is not constructed according to those rules of architecture which we seem to think ought to be implicitly followed; yet I can see no fault that offends taste. I am satisfied that even in Paris a church erected after the model of this temple would be admired, if only for its singular style of architecture, and its extraordinary appearance.

When reading travel accounts by these very early visitors to the East we should certainly try to resist the temptation, felt by so many historians, to project back onto it the stereotypes of Victorian and Edwardian behaviour and attitudes with which we are so familiar. For these attitudes were clearly entirely at odds with the actual fears and hopes, anxieties and aspirations of these vulnerable early travellers in India, who did not look at South Asia with the hauteur of the high colonial, as much as with the anxiety and occasionally the suspicion of the weak and defenceless wanderer.

Note the fear and helplessness experienced by Afanasy Nikitin threatened with death or conversion by a local ruler; or Cesare Federici robbed and beaten by dacoits; see how craven and grateful William Hawkins was when finally granted an audience by the Emperor Jahangir. Although the early European travellers were sometimes surprised or even disgusted by what they found in

India, their reactions seem to be far more the result of helpless vulnerability before this great Islamic power—one response to which was a retreat into self-conscious insularity—rather than the snide hauteur of some of the Victorians.

One of the most moving passages in this book is when the lonely Afanasy Nikitin worries that his Christian faith might have begun to ebb, living as he was surrounded by Muslims, so that before long he has begun to lose track of the Christian calendar and to calculate instead using that of the Muslim, substituting the Ramadan fast for that of Lent: 'I forgot the Christian faith', he writes, 'and Christian festivals, and know not Easter nor Christmas…and I am between the two faiths… O true believing Christians! He that travels through many countries will fall into many sins, and deprive himself of the Christian faith…'

Nikitin of course was not alone. As the English ambassador to the Ottoman Porte, Sir Thomas Sherley, pointed out in one of his despatches at this time, the more time Englishmen spent in the East, the closer they moved to adopting the manners of the Muslims: 'conversation with infidelles doeth mutch corrupte', he wrote. 'Many wylde youthes of all nationes, as well Englishe as others…in everye 3 yeere that they staye in Turkye they loose one article of theyre faythe.' Islam at this period overpowered Europeans more by its sophistication and power of attraction than by the sword.

This was certainly what happened to the Portuguese in Goa. Already, by the time the Portuguese Inquisition arrived in India in 1560, Goa much more closely resembled the Mughal capitals of Delhi and Agra than Lisbon or any city in Portugal. As one shocked Jesuit had reported back to Rome, 'the Inquisition is more necessary in these parts than anywhere else, since all the Christians here live together with the Muslims, the Jews and the Hindus and this causes laxness of conscience in persons residing therein.'

By 1560, Goa already had a population of 225,000, and had grown much larger than Madrid, Lisbon and all other contemporary European capitals with the exception of London and Antwerp. In public its grandees dressed ostentatiously in silks, shielding themselves with umbrellas, never leaving their houses except accompanied by vast retinues of slaves and servants. Travellers reported how the Goan aristocracy kept harems and that even the Christian women wore Indian clothes inside the house and lived as if in purdah 'little seene abroad'. If they had to go out, they did so veiled or in modestly covered palanquins.

Their men folk chewed betel nut, ate rice (but only with their right hand) and drank *arrack* distilled from palm sap; they rubbed themselves with 'sweet sanders', and their hospital doctors prescribed the old Hindu panacea of cow's urine three times a day to their patients 'in order to recover their colour, one glass in the morning, one at midday, and one in the evening'. They drank water from the pot in the Indian fashion 'and touch it not with their mouths, but the water running from the spout falleth into their mouthes, never spilling a drop…and when any man commeth newly from Portingall, and then beginneth to drink after this manner, because he is not used to this kinde of drinking, he spilleth it in his bosome, wherein they take great pleasure and laugh at him, calling him Reynol, which is a name given in jest to such as newlie come from Portingall.' Further, as the Venetian Federici reported: 'I have seene many [European] King's Courts, and yet have I seene none in greatness like this of Vijayanagar.'

Even the ecclesiastical establishment showed signs of taking on the ways of its Indian environment: from 1585 a bizarre edict was issued commanding that only Indo-Portuguese with Brahman (Hindu priestly) blood would be accepted in the colony's seminaries to train for the priesthood of the Roman Catholic Church: 'all this they have learned and received from the Indian heathens', wrote a surprised Dutch traveller, Jan van Linschoten, 'which have had these customs of long time.' All this is well worth bearing in mind when reading, for example, the harrumphing of by Father Antonio Monserrate about 'savage and degraded' Indian customs.

Perhaps partly because of the Inquisition, a surprisingly large number of Portuguese made the decision to emigrate from Portuguese territory and seek their fortunes at different Indian courts such as Vijayanagar, usually as gunners, cavalrymen and mercenaries. This was a process whose origins dated from the very beginning of the Portuguese presence in India: in 1498, on his famous first voyage to India, Vasco da Gama found that there were already some Italian mercenaries in the employ of the various rajahs on the Malabar Coast; and before he turned his prow homewards two of his own crew had left him to join the Italians in the service of a local rajah for higher wages. Sixty years later, by 1565, according to the Portuguese chronicler Joãn de Barros, there were at least two thousand Portuguese fighting in the armies of different Indian princes. By the early seventeenth century, another Portuguese writer thought the number must have reached at least five thousand. Not all of these converted to Islam, or changed their modes of living, but it is clear from the sources the great majority of them did.

Attached to the Adil Shahi court at the great Deccani Sultanate of Bijapur, for example, there was Gonçalo Vaz Coutinho, formerly a powerful landowner in Goa, who was imprisoned on a murder charge before escaping to Bijapur where he converted to Islam and was given 'lands with great revenues, where he remained as a perfect Moor, with his wife and children'. In Imperial Delhi, Dona Juliana Dias de Costa could be found supervising the harem of the Mughal Emperor; her father had been a court doctor and her descendants were still in Mughal service as late as 1761 when they fled to Lucknow to avoid the massacres that followed the fall of the city to the Afghan warlord Ahmad Shah Abdali.

Nor were the first English travellers any different from the Portuguese, as early accounts of life in the English factory in Surat—established shortly after the embassy of William Hawkins—make clear. Here the English traders, or 'factors' as they called themselves, inhabited a building that combined elements both of an Oxbridge college and a Mughal *caravanserai*. On one hand, the day started with prayers and ended at a communal meal presided over by both the President and the Chaplain, the latter whose job it was to monitor the behaviour of the factors, to assure regular attendance at chapel and to prevent un-Christian behaviour; on the other hand, this cosy English collegiate scene took place within a 'Moor's building' and after dinner the factors could wash and unwind in a 'hummum' [Turkish Bath] a facility not readily available on the banks of the Isis or Granta. As very few European goods were available, the factors quickly adapted themselves to the material culture of India. It is fascinating to see how soon such specifically Indian luxuries as 'a betle box, two pigdanes [from the Hindi *pikdan*, a spittoon], and a rosewater bottle' begin to turn up in the East India Company inventories.

Indian food also made an early appearance on the menu at the factory: 'ordinarily we have dopeage [*do-piyaza,* double-onion curry] and rice, kegeree and picked mangoes,' reported Peter Mundy, while other early accounts mention 'cabobs' [kebabs], 'dumpokes' [meat slow cooked in a *dampakht*, a sealed pot] and 'mango achar' [chutney]. By 1630, the factory's President, William Methwold, admitted that the factors had almost completely given up using the Western drugs that the Company was in the habit of sending out to Surat, preferring to take the advice of local Mughal doctors: 'The utility of the drugs is not to be doubted', writes Methwold, 'but being farr fecht and longe kept, applied by an unskilful hand, without the consideration of the temprature of a mans body by the alteration of climats, they peradventure have small or contrary effects.' Rather sheepishly he then admits: 'wee for our parts doe hold that in things indifferent it is safest for an Englishman to Indianize, and, so conforming himselfe in some measure to the diett of the country, the ordinarie phisick of the country will bee the best cure when any sicknesse shall overtake him.'

The further the factors went from the English base in Surat, the more they found themselves adapting to Indian ways, although occasionally you do get the odd hint of homesickness: in the small East India Company warehouse at Ahmedabad, for example, inventories show an almost complete lack of European furniture with the factors choosing instead to sit on the floor on five 'sitternegees' [presumably *shatranji*, chequered cotton carpets]; moreover they have a 'coho pott' at a time when coffee was regarded as a 'Moorish drink'. The only link with home are 'two pictures, one of the cittie of London and the other of the King in Parliament'. They also have 'an English coach', which oddly enough appears to have been pulled by oxen.

Elsewhere more dramatic transformations were taking place, as Britons found their national, racial and religious loyalties challenged by the Indian environment that surrounded and at times enveloped them. The letters of the English Factories contain many enigmatic entries such as that of 8th September 1647 about the death of Gilbert Harrison who was a factor at Thatta, the ancient port near the mouth of the Indus. Before he died, Harrison had made no will but verbally desired his assistant 'to give his dagger and most of his "Hiendoostane"' clothes to his servant. He also requested that a tomb, which was already under construction, be completed 'in the chiefe burying place about Nasserpore' where 'the chief men of Nasserpore' wanted him 'to lye there sepulized'. Would the elders of Nasserpore want a Christian buried in the main Muslim graveyard? It would seem unlikely as it would be against one of the fundamental tenets of Muslim law, so Harrison must have been regarded, in Thatta at least, as a Muslim.

There is very little hint of such assimilation in most post-colonial critiques of European travel writing. Indeed, reading some of critics it seems as if Victorians succeeded in colonising not just India but also, more permanently, the academic imagination, to the exclusion of all other images of the Indo-European encounter. As the texts here reproduced make very clear, during the four hundred years of European relations with India, the balance of power has shifted very radically at different periods leading to wide varieties of different relationships between the different peoples, and we must be careful not impose the ideas of a later era on that of an earlier one, when very different circumstances were in place.

We should also be aware too of the degree to which the Mughals also defied the stereotypes we tend to set up for them. Akbar's interest in Christianity, and his pleasure in wearing Portuguese clothes, is a case in point, and one that goes against the eternal anti-Christian hostility that commentators such as the influential Islamophobe Bernard Lewis would have us believe was always felt by Muslims in this period. Indeed, Mughal India is one of the many moments in the history of Islamo-Christian relations that defies the simplistic strictures of the 'Clash of Civilisations' theory, for both Akbar and his son Jahangir were enthusiastic devotees of both Jesus and his mother Mary, something they did not see as being in the least at variance with their Muslim faith or with ruling of one of the one most powerful Islamic Empires ever to exist.

In 1580, Akbar began this process by inviting to his court near Agra a party of Portuguese Jesuit priests from Goa, and allowing them to set up a chapel in his palace. There they exhibited two paintings of the Madonna and Child before a large and excited crowd. To the astonishment of the Jesuits, Akbar promptly prostrated himself before the images of Jesus, and later showed a particular pleasure in the Jesuit's Christmas festival, when a crib was set up in the imperial palace, adorned with velvet and sculptures of the Christ Child, and accompanied by placards proclaiming *'Gloria in Excelsis Deo'* in Persian. Akbar took a particular interest in Jesus's function as Messiah and questioned the Jesuits closely about the Last Judgement and whether Christ would be the judge. Akbar also showed his appreciation of his Jesuit guests by not only donning Portuguese garb, as described by Father Antonio Monserrate in a passage included in this book, but also by going as far as listening to madrigals.

Akbar's thesis was that 'the pursuit of reason' rather than 'reliance on the marshy land of tradition' was the proper way to address religious disputes. Attacked by Muslim traditionalists who argued in favour of instinctive faith in the Islamic tradition, Akbar told his trusted lieutenant Abu'l Fazl: 'The pursuit of reason and rejection of traditionalism are so brilliantly patent as to be above the need of argument. If traditionalism were proper, the prophets would merely have followed their own elders [and not come with new messages].'

Akbar also issued an edict of *sulh-i kul,* or universal toleration, forbade the forcible conversion of prisoners to Islam and married a succession of Hindu wives. At the same time that most of Catholic Europe was given over to the Inquisition, and in Rome Giordano Bruno was being burnt for heresy at the stake in the Campo dei Fiori, in India the sixteenth century Mughal Emperor Akbar was declaring that 'no man should be interfered with on account of religion, and anyone is to be allowed to go over to a religion that pleases him'. That Akbar's sentiments were more than hyperbole is shown by the interesting incident recorded by Friar Sebastian Manrique when one of his followers killed a sacred peacock in Orissa. When Manrique says that such actions are not forbidden by the Koran, the Mughal Governor replies that Akbar 'had given his word, taking his oath in the *Mosaffo* of his holy Prophet, that he and his successors would let them [the Hindus] live under their own laws and customs: he therefore allowed no breach of them.'

In this tolerant atmosphere, as Mughals and Hindus visited the same shrines, followed the same holy men and began to intermarry, as Father Antonio Monserrate noted, a spirit of toleration replaced the earlier habit of temple destruction, the dialogue between the rival religions reached its climax, the two cultures finally fused into one and flowered into a civilisation of breathtaking beauty and perfection.

Almost every aspect of the daily life and culture of Mughal India came to reflect that fusion. In music, the *qawwali,* the mystical love song of the Indian Sufi, mixed the indigenous musical systems of India with the new ideas brought to Hindustan from Persia and Central Asia; likewise the long-necked Persian lute was combined with the classical Indian *vina* to form the *sitar.* The architecture of the Mughals—most famously in the great Taj Mahal— reconciled the styles of the Hindus with the arch and dome of Islam to produce a fusion more astonishingly beautiful than either of the parent traditions. When that spirit of tolerant pluralism was finally cast aside by the sixth Great Mughal, Aurangzeb, the Empire shattered.

In these memoirs and accounts of European travellers we are presented with real, flawed, subjective portraits of a world that allow us to resurrect the ordinary individuals who lived in and travelled through one of the great Empires of history. Public, political and national history, after all, consist of a multitude of private, domestic and individual histories. It is perhaps through the human stories of the successes, struggles and excited discoveries of these travellers and the people they encounter that we can best bridge the great chasm of time and understanding separating us from the remarkably different world of Mughal India.

—William Dalrymple, Delhi

Introduction

Travels, Travel Writing
and Mughal India

What did the various Europeans 'on the road' in Mughal India actually see? How did they describe their discoveries? As the earliest among them explored India's interior, they entered largely unknown realms where the peoples and customs they encountered, the natural and built environments they experienced and the rulers and laws they accepted were unfamiliar and striking. Sharp wits and robust constitutions enabled these early travellers to explore whole new worlds. Beyond their rich accounts of India's monuments and astonishing wonders that have gradually become stereotypical in the West, these travellers also described their daily lives: who and what they saw around them, how exactly they journeyed and how they struggled and overcame unexpected challenges. Their visions fascinated and informed those who followed after them, as well as readers at home at the time—they continue to do so today. Through reading these ten diverse travel narratives penned by early European travellers from many homelands and backgrounds as they ventured through Mughal India, we can compare them to our own experiences of India, as actual or armchair travellers, three or four centuries later.

People travel for assorted reasons. Many of the travellers in this book ventured to India for commerce, seeking its abundant gold, silver and gems, as well as agricultural and crafted goods. For them, India seemed far wealthier than their own countries. Russian horse dealer Afanasy Nikitin and Venetian tourist Cesare Federici saw how imported horses could be exchanged for India's precious natural wealth and skilled crafts, so valued in Europe. Some of our travellers combined pleasure and exploration with business and diplomacy, like English ambassador and merchant William Hawkins and French ambassador and gem-dealer Jean-Baptiste Tavernier. As an employee of the East India Company, Peter Mundy struggled in frustration as he conveyed cart- and camel-loads of indigo dye and saltpetre from north India to the coast. Seeking religious and political influence, Catholic missionaries of rival kingdoms and monastic orders, including Portuguese Jesuit Father Antonio Monserrate, Portuguese Augustinian Friar Sebastien Manrique and Spanish Dominican Friar Domingo Fernández de Navarrete, sought to convert both emperors and commoners in India. Others, including Venetian Niccolao Manucci and Frenchman François Bernier, travelled in their employer's entourage, the former with a doomed English ambassador seeking the Mughal imperial court, the latter as physician, tutor in natural philosophy and conversation-partner with a Mughal nobleman crossing Punjab into Kashmir.

People also prepare themselves in dissimilar ways. Some of these travellers had already learned Persian or Turkish—languages spoken by the ruling Mughals and other (especially Muslim) elites. None, however, spoke fluently all the regional languages of the various peoples among whom they travelled. All therefore employed Indians who could translate for and guide them. Several were the first of their countrymen to reach India; most had no precursors or guides, written or oral, to prepare them.

A choice that all faced was what to wear: their own familiar garb or Indian-style clothing more suited to the often extreme environment of seasonal heats and monsoon rains. Manrique deliberately adopted the clothing of a Mughal merchant, in order to pass for one on the road. Only when he wished to impress high Mughal officials did he don his religious robes. Bernier adopted the appropriate outfit as attendant to a Mughal courtier. Manucci selected Turkish-style clothes, which, while not Indian, were also not European. Mundy described how for fellow Englishmen in Agra in 1632 'Our Habitt when we goe abroad is a *Shash* [turban] on our heads, a *Doopata* or white lynnen scarfe over our shoulders (this in Summer and Pummering [pashmina wool] in Winter); then a fine white lynnen Coate, a girdle to binde about us, breeches and shooes, our swords and daggers by our sides.'[1] In contrast, many other travellers steadfastly, and uncomfortably, dressed in their own national costume rather than adjust to local habits or conditions.

Other choices included what and how to eat and drink. Just as they wore Indian-style clothes, Mundy wrote that he and his English companions ate local-style dishes 'after the Custome of this place, sitting on the ground att our meate or discourse…[on] Carpetts with great round, high Cushions to leane on.'[2] Indian cuisine at that time was incorporating native American plants that Europeans had introduced—including tomatoes, chilli peppers, potatoes and tobacco—but the food still differed considerably from the travellers' accustomed tastes. The water available was not always safe from germs or parasites so some relied on wind. Several travellers remarked, sometimes with appreciation, sometimes with regret, on the plentiful supplies and intoxicating power of *toddy* (fermented palm sap), which was perfectly healthy unless excessively consumed.

Further, their contemporary European understandings of how human bodies were constituted and functioned often led them to diagnoses which we today would find curious. Following classical European 'humoral' theory, Bernier believed direct exposure to Lahore's night airs, unlike those of Delhi, caused a 'flux accompanied by acute pains in my limbs' which, fortuitously, 'dissipated my bad humours'. Manrique, when persistent fevers brought 'the inevitable and natural fear of death', detoured weeks out of his way for 'spiritual treatment…[by] the Sacraments of Penitence and the Eucharist' from 'missionary Brethren', plus 'simples and antidotes' for his wasted body.

Despite dire diseases, all our authors survived (at least long enough to pen their accounts), but a high proportion of their companions did not. Indeed, during this early period about half of the ships that sailed from Europe to India never returned; even fewer of the Europeans aboard reached home. Four of the ten authors—Nikitin, Monserrate, Hawkins and Manucci—died in India or on the return trip. To enjoy travel in Asia required fortitude, care and also good fortune.

These travellers all gained prolonged physical and personal experience of the lands and peoples of India. Those who walked or were carried on the shoulders of palanquin bearers, and even those who rode horses, camels, or bullocks, or in oxcarts or carriages, went at human-scale speeds, with no choice but to participate in the itinerant world around them. Indian travellers walked or rode alongside them; townspeople and villagers peered and called out at the slowly passing Europeans; officials and bandits searched the travellers' property—and occasionally confiscated it by force. Even those who went by river were pulled by trudging men or sailed slowly, mooring nightly next to unpredictably hospitable or threatening villages. Almost all the travellers went armed, both for roadside hunting of game and also to ward off any Indians their actions had offended or their property had tempted. Further, the periodic heat and rains—and the insect life that thrived in those conditions—affected all, while the technologies of ameliorating them were limited at best, even for the wealthy. At night, most travellers camped out—in a tent, *caravansarai*, village barn, or under the Indian stars—while the most fortunate among them lived at times in lavish palaces assigned to them by the Mughal emperor, a regional ruler, or their officials. Thus, all truly experienced life on the road, although sometimes and by some travellers more comfortably than others.

The Selections

This anthology balances representation with diversity, presenting an array of European views about many of India's regions over precisely two centuries— 1471-1671—from just before the advent of Mughal imperial rule through the peak of its power. The backgrounds and orientations of these authors differed considerably. They include a Russian, a Spaniard, two Englishmen, two Frenchmen, two Venetians and two Portuguese: men who were ambassadors, merchants, priests and adventurers seeking their fortunes in perilous India. Father Antonio Monserrate, William Hawkins, Niccolao Manucci and Jean-Baptiste Tavernier all personally pleaded with Mughal emperors for favour. Friar Sebastien Manrique and Cesare Federici were occasionally reduced to begging for shelter and food from poor Indians in villages or along the wayside.

These ten men travelled during two fascinating and tumultuous centuries; their narratives appear in chronological order, thus highlighting changing, as well as occasionally contradictory, European visions of India. The first of the travellers, Nikitin, predated the conquest by Mughal Emperor Babur (r. 1526-

30) who was descended from the legendary Mongol world-conqueror Genghis Khan and the fabled Turkman warlord Timur, 'Tamerlane'. Federici and Monserrate experienced the remarkable reign of Babur's grandson, Emperor Akbar (r. 1556-1605) as he conquered the multiplicity of raja-doms, sultanates and other states scattered across north India, consolidated the empire and created a synthetic Indo-Mughal culture. Hawkins described the mercurial Emperor Jahangir (r. 1605-27). Mundy, Manrique and Manucci experienced the glorious reign of Emperor Shahjahan (r. 1628-58, d. 1666). Bernier, Tavernier and Fernández de Navarrete observed Emperor Aurangzeb (r. 1658-1707) fight his way onto the throne and then extend his sovereignty southward across virtually all of India. At its peak, the Mughal Empire far exceeded in size and wealth any kingdom in Europe of the time, as many travellers noted. Even today, the Mughals remain potent symbols of India's past.

Indian cities have risen and fallen in prominence over the centuries. Fatehpur, Akbar's Mughal imperial capital, newly vibrant in Monserrrate's account around 1580, was soon almost abandoned, as noted by Mundy in 1632. Yet, many sites visited by the travellers will be recognized and experienced by us today.

All the travellers included here addressed European employers or friends rather than Indian readers. Most used the popular travel narrative genre of the day, although Bernier penned his account as a series of letters. Most wrote in their native languages, but Venetian Manucci chose Portuguese, French and Italian, while the two Portuguese priests, Monserrate and Manrique, selected the more cosmopolitan Latin and Spanish respectively, in light of their intended audiences. Given the range of languages they used, this collection depends on earlier translators. Englishmen Hawkins and Mundy wrote in the form of English current during the seventeenth century, with a distinctive grammar, vocabulary and inconsistent spelling, some of which have been intentionally preserved here. (The Glossary at the end of this book explains all italicised terms in this Introduction and in the selections themselves.)

Given the great richness of European accounts of Mughal India, this anthology has had to be selective. Some of our travellers were more concise, so virtually everything they wrote about India is included. Others wrote voluminously, so their chapters include only particularly engaging parts of their writing. In each case, a reference to the full original work appears at the end of the chapter. This anthology leaves for future reading accounts by Danish, Dutch, German, Icelandic and many other European travellers whose fascinating narratives accord somewhat less with our theme. I trust readers may be inspired to continue their explorations, begun with this anthology.

Indian Societies and Cultures in the Mughal Period

While we may today think of India as a single nation, it has historically included many lands. The South Asian 'sub-continent' is larger and more diverse in territory and population than the European 'continent'. Never in South Asia's history (except during the British Raj, 1858-1947) have all its regions come under a single sovereign. Thus, the travellers in this book witnessed the Mughal emperors extend their power further than any previous Indian rulers in history, dwarfing all its contemporary European kingdoms.

Each of India's many regions has its own culture. The travellers passed through the homelands of more than a dozen languages including: Bengali, Gujarati, Deccani (and its related Hindustani), Kannada, Kashmiri, Malayalam, Marathi, Oriya, Punjabi, Sindhi, Tamil and Telugu—each with many distinct dialects, rich oral traditions and an extensive written literature. In addition, the Mughal officials they encountered used Persian, Turkish and/or Arabic. Further, each region also has distinctive social formations and a mix of specific caste communities with particular jobs and customs. All of the travellers noted the stark economic and social differences that were present throughout Indian society. Indian elites were evidently fabulously rich, as expressed in their luxurious palaces, lavish lifestyles, many wives and slaves and huge armies. In contrast, some of the poor were so desperate that during famines they sold their children rather than see them starve. Mundy, for example, noted 'In this place the men and women were driven to that extremitie for want of food, that they sold their children for 12…pence a peece; yea, and to give them away to any that would take them, with manye thancks, that soe they might preserve them alive, although they were sure never to see them again.'[3]

Although all these Europeans came from countries where slavery was also practiced and social differences pronounced, they puzzled over India's fabled and complex caste system which divided people by birth and traditional occupation. Brahman elites explained society as consisting of four divisions (*varna*), as some of these travellers recorded. The reality of everyday life was much more variable, with thousands of smaller social groupings (*jati*, meaning 'birth') established hereditarily through intramarriage and reinforced through intradining. Tavernier, for example, described four *jati*s of peripatetic transporters (*banjara*), each specializing in different commodities carried long-distance on bullock-back. Several travellers felt excluded when they were not allowed to share—or even observe—the food or water of Hindus in their party. Some travellers could understand this for Indians of higher social class than themselves but Fernández de Navarrete and others found it particularly galling when they were excluded by people they employed and regarded as born into the low *Pariah jati*.

Struggling to explain in their own terms the physical differences among peoples, some travellers referred to themselves as 'white' versus some Indians as 'black' or 'dark'. But skin colour seems to have been less determining than other, often inconsistent, European categorizations. In several accounts, social status at birth, including religion, marked the most fundamental difference among people. But what were the effects of religious conversion and how were people, especially women, transformed by their weddings? The Mughal Emperor Jahangir offered Englishman Hawkins a fair Muslim noblewoman as his bride, pledging that she would convert to Christianity. Yet, neither her light skin colour nor becoming a Christian qualified her in Hawkins' mind to be his wife. In contrast, Hawkins accepted the Emperor's next offer, Mariam, an Armenian-Indian, whom Hawkins regarded as 'of the race of the most ancient Christians'. After Hawkins' death, Mariam was still accepted by London high society and married a second Englishman there in 1614. Conversely, Friar Fernández de Navarrete was most shocked that Catholics would 'pimp' for Catholic women by allowing them to marry *Gentiles* (meaning Hindus) or *Moors* (meaning Muslims). He also repeatedly talked of untrustworthy 'mongrels', including a Dutch East India Company high official who had a Japanese mother and a Dutch father. The Dutch East India Company clearly had different values since they had placed this official in charge of their Golconda outpost, with command over 'pure' Dutchmen.

Did India's climate or culture alter peoples' physical bodies, either in a few years or over generations, as several presupposed, so that a European domiciled in India would become Indianized? Nikitin at times bemoaned that his stay in India was stripping away his Russian Orthodox Christianity. Thus, today's ideas about race only gradually emerged after the inequities of the slave trade and colonialism empowered Europeans and Euro-Americans to think of Asians, Africans and indigenous Americans as essentially and naturally different from themselves.

All the travellers in this book were Christian. Yet they variously adhered to competing Russian Orthodox, Roman Catholic, Anglican and Huguenot denominations. Even within the Catholic Church, the monastic orders of Jesuit Father Monserrate, Augustinian Friar Manrique and Dominican Friar Fernández de Navarrete vied bitterly for prominence and power. Hence, their attitudes toward the multitude of religious traditions in India were quite complicated. For Monserrate and Manrique, 'blasphemous' Indian beliefs had exactly the same satanic origins as those of pre-Christian Greece and Rome 'For the Evil One, in order to avoid inconsistency, implanted in the minds of the men of ancient India the same ideas about the birth of the gods as he implanted in the minds of our own foolish ancestors.'[4] Several, including Bernier, recounted how they deliberately tested the alleged miracles of Hindu gods or Muslim saints, demonstrating how natural laws or Christian faith explained away or falsified them. Indian holy mendicants—especially those who obviously followed extreme asceticism, wandered naked, or allegedly indulged in drugs like opium—frequently inspired disapproval. Nonetheless, the strict vegetarianism and respect for all living things adhered to by some Indian sects could evoke admiration, wonder or scepticism. Many travellers remarked with awe about the lengths people—apparently followers of the Jain or Hindu Vaishnava traditions—went to avoid killing animals, even insects.

Particularly remarkable for the travellers was India's visual culture. As Christians, they saw the often multi-limbed, multi-headed representations of Hindu deities—some with animal features, many awesome in appearance—as inconceivably alien and difficult to understand. However, the unfamiliar but impressive architectural forms of unimagined extent and luxury—Hindu temples, sumptuous palaces and imposing urban strongholds—caught the eyes and spurred the pens of these men, eliciting admiration and favourable comparison with Europe's finest buildings. The Venetian Federici wrote 'I have seene many [European] Kings Courts, and yet have I seene none in greatnesse like to this of Vijayanagar.'

Beyond the constellation of beliefs we today call Hinduism (but which these travellers identified in various ways), Indians followed many other religious traditions as well. Some of these religions had evolved in India while others had come from abroad, including the small fire-worshipping Parsi Zoroastrian community from Iran (whom Manucci erroneously claimed rejoiced in having fire destroy their homes). Several travellers correctly believed that some Indian communities were Jewish, although Monserrate incorrectly asserted that Kashmiri people were among these. He also wrongly believed that a set of Jain statues were images of Christ and his Apostles and that Christian kings had ruled India in the thirteenth century, along the lines of the fabled 'Prester John'. By this period, about a quarter of the entire Indian population had converted to Islam. Each of the authors regarded Muslims generally in the context of Europe's centuries of conflict with Islam.

Three of the travellers were Catholic missionaries who had gone to Asia in order to spread their faith. Father Monserrate sought to convert the Mughal imperial family (although he expressed frustration at how Emperor Akbar appeared about to convert but never actually did so). Friar Manrique reported that his Muslim servant begged for conversion and arranged for his catechism. Friar Fernández de Navarrete brought with him a converted Chinese servant. Despite their efforts, these and other Christian missionaries had little success outside the small European enclaves on India's coasts, although the Syrian Christian Indians described by Federici and Fernández de Navarrete trace their conversion back to Saint Thomas the Apostle himself.

All these travellers were men, although sometimes women accompanied them. Hawkins, for instance, escorted his Indian wife, Mariam, to Europe. Some other Europeans, whether they mentioned this or not, had Indian women servants and mistresses. In Europe and India, few women were literate at that time and thus their accounts of their travels and lives remained oral, largely outside of written historical records. As men, the travellers described the behaviour of Indian women in ways that would soon become stereotypical in Europe. Indeed, they made many moral judgments, often based on their Christian faith and values about appropriate gender roles. Fernández de Navarrete, for instance, critiqued the King of Golconda for his 'Mahomet's Paradise among [his 900] Women, Musick, Dancing and other Sports, all unbecoming the duty of a King...without the least regard for government.'[5] Nonetheless, many of the orientalist images of India as a land of sexual pleasure and corruption which would become prevalent with European colonialism only occasionally surfaced in these earlier accounts. For example, the immolation of Hindu widows, the act of performing *sati* (literally being a 'true wife'), became something that virtually every male European visitor expected to see and describe—almost all of the travellers in this anthology did so (some in passages not included here). Monserrate and most later colonial commentators portrayed these burning widows primarily as symbols of Indian male, particularly Brahman, oppression and therefore indicative of the degraded condition of Indian society generally. In contrast, Federici and Hawkins attributed considerable choice and initiative to the women and reluctantly admired their courage.

Environmental Contexts

India's vast landscapes and wide climatic range create different conditions in each region during each season. These travel accounts range from cool Kashmir among the glacial Himalayas in the far north, over the often hot Gangetic plains, through the arid and rough hills of central India's Deccan highlands, to the mixed terrain of the peninsula's southern tip. All the travellers were impressed by the monsoon (Arabic for 'season'). The building heat, especially from March to May, draws winds from the southwest which drop heavy rains from June to September: India's first monsoon. The second monsoon, from October through December, drenches India's southeast coast. These inexorable seasons affected every aspect of life, from obtaining food, water and shelter, to avoiding temperature extremes, to waiting out floods or slogging over muddy and rutted roads.

India's fauna and flora also often proved arrestingly exotic to the travellers. Animals unknown to them appeared suddenly at hand, some apparently confirming legends, like the lizard whose glance killed, described by Monserrate. Elephants and peacocks stood out; Manrique and Manucci both nearly died over peacocks—the former for eating them, the latter for hunting them. Similarly, intoxicating plants also entered their lives, including *toddy*. The stimulating habit of chewing *betel* leaves (usually wrapped around a mixture of lime, chopped *areca* nut and other condiments), particularly since it produces a blood-red spittle, appeared a widespread and remarkable habit described by many of the travellers variously as health-giving, intoxicating, addictive, or lust-inducing.

Political Contexts

India had no single ruler or system of laws. Europeans sailed there even before the Mughal conquests and they interacted with each other and the indigenous populations and rulers in complex ways that shifted over time and space. In the period between the first two accounts of Nikitin and Federici, Vasco da Gama's Portuguese fleet arrived (1498), the Central Asian Mughals twice invaded (1526, 1555) and the once-powerful Deccani state of Vijayanagar was decisively defeated (1565). Throughout the period covered in this book, independent and semi-autonomous local rulers, warlords and Mughal officials, particularly in central and southern India, continued to make travel dangerous, while repeated tolls and differing currencies made it onerous. From opposing sides, both Hawkins and Manucci personally participated in the deep conspiracies rife among Mughal courtiers who variously allied with or opposed competing Indian and European powers. Both Manucci and Fernández de Navarrate reported the growing challenges to Mughal power and authority, particularly from Maratha Maharaja Shivaji (1627-80), who repeatedly sacked the key port of Surat and established a confederacy that conquered central India over the early eighteenth century.

Those venturing in regions outside Mughal authority, particularly in the Deccan, had very different political reference points to those who experienced its rapid imperial expansion and rule. Avoiding conquering armies, rapacious rulers and officials and marauding bandits remained an ever-present concern for all the travellers. Some, like Nikitin, Federici, Mundy and Manucci, repeatedly fell victim to roadside robbers. Even *caravansarai*, in which all of these travellers stayed, had to bar their gates nightly, as did most walled cities. The travellers recognized and submitted to the authority and power of not only the Mughal emperor but every governor and local ruler whose territories they entered. As in Europe, the moods and relations of royalty and office-holders could decide the fate of those under their power. Manrique, for instance, used 'a piece of green flowered Chinese taffeta, worked with white, pink and yellow flowers' to bribe the wife of a town governor in order to induce her husband to allow an escape from prison. Hawkins, Manucci, Bernier, Tavernier and others tried to use personal relations with officials, even with the emperor himself, to advance their causes or swell their profits. None of the travellers, however, called for the replacement of Indian rulers by European ones, as would later become a frequent theme in justifying colonialism as preferable to Indians than rule by so-called 'oriental despots'. Rather, many of these travellers wished Indian rulers were stronger and would enforce uniform laws across more of India for the protection of travellers like themselves.

The political, theological and commercial struggles among European kingdoms, Christian sects and competing corporations which extended to India added further danger for all travellers. Manucci believed his employer, representing deposed English Catholic King Charles II, was assassinated by East India Company officials loyal to King William, a Protestant. Several Catholic travellers derided Protestants as 'heretics', while some Protestants deemed Catholics (like Hindus) as 'idol-worshippers'. There were even internecine struggles, not only Portuguese versus English versus French, but also among Catholic monastic orders: Jesuit, Augustinian, Dominican. Despite this, when Europeans from (even temporarily) friendly kingdoms met, they often embraced and toasted each other as fellow-travellers.

At the height of Mughal power, rival northern European joint-stock East India trading corporations began to arrive, including the English (established

1600), Dutch (1602), Danish (1616) and French (1664). Many of the travellers in this anthology worked for one or another of these East India companies—as envoys petitioning for trade privileges or tax exemptions, as merchants trying to strike the best deals for Indian goods or as conveyors of hard-won acquisitions safely to their company's ships on the coast. When the Mughal Empire fragmented during the eighteenth century, the English forced out the French, marginalized the other East India companies and began to establish their own empire in India. None of the travellers in this book or the people they observed considered their relationships and roles in India as we do today, with a knowledge of what colonialism would bring.

For many Indians, including rulers, merchants, brokers, translators, export-oriented artisans, seamen and servants, the various squabbling Europeans represented opportunities laced with danger. Growing numbers of Indians found employers, consumers and allies among those who reached India, but at the cost of involvement in intra-European struggles and alienation from other Indians. During this period, Europe produced few goods that had value in India and could offer little except gold and silver (much of which was originally looted by Iberians from the Americas) and what they called 'toys', meaning curiosities and unusual artefacts, including intricate jewellery such as Hawkins, Tavernier and others purveyed. Each European envoy proffered expensive gifts to influential courtiers who would side with him. The travellers also offered Indians exotic knowledge of the outside world, although many conflicting travellers' tales had to be assessed against each other. For example, Monserrate and other Portuguese warned Mughal emperors that perfidious England was a tributary of Portugal. Hawkins denied this and, in turn, warned the Mughals against Portuguese duplicity.

While the growth of European colonial empires that later dominated world affairs for centuries lay far in the future, in retrospect we can perceive their seeds in these accounts. Following da Gama, the Portuguese crown had established the *Estado da India*: a network of royal enclaves along the coasts of India and southeast Asia (Portuguese colonies in India, including Goa, survived until 1961 when independent India seized them). Moving inland militarily against the dynamic Mughal Empire, however, was neither within Portuguese capacity nor interest. Rather, we find the optimistic efforts of Father Monserrate to bring India within the Christian world through conversion of the Mughal imperial family. From 1580-1640, as bemoaned by Portuguese Friar Manrique, the Spanish king ruled Portugal, reducing its power in India. From the early seventeenth century onward, the arrival of competing northern European merchant adventurers and joint-stock corporations further threatened the Portuguese. Indeed, some Portuguese prophetically warned the Mughals that, given a foothold in India, the English would not rest until they conquered it all. Violently opposing this accusation, English ambassador Hawkins denied 'with my life, and that we were not so base a nation' as even to consider colonial conquest. Nonetheless, Hawkins and Mundy worked to advance English political and commercial advantages, while Frenchmen Bernier and Tavernier promised riches to their king if only he would intervene in India. Of all the travellers, only Russian Nikitin and Venetian Federici had no political ambitions toward India.

The Significance of Travel Writing of the Period

Most people travel, some only in their own countries but many in the distant lands of others, for diverse and complex reasons. Even today, let alone in earlier centuries, proportionately few write extended accounts or books about the places and peoples they observe. Each of the authors in this anthology thus stands out as distinctive since he chose to write about his experiences. Each replicates, as well as varies from, those of other travellers of his day. Each is sufficiently long for today's reader to get a sense of the author as an individual. His extended observations, both accurate and misapprehending, can be compared to other writers' views of Indian people and places, including our own.

As with all accounts, we learn as much about the author and his culture as we do about the objects of his gaze and commentary. He envisioned particular readers of his time—none could have imagined us as readers in the twenty-first century. His intended readership led to some of his choices about the language and form of his account, which, in turn, shape the way we can understand it today. Some remained more factual and business-like, writing little about themselves personally; others chose more literary language, with or without overt inclusion of their personal thoughts and emotions. Some wrote to persuade; others to astound. Some wrote a daily diary, some retrospectively composed more synthetic narratives based on their memories of earlier experiences. Bernier, for example, wrote to a French friend describing his outfit, the customs of the imperial encampment and his personal reactions to Punjab and Kashmir. Mundy kept two accounts, one more descriptive, one more factual: the selection draws from both. Monserrate (while later imprisoned in Ethiopia) had time to rewrite his daily notes into a unified Latin narrative. He thus had the scope to consider self-reflectively, for example, how he and his fellow Jesuits, black-robed and tonsured, might appear as alien curiosities in the eyes of the Indians whom they themselves observed. Several travellers, including Federici, explicitly stated what they actually saw, what they learned from others and noted errors in earlier accounts disproved by the author's direct observation.

In addition to reflecting the values of their time and of each individual author, these accounts had profound effects on Europe's perception of India. Many of today's scholars have pointed out how the genre of the travel narrative developed in post-Enlightenment Europe, resonating with larger trends.[6] The explicit desire to identify oneself as an individual, distinguished from others as one makes progress through life appeared increasingly in European travel narratives (including the *itinerário* genre) from the sixteenth century onward, spreading to other individualistic genres like novels and autobiographies.[7] Throughout this period, growing numbers of people in Europe proved fascinated by exploration narratives written by their countrymen. Foreign travel in particular gradually appeared to many Europeans to elevate and broaden both traveller and reader since discovering new lands and peoples opened new possibilities and also reconfirmed the values of 'home'. Written accounts of such distant travels seemed to enlighten readers who could participate vicariously, without facing the actual hazards of the journey. The twin concepts of exploration and discovery of the new and different, and then the mastery of those, became marks of reputed virtue. Eric Leed argues that for European humanists of this period 'The new notion of the journey itself as an education, as a civilizing and cultivating process, implied its systematisation as a curriculum.'[8] Thus, many European authors of travel texts deliberately conveyed the sense of self-improvement, often achieved through a valorised contrast with others from whose bad, as well as good, examples one should learn. The traveller's direct (and the reader's indirect) engagement with foreignness also brought contact and/or confrontation with people who appeared both dangerously and attractively exotic.

Many European travel-writers of the period, in order to publicise their own accomplishments, sought wider distribution of their narratives. Instead of leaving them in manuscript form to circulate among acquaintances, authors increasingly printed their works so that a wider range of readers could appreciate them (and their authors). Additionally, European compliers sought out and republished these accounts and also printed private manuscripts not intended by their authors to be published. In England, for example, editors like Richard Hakluyt (1552-1616) and Samuel Purchas (c. 1577-1626) started printing and selling vast compilations of travel narratives, first to celebrate English achievements and then also as comprehensive documentation of European exploration throughout the world. Some selections in our anthology come from translations first published in Hakluyt's collection. Public interest in reading from the travel narrative genre spread beyond the English aristocracy into the bourgeoisie from the late seventeenth century onward as joint-stock East India companies were launching mercantile fleets into Asia. These publications thereby reinforced the national desire to explore and profit from distant lands; they inspired European soldiers, merchants and colonial administrators to go to India for personal and national gain. From their early travels in India, Europeans have written and variously disseminated their accounts of their journeys and of the Indians they observed, in ways that advanced European intellectual and cultural agendas.

The travel-narrative, some scholars argue, reflected the creation of modernity in Europe alone. The genre also served as hand-maiden to exploitative European colonialism and racism, as the imperious European traveller abroad and the Orientalist at home both gazed on the 'othered' non-White subject and then enshrined his description as the sole truth about the

East.[9] Such travel narratives also made gender inherent in this distancing: mostly male Europeans surveilled and unveiled Asian or African women or effeminised Asian men. These chapters show that simple dichotomies fail to represent accurately the complexity of these early travellers' experiences or the diverse content of their accounts. Nor could any have imagined the spread of colonialism that would follow in subsequent centuries.

Each author in this anthology travelled with different companions and wrote for different readers. How and with whom each author travelled clearly affected his experiences. Some journeyed with European coreligionists or fellow-countrymen; others travelled alone except for Indian servants. Further, their written visions of India reflected their intended audiences, all of whom were European, albeit of various stripes. While some of these authors used 'we' and 'us' only for companions or readers from their own homeland, most had more ambivalent self-identifications. The Venetian Manucci served a fellow Catholic, although the master was an Englishman who was currently battling Protestant Englishmen. Manucci and Tavernier both at times served Mughal Prince Dara Shukoh (1615-59), who was then executed as an alleged infidel by his younger brother Aurangzeb. The Catholic Bernier sometimes linked himself as 'we' with Mughal courtiers he served and among whom he lived, but other times he meant only Frenchmen like himself. Yet, he also travelled and partied with his fellow Frenchman Tavernier, even though the latter was Protestant. The Anglican Hawkins accepted his Christian Armenian-Indian bride, Mariam, as a woman bound by marriage to him for life, even as he clashed with Portuguese Catholic men, especially Jesuits. Monserrate, Manrique and Fernández de Navarrete each regarded their Indian, Chinese and Filipino converts (or near converts) as Catholics, but different from themselves. Thus, the inclusive and exclusive boundaries that these authors presupposed around themselves varied by context, only occasionally dividing as Europeans against Indians by race—something that would emerge as a central distinction later under colonialism.

While none of the travellers in this book wrote for Indian readers, Europeans were not the only ones writing travel narratives at this time. Various Asians, both Indian and others, also composed accounts during this period about their adventures in India. Indeed, throughout the period considered in this book, Indians also travelled to Europe by land and on European ships.[10] Yet, strikingly, while Europeans composed and then compiled and published their accounts of India, Indians did not publish their travel accounts either in India or Europe until the late eighteenth century. Only six out of the several thousands of people from India who had travelled to Britain by 1800 actually wrote books (that have survived) about their journeys. Of these, the only two that published their books did so in English, in Britain. This modest production, contrasted with the rich array of European travel accounts about India, suggests that Europeans were much more interested in reading and mastering knowledge about Indians than vice versa.

Writing and publishing European travel narratives about Asia thus aligns with the asymmetries of exploration and colonialism that would follow. The travellers in this anthology were unwitting contributors to later colonialism but their complex accounts of their personal experiences in the Mughal Empire remain significant and fascinating first-hand evidence about an early phase in the connected histories of Europe and India.

Principles of editing

In order to make these texts, some of which were written in archaic English, as accessible as possible while retaining the flavour of the originals, I have modernised all proper names (indicated in the first appearance in square brackets but silently thereafter). Unless foreign terms are clear in the context, I have italicised them, with a brief definition in the Glossary. I have generally preserved the author's or translator's original spellings, but have made consistent his often inconsistent spellings of common English words. Ellipses indicate omitted passages. Purists will, I trust, forgive these editorial changes.

The author has made every effort to contact copyright holders of these selections. Perceived omissions, if brought to the publisher's notice, will be rectified in the next printing.

Notes

[1] Peter Mundy, *Travels*, ed. Richard Carnac Temple (Cambridge: Hakluyt Society, 1907-25), vol. 2, p. 218.

[2] Ibid.

[3] Ibid, p. 42.

[4] Father Antonio Monserrate *The Commentary of Father Monserrate, S. J., on His Journey to the Court of Akbar, tr. John S. Hoyland, annotated S. N. Banerjee (London: Oxford University Press, 1922), p. 91.*

[5] Friar Domingo Fernández de Navarrete, *Tratados historicos, politicos, ethicos y religiosos de la monarchia de China*, tr. and ed. in *A Collection of Voyages and Travels*, vol. 1, (London: John and Awnsham Churchill, 1744, 3rd edition), pp. 281-2.

[6] See Mary Louise Pratt, *Imperial Eyes: Travel Writing and Transculturation* (London: Routledge, 1992) and Tony Ballantyne and Antoinette Burton, eds., *Bodies in Contact: Rethinking Colonial Encounters in World History* (Durham, Duke University Press 2005).

[7] Joan-Pau Rubies, *Travel and Ethnology in the Renaissance* (Cambridge: Cambridge University Press, 2000), p. 25.

[8] Eric Leed, *The Mind of the Traveller* (New York: Basic Books, 1991), p. 185.

[9] For the seminal study see Edward Said, *Orientalism* (New York: Vintage, 1978).

[10] See Michael H. Fisher, *Counterflows to Colonialism: Indian Travellers and Settlers in Britain, 1600-1857* (Delhi: Permanent Black, 2006).

Chapter One

Afanasy Nikitin

I n 1468, the Russian horse dealer Afanasy (or Athanasius) Nikitich Nikitin left his native Twer (now Kalinin, near Moscow, then the capital of an independent principality) to make his fortune. Moving south down the Volga River, he endured years of misadventures, robberies, captures and escapes in Muslim kingdoms around the Caspian Sea. After haltingly passing the Khorassan region of Iran, he sailed from Hormuz across the Indian Ocean via Muscat to India's west coast. Nikitin stopped at Cambay (now Khambhat) in Gujarat before continuing to Chaul, where he landed with little but his skill as a horse-trader to sustain him. Horses, which do not thrive in India, were in constant demand by warriors and rulers there, nonetheless, he found he could barely profit from his trade.

As the first Russian ever to record his travels in India, Nikitin had little knowledge of what he would find and he feared falling under the power of Muslims there. As he colourfully recounts, he was awed by the huge armies, vast power and lavish wealth of the Muslim Sultan of Bidar and his commanders. The Sultan lorded over 'kafirs'—the majority Hindu population—and also attacked rival rulers like the Hindu Maharaja of Vijayanagar. The complexity of Hindu deities and forms of worship, which Nikitin implicitly compared to Russian Orthodox saints, also fascinated him. Nikitin constantly strove to reassure himself that Russia was more civilised, remarking repeatedly on the relatively unclothed state of Indian women, children and deities, for example. During his three year journey around western and central India, he struggled to avoid losing his Russian Orthodox Christianity.

Nikitin's account provides us with a fascinating picture of India, its peoples and its customs on the eve of two dramatic changes. He travelled just prior to the arrival of the Portuguese fleet under Vasco da Gama in 1498 that conventionally marks the earliest beginnings of European colonialism there. Nikitin also observed India prior to the invasion of Mughal emperor-to-be Babur in 1526. While Nikitin was not the first European to visit India, his Russian perspective adds a unique dimension to his struggles to understand, and profit from, the India of his day. In 1473, Nikitin finally gave up and began his dangerous

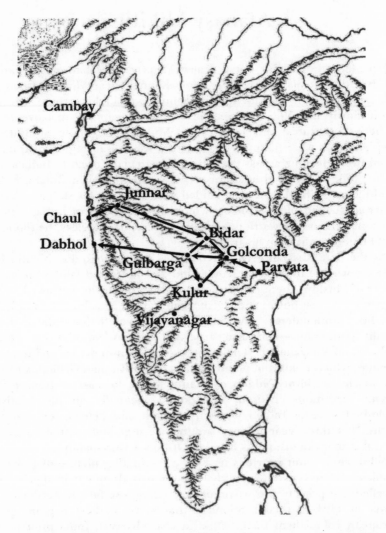

Afanasy Nikitin's travels by land in west and central India, 1471-73

journey home via Ethiopia, Arabia and the Black Sea; he died in 1474, before reaching his native Twer.

⤜

By the prayer of our holy fathers, O Lord Jesus Christ, Son of God, have mercy upon me, Thy sinful servant, Athanasius, son of Nikita.

This is, as I wrote it, my sinful wandering beyond the three seas: the first, the sea of Derbend [the Caspian]...; the second, the India Sea—Doria Hondustanskaia; the third, the Black Sea...

I started from the church of our holy Saviour of Zlatoverkh, with the kind permission of the Grand-Duke Michael Borissowich and the bishop Gennadius of Twer; went down the Volga, came to the convent of the holy life-giving Trinity, and the holy shrines of Boris and Gleb the martyrs...

I have not named the many and large cities through which I passed. At Hormuz the sun is scorching and burns man. I stopped there a month. On the first week after the great day [Easter], I shipped my horses in a *tava*, and sailed across the Indian Sea in ten days to Moshkat. Thence in four days to Degh; and farther to [Gujarat] and [Cambay], where the indigo grows; and lastly to [Chaul]. We sailed six weeks in the *tava* till we reached Chaul, and left Chaul on the seventh week after the great day.

This is an Indian country. People go about naked, with their heads uncovered and bare breasts; the hair tressed into one tail, and thick bellies. They bring forth children every year and the children are many; and men and women are black. When I go out many people follow me, and stare at the white man.

Their [prince] wears a *fata* on the head; and another on the loins; the boyars wear it on the shoulders and on the loins; the [princesses] wear it also round the shoulders and the loins. The servants of the prince and of the boyars attach the *fata* round the loins, carrying in the hand a shield and a sword, or a scimitar, or knives, or a sabre, or a bow and arrows—but all naked and barefooted. Women walk about with their heads uncovered and their breasts bare. Boys and girls go naked till seven years, and do not hide their shame.

We left Chaul, and went by land in eight days to Pilee, to the Indian mountains; thence in ten days to Oomri, and from that Indian town to [Junnar] in six days. Here resides Asad, khan of Indian Junnar, a tributary of Melik-Tuchar [Malik at-Tujjar Muhammad Gavan, Chief Minister of Bidar Sultanate]. I hear he holds [70,000] troops of Malik at-Tujjar, while Malik at-Tujjar himself presides over [200,000]. He has been fighting the *kafirs* for twenty years, being sometimes beaten, but mostly beating them.

The khan rides on men, although he has many good elephants and horses. Among his attendants are many Khorassanians... They all are brought over by sea in *tavas* or Indian ships.

17

And I, poor sinner, brought a stallion to the land of India; with God's help I reached Junnar all well, but it cost me a hundred roubles.

The winter began from Trinity day [June], and we wintered at Junnar and lived there two months; but day and night for four months there is but rain and dirt. At this time of the year the people till the ground, sow wheat, *tuturegan*, peas, and all sorts of vegetables. Wine is kept in large skins of Indian goat…

Horses are fed on peas; also on *kichiris*, boiled with sugar and oil; early in the morning they get [rice-cakes]. Horses are not born in that country, but oxen and buffaloes: and these are used for riding, conveying goods, and every other purpose.

Junnar stands on a stony island; no human hand built it—God made the town. A narrow road, which it takes a day to ascend, admitting of only one man at a time, leads up the hill to it.

In the land of India it is the custom for foreign traders to stop at inns; there the food is cooked for the guests by the landlady, who also makes the bed and sleeps with the stranger. Women that know you willingly concede their favours, for they like white men. In the winter, the people put on the *fata* and wear it round the waist, on the shoulders, and on the head; but the princes and nobles put trousers on, a shirt and a kaftan, wearing a *fata* on the shoulders, another as a belt round the waist, and a third round the head.

O God, true God, merciful God, gracious God.

At Junnar the khan took away my horse, and having heard that I was no Mahommedan, but a Russian, he said: 'I will give thee the horse and a 1000 pieces of gold, if thou wilt embrace our faith, the Mahommedan faith; and if thou wilt not embrace our Mahommedan faith, I shall keep the horse and take a 1000 pieces of gold upon thy head.' He gave me four days to consider, and all this occurred during the fast of the Assumption of our Lady, on the eve of our Saviour's day [18 August].

And the Lord took pity upon me because of his holy festival, and did not withdraw his mercy from me, his sinful servant, and allowed me not to perish at Junnar among the infidels. On the eve of our Saviour's day there came a man from Khorassan, Khozaiocha Mahmet [Khwaja Muhammad], and I implored him to pity me. He repaired to the khan into the town, and praying him delivered me from being converted, and took from him my horse. Such was the Lord's wonderful mercy on the Saviour's day.

Now, Christian brethren of Russia, whoever of you wishes to go to the Indian country may leave his faith in Russia, confess Mahomet, and then proceed to the land of Hindostan. Those *Mussulman* dogs have lied to me, saying I should find here plenty…but there is nothing for our country. All goods are for the land of *Mussulmans*, as pepper and colours, and these are cheap.

Merchandise conveyed by sea is free from duty, and people that would bring it to us will give no duty; but the duties [on us] are many. The sea is infested with pirates, all of whom are *Kafirs*, neither Christians nor *Mussulmans*; they pray to stone idols and know not Christ.

We left Junnar on the eve of the Assumption of the very holy [Virgin, late August] for [Bidar], a large city, and we were a month on the road. From there we went in five days to Kulongher, and in five days from the latter to [Gulbarga]. Between these large towns there are many small ones: three for each day, and occasionally four; so many *kos*, so many towns. From Chaul to Junnar it is 20 *kos*; from Junnar to Bidar, 40; from Bidar to Kulongher, 9 *kos*; and from Bidar to Gulbarga, 9.

In Bidar there is a trade in horses, goods, stuffs, silks, and all sorts of other merchandise, and also in black people; but no other article is sold but Indian goods, and every kind of eatables; no goods, however, that will do for Russia. And all are black and wicked, and the women all harlots, or witches, or thieves and cheats; and they destroy their masters with poison.

The rulers and the nobles in the land of India are all Khorassanians. The Hindostanis walk all on foot and walk fast. They are all naked and barefooted, and carry a shield in one hand and a sword in the other. Some of the servants are armed with straight bows and arrows.

Elephants are greatly used in battle. The men on foot are sent first, the Khorassanians being mounted in full armour, man as well as horse. Large scythes are attached to the trunks and tusks of the elephants, and the animals are clad in ornamental plates of steel. They carry a citadel, and in the citadel twelve men in armour with guns and arrows.

There is a place Shikhbaludin Peratyr, a *bazaar* [Alland], and a fair once a year, where people from all parts of India assemble and trade for ten days. As many as 20,000 horses are brought there for sale from Bidar, which is 20 *kos* distant, and besides every description of goods; and that fair is the best throughout the land of Hindostan. Every thing is sold or bought in memory of Shikhbaludin, whose fete falls on the Russian festival of the Protection of the Holy Virgin [l October].

In that Alland, there is a bird, gookook, that flies at night and cries 'gookook', and any roof it lights upon, there the man will die; and whoever attempts to kill it, will see fire flashing from its beak. Wild cats rove at night and catch fowls; they live in the hills and among stones. As to monkeys they live in the woods and have their monkey prince, who is attended by a host of armed followers. When any of them is caught they complain to their prince, and an army is sent after the missing; and when they come to a town they pull down the houses and beat the people; and their armies, it is said, are many. They speak their own tongues and bring forth a great many children; and, when a child is unlike its father or its mother, it is thrown out on the high road. Thus they are often caught by the Hindostanis, who teach them every sort of handicraft, or sell them at night, that they may not find their way home, or teach them dancing.

Spring begins from the Protection of the Holy Virgin. A fortnight after this festival they celebrate Shikhbaludin and the spring during eight days. They make the spring three months, the summer three months, the winter three months, and the autumn three months. Bidar is the chief town of the whole of Mahommedan Hindostan; the city is large, and contains a great many people.

The sultan [of Bidar, Muhammad II, Bahmani] is a little man, twenty years old, in the power of the nobles. Khorassanians rule the country and serve in war. There is a Khorassanian Boyar, Malik at-Tujjar, who keeps an army of 200,000 men; Melik Khan keeps 100,000; Kharat Khan, 20,000, and many are the khans that keep 10,000 armed men.

The sultan goes out with 300,000 men of his own troops.

The land is overstocked with people; but those in the country are very miserable, whilst the nobles are extremely opulent and delight in luxury. They are wont to be carried on their silver beds, preceded by some twenty chargers caparisoned in gold, and followed by 300 men on horseback and 500 on foot, and by horn-men, ten torchbearers and ten musicians.

The sultan goes out hunting with his mother and his lady, and a train of 10,000 men on horseback, 50,000 on foot; 200 elephants adorned in gilded armour, and in front 100 horn-men, 100 dancers, and 300 common horses in golden clothing, 100 monkeys, and 100 concubines, all foreign.

The sultan's palace has seven gates, and in each gate are seated 100 guards and 100 Mahommedan scribes, who enter the names of all persons going in and out. Foreigners are not admitted into the town. This palace is very wonderful; everything in it is carved or gilded, and, even to the smallest stone, is cut and ornamented with gold most wonderfully. Several courts of justice are within the building.

Throughout the night the town of Bidar is guarded by 1000 men, mounted on horses in full armour, carrying each a light.

I sold my stallion at Bidar, and got by him 60 and 8 *footoons*, having kept him a whole year.

Snakes crawl about in the streets of Bidar, in length [fourteen feet].

I came to Bidar from Kulongher on the day of St. Philip [14 November]; sold my horse about Christmas and stayed at Bidar till Lent; and made acquaintance with many Hindoos, told them what was my faith; that I was neither Mahommedan nor [?], but a Christian; that my name was Afanasy, and my Mahommedan name Khoza Issuf [Khwaja Yusuf] Khorossani. After that they no more endeavoured to conceal anything from me, neither their meals, nor their commerce, nor their prayers, nor other things; nor did they try to hide their women. And I asked them all about their religion, and they said: 'We believe in Adam'; and they hold the *Boots* to be Adam and his race. There are in all eighty-four creeds, and all believe in *Boot*, and no man of one creed will drink, eat, or marry with those of another. Some of them feed on mutton, fowls, fish, and eggs, but none on beef.

Having spent four months at Bidar, I agreed with some Hindoos to go to Parvata, which is their Jerusalem; its Mahommedan name is Gkhat Deikh *Bootkhana*. We were a month on the route. A fair is held there during five days.

Bootkhana is a very extensive building, about the half of Twer, built in stone, and exhibiting in carvings on the walls the deeds of *Boot*. All around it are cut out twelve wreaths, in which are shown how *Boot* achieved miracles; how he appeared in different forms; first in the shape of a man, then as a man with an elephant's nose, then as a man with a monkey's face, and again as a man with the appearance of a savage beast and a tail rising [two feet] above him.

People from all parts of the land of India congregate at *Bootkhana*, to witness the wonders of *Boot*. Old women and girls shave their hair at *Bootkhana*, and everyone coming there shaves his beard and head and whatever hair is on his body; and a tribute of two mekshenies is levied on each head for the sake of *Boot*, and also of four *fonties* on each horse. Twenty thousand people assemble at *Bootkhana*, but sometimes a hundred thousand.

At *Bootkhana*, *Boot* is sculptured in stone of an immense size, his tail rising over him. His right hand is lifted up high and extended like that of Justinian, emperor of Constantinople; his left holding a sword; he is quite uncovered, with only a small cloth round the loins, and has the appearance of a monkey. Some other *boots* are naked, without anything on their hinder parts, and the wives of *Boot* and their children are also sculptured naked.

A huge bull, carved in black stone and gilded, stands before *Boot*; people kiss his hoof and adorn him with flowers as well as *Boot*.

The Hindoos eat no meat, no cow flesh, no mutton, no, chicken. The banquets were all on pork; and pigs are in great abundance. They take their meals twice a day, but not at night, and drink no wine nor mead; but with Mahommedans they neither eat nor drink. Their fare is poor. They eat not with one another nor with their wives, and live on Indian corn, carrots with oil, and different herbs. Always eating with the right hand, they will never set the left hand to anything nor use a knife; the spoon is unknown. In travelling every one has a stone pot to cook his broth in. They take care that Mahommedans do not look into their pot, nor see their food, and should this happen they will not eat it; some, therefore, hide themselves under a linen cloth lest they should be seen when eating.

They offer their prayers towards the east, in the Russian way, lifting both hands high and putting them on the top of the head; then they lie down with the face to the ground, stretching their body to its full length, and such is their law.

They sit down to eat, and wash their hands and feet, and rinse their mouths before they do so.

Their *Bootkhanas* have no doors, and are situated towards the east; and the *boots* also stand eastward.

The bodies of the dead are burnt, and the ashes scattered on the waters.

When a woman is confined, her husband acts the midwife. He gives the name to a son, but the mother gives it to a daughter. Still there is no good about them, and they know not what is shame.

On meeting together, they bow to each other like the monks, touching the ground with both hands, but say nothing.

During Lent they go to Parvata, their Jerusalem. In Mahommedan it is named Mecca, in Russian Jerusalem, in the Hindoo tongue Parvata.

They come hither all naked, with only a small linen round their loins; and the women also naked, with a *fata* round the middle; but some are dressed in *fatas*, wearing necklaces of sapphire, bracelets round the arms, and golden rings.

They drive into the *Bootkhana* on bulls, the horns of which are cased in brass. These animals, called 'ach-chee', have their feet shod, and carry round the neck 300 bells. The Hindoos call the bull father, and the cow mother; with their excrements they bake bread and boil food, and with their ashes sign the images of these animals on their own faces, foreheads, and whole bodies.

On Sundays and Mondays they only eat once in the day...

From Parvata we returned to Bidar, a fortnight before the great Mahommedan festival. But I know not the great day of Christ's Resurrection; however, I guess by different signs, that the great Christian day is by nine or ten days sooner than the Mahommedan *Bairam*. I have nothing with me; no books whatever; those that I had taken from Russia were lost when I was robbed. And I forgot the Christian faith and the Christian festivals, and know not Easter nor Christmas, nor can I tell Wednesday from Friday, and I am between the two faiths. But I pray to the only God that he may preserve me from destruction. God is one, king of glory and creator of heaven and earth.

On my return to Russia I again adopted the Russian law.

The month of March passed, and I had not eaten any meat for one month, having begun to fast with the Mahommedans on a Sunday. Abstaining from all animal or Mahommedan food, I fed myself twice a day with bread and water, abstained from female society, and prayed to God Almighty, who made heaven and earth; and no other god of any other name did I invoke...

I kept the great day in May at Bidar, the Mahommedan residence in Hindostan, having begun to fast on the first day of April; but the Mahommedans kept the *Bairam* in the middle of May.

O true believing Christians! He that travels through many countries will fall into many sins, and deprive himself of the Christian faith...

Four great Lent fastings and four great days [Easter days] have already passed by, but I, sinful man, do not know which is the great day, or when is Lent, or Christmas, or any other holiday, or Wednesday or Friday. I have no books; they were taken by those that plundered us. Driven by this great misfortune I went to India, for I had nothing to return with to Russia, being robbed of all my goods...

On the Mahometan *Bairam*, the sultan went out [in procession], and with him twenty high-viziers, three hundred elephants, clad in Damask steel armour, carrying citadels equally fitted in steel, and each holding six warriors with guns and long muskets. The big elephants are mounted by twelve men. Each animal has two large flags and a heavy sword, weighing a *kentar*, attached to its tusks, and large iron weights hanging from the trunk. A man in full armour sits between the ears, holding in his hand a large iron hook wherewith he guides the animal.

But besides this there may be seen in the train of the sultan about a thousand ordinary horses in gold trappings, one hundred camels with torchbearers, three hundred trumpeters, three hundred dancers, and three hundred slaves.

The sultan, riding on a golden saddle, wears a habit embroidered with sapphires, and on his pointed headdress a large diamond; he also carries a suit of gold armour inlaid with sapphires, and three swords mounted in gold. Before him runs a *Mussulman*...and behind a great many attendants follow on foot; also a mighty elephant, decked with silk and holding in his mouth a large iron chain. It is his business to clear the way of people and horses, in order that none should come too near the sultan.

The brother of the sultan rides on a golden bed, the canopy of which is covered with velvet and ornamented with precious stones. It is carried by twenty men.

[Sultan] Muhammad sits on a golden bed, with a silken canopy to it and a golden top, drawn by four horses in gilt harness. Around him are crowds of people, and before him many singers and dancers, and all of them armed with bare swords or sabres, shields, spears, lances, or large straight bows; and riders and horses are in full armour. Some are naked, but wear a small garment round the waist.

At Bidar the moon remains full three days. I found there no fresh vegetables.

The heat in Hindostan is not great; it is great at Hormuz...

May God preserve the Russian land, God preserve this world, and more especially from hell; may He bestow his blessing on the dominions of Russia and the Russian nobility, and may the Russian dominion increase. O Lord, I rely upon Thee; spare my life. I have lost my road and know not where to go!...

If you proceed to Mecca you must take the Mahommedan faith, and on account of this Christians do not like to go to Mecca. On the other hand, living in India is very expensive. I have spent the whole of my money, and being alone I spend daily for my food one-sixth of an *altyn*; nor do I drink wine...

On the fifth great day, I thought of returning to Russia, and I set out from Bidar a month before the Mahommedan *Bairam*... Knowing no more the great Christian day, the day of Christ's resurrection, I kept Lent time with the *Mussulmans* and broke fasting with them on Easter day, which I did at Gulbarga...

The sultan moved out with his army on the fifteenth day after the *Ulu Bairam* to join Malik at-Tujjar at Gulbarga. But their campaign was not successful, for they only took one Indian town, and that at the loss of many people and treasures.

The Hindoo sultan Kadam is a very powerful prince. He possesses a numerous army, and resides on a mountain at [Vijayanagar]. This vast city is surrounded by three forts, and intersected by a river, bordering on one side on a dreadful jungle, on the other on a dale; a wonderful place, and to any purpose convenient. On one side it is quite inaccessible; a road goes right through the town, and as the mountain rises high with a ravine below, the town is impregnable.

The enemy besieged it for a month and lost many people, owing to the want of water and food. Plenty of water was in sight, but could not be got at.

This Indian stronghold was ultimately taken by Melikh Khan Khoda, who stormed it, having fought day and night to reduce it. The army that made the siege with heavy guns, had neither eaten nor drunk for twenty days. He lost five thousand of his best soldiers. On the capture of the town twenty thousand inhabitants, men and women, had their heads cut off; twenty thousand, young and old, were made prisoners, and sold afterwards at ten *tankas* and also at five *tankas* a head; the children at two *tankas* each. The treasury, however, having been found empty, the town was abandoned.

From Gulbarga I went to [Kulur], where the cornelian is produced and worked, and from whence it is exported to all parts of the world. Three hundred dealers in diamonds reside in this place…

I stopped there five months and then proceeded…to Dabhol, a port of the vast Indian Sea. It is a very large town, the great meeting-place for all nations living along the coast of India and of Ethiopia.

And there it was that I, Athanasius, the sinful servant of God the creator of heaven and earth, bethought myself of the Christian religion, of the baptism of Christ, of the Lent fastings ordained by the holy fathers, and of the precepts of the Apostles, and I made up my mind to go to Russia. So I embarked in a *tava*, and settled to pay for my passage to Hormuz two pieces of gold.

We sailed from Dabhol three months before the great day of the Mahommedan Lent…

Nikitin reached Russian-speaking lands but died just short of Twer. Nor did his account of his travels circulate much among his fellow Russians, as he had intended. His dispirited description of commercial opportunities for Russians in India may have discouraged any who did read his story.

In recent times, however, Nikitin's pioneering accomplishments have been celebrated in both Russia and India, especially as these two nations have sought ways to symbolically strengthen their political alliances. In addition to stamps, coins and railroad trains in Russia commemorating Nikitin, the Russian consulate in Mumbai recently installed a monument to him. In 2003, an undersea mountain in the Indian Ocean was named after him.

Reportedly, only two somewhat corrupted copies of his manuscript have survived, both in Russia. Nikitin's dates of travel had been established as 1466-72 until the scholarship of Leonid S. Semenov authoritatively revised them to 1468-74 on the basis of extensive new research (Semenov, *Puteshestvie Afanasiia Nikitina*, Moscow: Nauka, 1980). Our translation is by a Russian diplomat posted in London: Count Michat Michatovich Wielhorsky-Matuszkin, published as *The Travels of Athanasius Nikitin, A Native of Twer* in a collection *India in the Fifteenth Century*, edited by R. H. Major (London: Hakluyt Society, 1857). There are also other translations into English, one by I. G. Verite, Nikolai Sergeevich Chaev, et al., entitled *Voyage Beyond Three Seas* (Moscow: Gos. izd-vo geogr. lit-ry, 1960) and another by Stephan Apresyan, entitled *Afansy Nikitin's Voyage Beyond Three Seas* (Moscow: Raduga, 1985). His account was also translated into various other European languages.

Chapter Two

Cesare Federici

In 1563, Cesare Federici left his native Venice 'very desirous to see the East parts of the World'. He travelled via Aleppo and Hormuz and then crossed the Indian Ocean. Patrolling Portuguese warships demanded that Portuguese licences be purchased by all who sailed, on pain of seizure of their goods, ships and, occasionally, themselves. Federici, who had no licence, was captured and carried by the Portuguese to their coastal enclave at Diu in Gujarat and then to their colonial capital, Goa.

After extricating himself from Portuguese confinement, Federici ventured inland in 1567 through dangerous territory toward Vijayanagar. The embattled kingdom was still struggling to recover from assaults begun decades earlier by the Sultan of Bidar and his allies (described by Nikitin in Chapter One). These multisided conflicts also opened central India to conquest from the north by the expanding Mughal Empire. Meanwhile, merchants and travellers like Federici faced daily threats to their merchandise and lives; he himself was repeatedly robbed on the road by petty bandits. Nonetheless, the lure of profit sustained extensive and lucrative commerce in imported horses and in Indian-made goods and commodities.

As he explored India's interior, Federici noted intriguing features of the societies and cultures he found there. He identified people as either Moors or Gentiles and provides us with one of an increasing number of European accounts of a *sati*. While moving by sea along India's southern coasts, he wondered at the matrilineal Nair caste of fierce warriors. He detailed the prosperous pearl fisheries of the Gulf of Mannar, located between India and Ceylon/Sri Lanka. He also visited Christians who claimed to have been converted by the Apostle Saint Thomas in person, and who followed the Syrian branch of eastern Christianity. The shrine at Saint Thome outside Madras/Chennai, where Saint Thomas' body is believed to lie, may earlier have been a Hindu temple; indeed, it still reflects both Christian and Hindu devotional motifs. After three years in India, his thirst for new experiences unquenched, Federici sailed to explore more Asian lands further to the east.

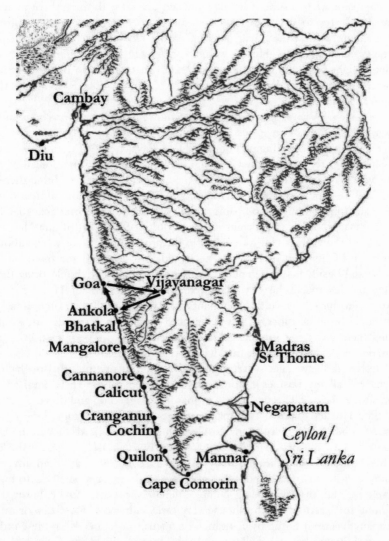

Cesare Federici's travels by land in central and south India, 1563-66

❧

In the yeer of our Lord 1567, I went from Goa to [Vijayanagar] the chiefe Citie of the Kingdom of Narsinga eight days journey from Goa, within the Land, in the companie of two other Merchants which carried with them three hundred Arabian Horses to that King; because the Horses of that Countrie are of a small stature; and at the going out of Goa the Horses pay custome, two and forty *Pagodies* for every Horse, which *Pagody* may be of sterling money six shillings eight pence; they be pieces of gold of that value. So that the Arabian Horses are of great value in those Countries, as 300, 400, 500, and to 1000 *Ducats* a Horse.

The Citie of Vijayanagar was sacked in the yeer 1565 by four Kings of the *Moores*, which were of great power and might... When the kings were departed from Vijayanagar, Temiragio [Tirumala Deva Raya, r. 1568-72, brother of the defeated king] returned to the Citie, and then beganne for to repopulate it, and sent word to Goa to the Merchants, if they had any Horses, to bring them to him, and he would pay well for them, and for this cause the aforesaid two Merchants that I went in companie withal, carried those Horses that they had to Vijayanagar. Also this Tyrant made an order of law that, if any Merchant had any of the Horses that were taken in the aforesaid battle or wars, although they were of his own marke, that he would give as much for them as they would; and beside he gave general safe conduct to all that should bring them. When by this means he saw that there were great store of Horse brought thither unto him, he gave the Merchants faire words, until such time as he saw they could bring no more. Then he licenced the Merchants to depart, without giving them any thing for their Horses, which when the poor men saw, they were desperate, and as it were mad with sorrow and griefe.

I rested in Vijayanagar seven months, although in one month I might have discharged all my businesse, for it was necessarie to rest there until all the wayes were cleer of Theeves, which at that time ranged up and downe. And in the time I rested there, I saw many strange and beastly things done by the *Gentiles*. First, when there is any Noble man or woman dead, they burne their bodies; and if a married man die, his wife must burne herself alone, for the love of her husband, and with the body of her husband; so that when any man dyeth, his wife will take a month's leave, two or three, or as she will, to burne herself in, and that day being come, wherein she ought to be burnt, that morning she goeth out of her house very early, either on Horseback or on an Elephant, or else is borne by eight men on a small stage; in one of these orders she goeth, being appareled like to a Bride, carried round the Citie, with her haire downe about her shoulders, garnished with Jewels and Flowers, according to the estate of the partie, and they goe with as great joy as Brides doe in Venice to their Nuptials; she carrieth in her left hand a looking-glasse, and in her right hand an arrow, and singeth through the Citie as she passeth, and saith, that she goeth to sleep with her deer spouse and husband. She is accompanied with her kindred and friends until it be one or two of the clocke in the afternoon, then they goe out of the Citie, and going along the River's side called Nigondin, which runneth under the walls of the Citie, until they come unto a place where they use to make this burning of Women, being widdowes, there is prepared in this place a great square Cave, with a little pinnacle hard by it, four or five steps up; the aforesaid Cave is full of dryed wood. The woman being come thither, accompanied with a great number of people which come to see the thing, then they make ready a great banquet, and she that shall be burned eateth with as great joy and gladnesse, as though it were her Wedding day; and the feast being ended, then they goe to dancing and singing a certain time, according as she will. After this, the woman of her own accord commandeth them to make the fire in the square Cave where the drie wood is, and when it is kindled, they come and certifie her thereof, then presently she leaveth the feast, and taketh the nearest kinsman of her husband by the hand, and they both goe together to the banke of the foresaid River, where she putteth off all her jewels and all her clothes, and giveth them to her parents or kinsfolke, and covering herself with a cloth, because she will not be seen of the people being naked, she throweth herself into the River, saying: O wretches, wash away your sinnes. Coming out of the water, she rowleth herself into a yellow cloth of fourteen braces long; and againe she taketh her husband's kinsman by the hand, and they goe both together up to the pinnacle of the square Cave wherein the fire is made. When she is on the pinnacle, she talketh and reasoneth with the people, recommending unto them her children and kindred. Before the pinnacle they use to set a Mat, because they shall not see the fiercenesse of the fire, yet there are many that will have them plucked away, shewing therein an heart not fearefull, and that they are not afraid of that sight. When this silly woman hath reasoned with the people a good while to her content, there is another woman that taketh a pot with oyle, and sprinkleth it over her head, and with the same she annointeth all her body, and afterwards throweth the pot into the fornace, and both the woman and the pot goe together into the fire, and presently the people that are round about the fornace throw after her into the cave great pieces of wood, so by this meanes, with the fire and with the blowes that she hath with the wood thrown after her, she is quickly dead, and after this there growth such sorrow and such lamentation among the people, that all their mirth is turned to howling and weeping, in such wise, that a man could scarce beare the hearing of it. I have seen many burnt in this manner, because my house was neer to the gate where they goe out to the place of burning; and when dyeth any Great man, his Wife with all his Slaves with whom he hath had carnal copulation, burne themselves together with him. Also in this Kingdome I have seene amongst the base sort of people this use and order, that the man being dead, he is carried to the place where they will make his sepulcher, and setting him as it were upright, then commeth his wife before him on her knees, casting her armes around his necke, with imbracing and clasping him, until such time as the Masons have made a wall round them, and when the wall is as high as their neckes, there commeth a man behind the woman and strangleth her; then when she is dead, the workmen finish the wall over their heads, and so they lie buried together…

There are many Kings, and great division in the Kingdome, and the Citie of Vijayanagar is not altogether destroyed, yet the houses stand still, but emptie, and there is dwelling in them nothing, as is reported, but Tygres and other wild beasts. The circuit of this Citie is four and twentie miles about, and within the walls are certain Mountaines. The houses stand walled with earth, and plaine, all saving the three Palaces…and the Pagodes which are Idol houses; these are made with Lime and fine Marble. I have seene many King's Courts, and yet have I seene none in greatnesse like to this of Vijayanagar, I say, for the order of his Palace, for it hath nine gates or ports. First when you goe into the place where the King did lodge, there are five great ports or gates; these are kept with Captains and Souldiers; then within these there are four lesser gates, which are kept with Porters. Without the first gate there is a little porch, where there is a Captaine with five and twentie Souldiers, that keepeth watch & ward night and day; and within that another with the like guard, where thorow they come to a very faire Court, and at the end of that Court there is another porch as the first, with the like guard, and within that another Court. And in this wise are the first five gates guarded and kept with those Captaines; and then the lesser gates within are kept with a guard of Porters, which gates stand open the greatest part of the night, because the custome of the *Gentiles* is to doe their businesse, and make their feasts in the night, rather then by day. The Citie is very safe from Theeves, for the Portugal Merchants sleep in the streets, or under Porches, for the great heat which is there, and yet they never had any harme in the night. At the end of two months, I determined to goe for Goa in the company of two other Portugal Merchants, which were making ready to depart, with two *palanchines* or little litters, which are very commodious for the way, with eight *Falchines* which are hired to carry the *palanchines*, eight for a *palanchine*, four at a time; they carry them as we use to carry Barrowes. And I bought me two bullocks, one of them to ride on, and the other to carry my victuals and provision, for in that Countrey men ride on bullocks with pannels, as we terme them 'girths and bridles', and they have a very good commodious pace.

From Vijayanagar to Goa in Summer it is eight days journey, but we went in the midst of Winter, in the month of July, and were fifteen days coming to Ankola on the Sea coast, so in eight days I had lost my two bullocks, for he that carried my victuals was weake and could no goe, the other, when I came unto a River, where a little bridge to passe over, I put my bullocks swimming and in the middest of the River there was a little Iland unto the which my bullock went, and finding pasture, there he remained still, and in no wise we could come to him; and so perforce, I was forced to leave him, and at that time there was much raine, and I was forced to goe seven days a foot with great paines; and by great chance I met with *Falchines* by the way, whom I hired to carry my clothes and victuals.

We had great trouble in our journey, for that every day we were taken Prisoners, by reason of the great dissention in that Kingdome; and every morning at our departure we must pay rescue four or five *Pagies* a man. And another trouble we had as bad as this, that when as we came into a new Governour's Country, as every day we did, although they were all tributarie to the King of Vijayanagar, yet everyone of them stamped a several coyne of Copper, so that the money that we tooke this day would not serve the next; at length, by the helpe of God, we came safe to Ankola, which is a Countrey of the Queen of Gargopam, tributarie to the King of Vijayanagar. The Merchandize that went every yeer from Goa to Vijayanagar were Arabian Horses, Velvets, Damaskes, and Sattens, *Armesine* of Portugal, and pieces of China, Saffron and Scarlets; and from Vijayanagar they had in Turkie for their commodities, Jewels, and *Pagodies* which be *Ducats* of gold; the apparel that they use in Vijayanagar is Velvet, Satten, Damaske, Scarlet, or white Bumbast cloth, according to the estate of the person, with long Hats on their heads, called Colae, made of Velvet, Satten, Damaske, or Scarlet, girding themselves instead of girdles with some fine white Bumbast cloth; they have breeches after the order of the Turkes; they weare on their feet plaine high things called of them Aspergh, and at their eares they have hanging great plentie of Gold.

Returning to my voyage, when we were together in Ankola, one of my companions that had nothing to lose, tooke a guide, and went to Goa, whither they goe in four days, the other Portugal not being disposed to goe, tarried in Ankola for that Winter. The Winter in those parts of the Indies beginneth the fifteenth of May, and lasteth unto the end of October; and as we were in Ankola, there came another Merchant of Horses in a *palanchine*, and two Portugal Souldiers which came from [Ceylon], and two carriers of Letters, which were Christians borne in the Indies; all these consorted to goe to Goa together, and I determined to go with them, and caused a *palanchine* to be made for me very poorely of Canes; and in one of them Canes I hid privily all the Jewels I had, and according to the order, I tooke eight *Falchines* to carrie me; and one day about eleven of the clocke we set forwards on our journey, and about two of the clocke in the afternoone, as we passed a Mountaine, which divideth the territorie of Ankola and Dialcan, I being a little behind my company, was assaulted by eight theeves, four of them had swords and targets, and the other four had bowes and arrowes. When the *Falchines* that carried me understood the noise of the assault, they let the *palanchine* and me fall to the ground, and ranne away and left me alone, with my clothes wrapped about me; presently the theeves were on my necke and rifling me, they stripped me starke naked, and I fained my selfe sicke, because I would not leave the *palanchine*, and I had made me a little bed of my clothes; the theeves sought it very narrowly and subtilly, and found two Purses that I had, well bound up together, wherein I had put my Copper money which I had changed for four *Pagodies* in Ankola.

The theeves thinking it had been so many *Ducats* of gold, searched no further; then they threw all my clothes in a bush, and hied them away, and as God would have it, at their departure there fell from them an hankercheef, and when I saw it, I rose from my *palanchine* or couch, and tooke it up, and wrapped it together within my *palanchine*. Then these my *Falchines* were of so good condition, that they returned to seek me, whereas I thought I should not have found so much goodnesse in them; because they were payed their money aforehand, as is the use, I had thought to have seen them no more. Before there coming I was determined to plucke the Cane wherein my Jewels were hidden, out of my couch, and to have made me a walking staffe to carry in my hand to Goa, thinking that I should have gone thither on foot, but by the faithfulnesse of my *Falchines*, I was rid of that trouble, and so in four days they carried me to Goa, in which time I made hard fare, for the theeves left me neither money, gold, nor silver, and that which I did eate was given me of my men for God's sake; and after at my coming to Goa I payed them for everything royally that I had of them.

From Goa, I departed for Cochin, which is a voyage of three hundred miles, and between these two Cities are many holds of the Portugals, as [Honavar], Mangalore, Barzelor, and Cannanore. The Hold or Fort that you shall have from Goa and Cochin that belongeth to the Portugals, is called Honavar, which is in the Kingdom of the Queen of [Bhatkal], which is tributarie to the King of Vijayanagar; there is no trade there, but only a charge with the Captaine and companie he keepeth there. And passing this place, you shall come to another small Castle of the Portugals called Mangalore, and there is very small trade but only for a little Rice; and from thence you goe to a little Fort called Barzelor, there they have good store of Rice which is carried to Goa; and from thence you shall goe to a Citie called Cannanore, which is a *Harquebush* shot distant from the chiefest Citie that the King of Cannanore hath in his Kingdome being a King of the *Gentiles*; and he and his are very naughtie and malicious people, always having delight to be in wars with the Portugals, and when they are in peace, it is for their interest to let their Merchandise passe; there goeth out of this Kingdom of Cannanore, all the Cardamomum, great store of Pepper, Ginger, Honie, ships laden with great Nuts, great quantitie of *Areca*, which is a fruit of the bignesse of Nutmegs, which fruit they eate in all those parts of the Indies, and beyond the Indies, with the leafe of an Herbe which they call *Bettell*, the which is like unto our Ivie leafe, but a *Bettell* is a little lesser and thinner; they eate it made in plaisters with lime made of Oistershells, an thorow the Indies they spend great quantitie of money in this composition, and it is used daily, which thing I would not have beleeved, if I had not seen it. The customers get great profit by these Herbes, for that they have custome for them. When this people eate and chawe this in their mouthes, it maketh their spittle to be red like unto blood, and they say, that it maketh a man to have a very good stomacke and a very sweet breath, but sure in my judgement they eate it rather to fulfill their filthie lusts, and of a knaverie, for this Herbe is moist and hot, and maketh a verie strong expulsion.

From Cannanore you goe to Cranganur, which is another small Fort of the Portugals in the land of the King of Cranganur, which is another King of the *Gentiles*, and a Countrey of small importance, and of an hundreth and twentie miles, full of Theeves, being under the King of Calicut, a King also of the *Gentiles* and a great enemie to the Portugals which when he is always in wars; he and his Countrie is the nest and resting for stranger Theeves, and those be called *Moores* of Carposa, because they weare on their heads long red Hats, and these Theeves part the spoiles that they take on the Sea with the King of Calicut, for he giveth leave unto all that will goe a roving, liberally to goe, in such wise, that all along that Coast there is such a number of Theeves, that there is no sailing in those Seas but with great ships and very well armed, or else they must goe in companie with the armie of the Portugals. From Cranganur to Cochin is fifteen miles.

Cochin is next unto Goa, the chiefest place that the Portugals have in the Indies, and there is great trade of Spices, Drugges, and all other sorts of Merchandize for the Kingdome of Portugal, and there within the land is the Kingdome of Pepper, which Pepper the Portugals lade in their shippes by bulke, and not in Sackes; the Pepper that goeth for Portugal is not so good as that for Mecca, because that in times past, the Officers of the King of Portugal made a contract with the King of Cochin in the name of the King of Portugal, for the prices of Pepper, and by reason of that agreement between them at that time made, the price can neither rise nor fall, which is a verie low and base price, and for this cause the villaines bring it to the Portugals, green and full of filth. Cochin is two Cities, one of the Portugals, and another of the King of Cochin; that of the Portugals is situate neerest unto the Sea, and that of the King of Cochin, is a mile and a halfe up higher in the land, but they are both set on the bankes of one River which is verie great and of a good depth of water, which River commeth out of the Mountaines of the King of the Pepper, which is a King of the *Gentiles*, in whose Kingdome are many Christians of Saint Thomas order; the King of Cochin is also a King of the *Gentiles*, and a great faithfull friend to the King of Portugal, and to those Portugals which are married and are Citizens in the Citie of Cochin of the Portugals. And by this name of Portugals throughout all the Indies, they call all the Christians that come out of the West, whether they be Italians, Frenchmen, or [Germans], and all they that marrie in Cochin doe get an Office according to the Trade he is of; this they have by the great priviledges which the Citizens have of that Citie, because there are two principal commodities that they deale withall in that place, which are these: The great store of Silke that commeth from China and the great store of Sugar which commeth from Bengal; the married Citizens pay not any custome for these two commodities; for all other commodities they pay four per cent custome to the King of Cochin, rating their goods at their owne pleasure. Those which are not married and Strangers, pay in Cochin to the King of Portugal eight per cent of all manner of Merchandise.

This King of Cochin is of a small power in respect of the other Kings of the Indies, for he can make but seventie thousand men of Armes in his Campe; he hath a great number of Gentlemen which he calleth *Amochi*, and some are called *Nair*, these two sorts of men esteeme not their lives anything, so that it may be for the honour of their King, they will thrust themselves forward in every danger, although they know they shall die. These men goe naked from the girdle upwards, with a cloth rolled about their thighes, going bare-footed, and having their haire very long and rolled up together on the top of their heads, and always they carrie their Bucklers or Targets with them and their Swords naked, these *Nair* have their wives common amongst themselves, and when any of them goe into the house of any of these women, he leaveth his Sword and Target at the doore, and the time that he is there, there dare not any be so hardie as to come into that house. The Kings children shall not inherite the Kingdome after their Father, because they hold this opinion, that perchance they were not begotten of the King their Father, but of some other man; therefore they accept for their King, one of the sonnes of the King's sisters, or of some other woman of the blood Royal, for that they be sure they are of the blood Royal.

The *Nair* and their Wives use for a braverie to make great holes in their Eares, and so big and wide, that it is incredible, holding this opinion, that the greater the holes be, the more Noble they esteeme themselves. I had leave of one of them to measure the circumference of one of them with a thread, and within that circumference I put my arme up to the shoulder, clothed as it was, so that in effect they are monstrous great. Thus they doe make them when they be little, for then they open the eare, and hang a piece of gold or lead thereat, and within the opening, in the hole they put a certaine leafe that they have for that purpose, which maketh the hole so great.

The ships every yeer depart from Cochin to goe for Portugal, on the fifth day of December, or the fifth day of January. Now to follow my voyage for the Indies: From Cochin I went to [Quilon], distant from Cochin seventie and two miles, which Quilon is a small Fort of the King of Portugals, situate in the Kingdome of Quilon, which is a King of the *Gentiles*, and of small trade; at that place they lade only halfe a ship of Pepper, and then she goeth to Cochin to take in the rest, and from thence to Cape Comorin is seventie and two miles, and there endeth the coast of the Indies; and alongst this Coast, neer to the water side, and also to Cape Comorin, downe to the low land of Chilao, which is about two hundred miles, the people there are as it were all turned to the Christian Faith; there are also Churches of the Friers of Saint Paul's order, which Friers doe very much good in those places in turning the people, and in converting them, and take great paines in instructing them in the law of Christ.

The Sea that lyeth between the Coast which descendeth from Cape Comorin, to the low land of Chilao, and the Iland Ceylon, they call the fishing of Pearles, which fishing they make every yeer, beginning in March or April, and it lasteth fiftie days, but they doe not fish every yeer in one place, but one yeer in one place, and another yeer in another place of the same Sea. When the time of this fishing draweth neer, then they send very good Divers, that goe to discover where the greatest heapes of Oysters be under water, and right against that place where greatest store of Oysters be, there they make or plant a Village with houses and a *Bazar*, all of stone, which standeth as long as the fishing time lasteth, and it is furnished with all things necessarie, and now and then it is neer unto places that are inhabited, and other times farre off, according to the place where they fish. The Fishermen are all Christians of the Countrey, and who so will may goe to fishing, paying a certain dutie to the King of Portugal, and to the Churches of the Friers of Saint Paul, which are in that Coast. All the while that they are fishing, there are three or four *Fusts* armed to defend the Fishermen from Rovers. It was my chance…to be there one time in my passage, and I saw the order that they used in fishing, which is this. There are three or four Barkes that make consort together, which are like to our little Pilot boates, an a little less, there goe seven or eight men in a Boat; and I have seen in a morning a great number of them goe out, and anker in fifteen or eighteen fathom of water, which is the ordinarie depth of Coast. When they are at anker, they cast a rope into the Sea, and at the end of the rope, they make fast a great stone, and then there is readie a man that hath his nose and his eares well stopped, and annointed with Oyle, and a basket about his necke, or under his left arme, then he goeth down by the rope to the bottom of the Sea, and as fast as he can he filleth the basket; and when it is full, he shaketh the rope, and his fellowes that are in the Barke hale him up with the Basket; and in such wise they goe one by one until they have laden their Barke with Oysters; and at evening they come to the Village, and then every companie maketh their mount or heape of Oysters, one distant from another, in such wise that you shall see a great long row of mounts or heapes of Oysters; and they are not touched until such time as the fishing be ended; and at the end of the fishing every companie sitteth round about their mount or heape of Oysters, and fall to opening of them, which they may easily doe because they be dead, drie and brittle; and if every oyster had pearles in them, it would be a very good purchase, but there are very many that have no pearles in them; when the fishing is ended, then they see whether they weigh, it be a good gathering or a bad; there are certaine expert in the Pearles, whom they call *Chitini*, which set and make the price of Pearles according to their carrats, beautie and goodnesse, making four sorts of them. The first sort be the round Pearles, and they be called Aja of Portugal, because the Portugals doe buy them. The second sort which are not round, are called Aja of Bengal. The third sort which are not so good as the second, they call Aja of Canara, that is to say, The Kingdome of Vijayanagar. The fourth and last sort, which are the least and worst sort, are called Aja of Cambay. Thus the price being set, there are Merchants of every Countrey which are readie with their money in their hands, so that in few days all is bought up at the prices set according to the goodnesse and carracts of the Pearles.

In this Sea of the fishing of Pearles, is an Iland called Mannar, which is inhabited by Christians of the Countrey which first were *Gentiles*, and have a small hold of the Portugals being situate over against Ceylon; and between these two Ilands there is a Channel, but not very bigge, and hath but a small depth therein; by reason whereof there cannot any great Ship passe that way, but small Ships, and with the increase of the water which is at the change, or the full of the Moone, and yet for all this they must unlade them and put their goods into small vessels to lighten them before they can passe that way for feare of Shoals that lie in the Channel; and after lade them into their ships to goe for the Indies, and this doe all small ships that passe that way, but those ships that goe for the Indies Eastwards, passe by the Coast of Coromandel, on the other side by the land of Chilao, which is between the firme land and the Iland Mannar. From Cape Comorin to the Iland Ceylon is one hundred and twentie miles overthwart...

From Negapatam following my voyage towards the East an hundred and fiftie miles, I found the House of blessed Saint Thomas, which is a Church of great devotion, and greatly regarded of the *Gentiles*, for the great Miracles they have heard to have been done by that blessed Apostle; neer unto this Church the Portugals have builded them a Citie in the Countrey subject to the King of Vijayanagar, which Citie although it be not very great, yet in my judgement it is the fairest in all that part of the Indies. It is a marvellous thing to them which have not seen the lading and unlading of men and merchandize in Saint Thome as they doe; it is a place so dangerous, that a man cannot be served with small Barkes, neither can they doe their businesse with the Boates of the ships, because they would be beaten in a thousand pieces, but they make certaine Barkes (of purpose) high, which they call *Masadie*, they be made of little boards; one board being sowed to another with small cordes, and in this order are they made. And when they are thus made, and the owners will embarke any thing in them, either men or goods; they lade them on land, and when they are laden, the Barke-men thrust the Boate with her lading into the streame, and with great speed they make hast all that they are able to row out against the huge waves of the Sea that are on that shore until that they carrie them to the ships; and in like manner they lade these *Masadies* at the ships with merchandise and men. When they come neer the shore, the Bark-men leap out of the Bark into the Sea to keep the Bark right that she cast not athwart surge and the shore, and being kept right, the Surfe of the Sea setteth her lading drie on land without any hurt or danger, and sometimes there are some of them that are overthrown, but there can be no great losse, because they lade but a little at a time. All the Merchandize they lade outwards, they emball it well with Oxe hides, so that if it take wet, it can have no great harme.

Federici carried on from India to Southeast Asia. After his eventual return to his native Venice, he published his account in 1587. It was almost immediately translated into English by T. Hickok as *Voyage and Travaile of M. C. Federici, Merchant of Venys.* (London: T. Hickok, 1588). Our selection comes from this first translation, which was later republished inter alia in Samuel Purchas, ed., *Hakluyt Posthumus or Purchas His Pilgrimes*, vol. 10 (Glasgow: James MacLehose, 1905 ed.), pp. 88-108, and in facsimile as Cesare Federici, *The Voyage and Travaile into The East India* (Amsterdam: Da Capo Theatrum Orbis Terrarum, 1971).

Chapter Three

Father Antonio Monserrate

In 1579, Portuguese Father Antonio Monserrate (1536-1600) travelled with fellow Jesuits at the request of Mughal Emperor Jalal al-Din Akbar (r. 1556-1605) from Goa to the imperial court at Fatehpur, near Agra. Even with the escort of a high Mughal official and armed troops, the journey proved perilous, underlining the political instability and endemic martial conflicts revealed in previous selections. Once at the imperial court, Monserrate and his companions struggled to convert the Emperor and members of his family to Catholicism. Emperor Akbar seems to have played on the eagerness of these Jesuits for such conversions in order to extract from them edifying and entertaining knowledge of Europe. The rising rivalries among the Portuguese, other Europeans and various factions in the Mughal court and administration thus come through powerfully in Monserrate's account. However, his sectarian missionary perspective colours his observations of Hindus, Bhil Adivasis (tribesmen, whom he calls 'mountaineers') and Muslims (whom he calls 'Agarenus'—descendants of Hagar and her son Ishmael), as well as of European Protestants (whom he refers to as 'certain abandoned creatures of our own age' and 'wicked renegades from the Christian Faith'). He also identifies the Mughals as Mongols, stressing their ancestry from Genghis Khan.

After two years of frustrating efforts at the imperial court, Monserrate joined Akbar's punitive expedition across north India and the Punjab against Akbar's rebellious half-brother, Mirza Muhammad Hakim (1554-85) in Kabul. As we will see in the later account by Bernier (Chapter Eight) such Mughal military campaigns were vast and elaborate—virtual cities moving across the countryside. Eventually, Monserrate returned to Goa but, captured on his way back to Rome, composed his account in Latin while imprisoned in East Africa. He described his adventures in the third person.

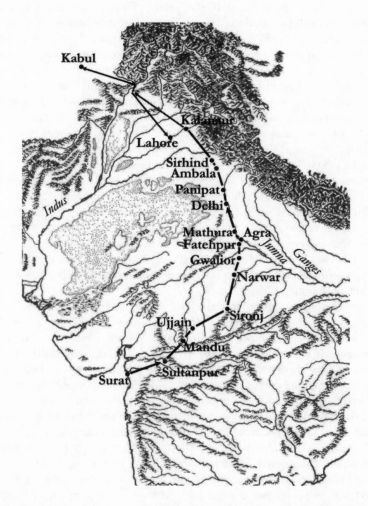

Father Antonio Monserrate's travels by land in west and north India and Punjab, 1579-82

ॐ

[*After a month's delay, their Mughal escort, Sayyid Abdullah Khan*], having got favourable auspices from the moon, led his company out of Surat, and pitched his camp outside the town near the gates. Camels and other means of transport had been provided to carry provisions and merchandise. On the next day, i.e., January 24th [1579], they set out, greatly to the delight of the Fathers, who did not approve of this delay and its superstitious cause, and were inexpressibly eager to reach the King's court; for they were confident that he would embrace Christianity. Having moved one mile, across the river [Sabarmati], to a spot near [Rander], the company encamped. This Rander, which is commonly called Raynel by the Portuguese, is a celebrated military fortress opposite Surat... Its citizens have frequently defended themselves most manfully against the Portuguese, although they have been overcome.

On the next day the travellers set out from this place, whereupon two of the Fathers and the rest of the Christians fell into no small danger. One of the priests was being carried in a litter, as he was ill. His bearers, eager to get rid of their burden, had gone on at a rapid pace far ahead of the rest of the company. The governor of Surat met them, surrounded by a band of guards. The priest saluted the governor, who asked him what party was coming behind. Meanwhile the governor's followers went on ahead, and perceiving the foreign appearance of the rest of the company fell upon them savagely, with intent to kill them all, shouting 'Franks, Franks'.

However, the governor and the ambassador whipped up their horses, reached the spot from opposite directions, and, by the mercy of God, succeeded in quelling the riot before a single *Musalman* had been slain by the Portuguese. If one had so perished, we should all have been killed. The two Fathers who had been in such danger thought that the one who had gone on ahead must certainly have been killed. When they caught him up they embraced him as though he had been restored to them from heaven.

On the next day they came to a fort built out of the debris of some Hindu temples which the *Musalmans* had destroyed. Such destruction would have been a praiseworthy action if many of their other actions had not been so abominable. The camp was pitched on the bank of the Tapti. On the same day the Hindus expatiate their sins of the past years in the following manner. A cocoanut shell is scraped out and filled with oil. A wick inserted and lighted. The Hindu then strips off his clothes and enters the river with the lighted lamp on his head. He slowly submerges himself till the lamp, caught by the current, is carried away. They regard themselves as purified from sin by this process. This festival is called by the Hindus the Satamia because it is held on the seventh day of the moon in the eleventh month, which in their reckoning is January.

Leaving the bank of the river the company reached Sultanpur on the ninth day from Surat. This was the day on which the Musulmans perform their sacrifices. A three days' halt was made at Sultanpur, as the ambassador desired to wait there on account of this festival. Thence they crossed the [Satpura] range and reached [Sindwa] four days later. The Satpura extends for 75 miles eastward from the sea, and is 16 miles wide. It is crossed by a narrow and difficult track. The camels have to be led in single file; and the carts are carried on men's shoulders. The jungle on each side is exceedingly dense, and the ground broken and rough. There one of the ambassador's guards was killed by robbers, and no revenge could be taken. The inhabitants of these mountains worship ghosts. They are ruled by three kings, of whom one is the master of the other two and is as it were their emperor. They are constantly at war with the *Mongols*. When one of their tribes is pacified, and a treaty made with the *Mongols*, the other two tribes carry on the wild and savage warfare, and frequently defeat their great enemy. Occasionally these battles are drawn; but the *Mongols* can never inflict on the mountaineers a decisive defeat. These mountaineers are wild, barbarous and degraded. They are addicted to brigandage, and have no weapons except bows made of bamboo and short arrows with rusty points. Yet they are exceedingly fierce, intractable, greedy of spoil, and headstrong. They have no cavalry and no artillery, but are vastly aided by the nature of their country, which is remarkable for its deep jungles and precipitous crags. They fortify these natural strongholds with intrenchments and stockades. They assail the enemy from ambuscades, which they lay in thickets and thorny places. Their attack may be open or concealed; but they hesitate to come to close quarters. The extreme narrowness of the tracks, and the steep cliffs on either side, enable a very few of them easily to hold the enemy at bay. If in spite of this a determined attack is made upon them which they cannot withstand, they successfully conceal themselves in the dense and craggy jungle.

The principal town of this tract of country, in which the emperor of these mountaineers himself resides, is called Satpura, just as the mountains are. The circuit of its walls is indeed great, but its huts are very mean and wretched.

At last, having crossed the mountains and penetrated the defiles along a rough and dangerous track, we reached Surana. While we were there, at 11 P.M. on January 31st, there was an eclipse of the moon. In the following year we learnt that at that very time the pious and devout King Henry of Portugal, the royal pontiff, had passed away. This exalted and mighty monarch died on his own birthday. Many people also regard it as a portent that, on the day when he was born, the district of Ulyssipon was whitened with snow; for it is very unusual for it to snow in that province, on account of the mildness of the climate. At any rate on the day of his death, the moon suffered eclipse. In regard to the life and character of King Henry, he was a signally pious and devout man. This eclipse may also be reckoned to have foreshadowed the trials and griefs in which came upon Portugal after the death of King Henry.

Not very far from Surana, the river [Narmada] is crossed… In the stormy season the very wide and deep bed of this river is filled with rapidly-flowing muddy water, so that it can only be crossed by means of a bridge or a boat. But in the summer, when the water of the rains has subsided, it can be crossed on foot. It is full of fish, and its water is so clear that the fish and turtles, and even the smallest pebbles, can be counted. Its banks are covered with thick reed-beds, and with the health-giving herb marjoram.

Two days after crossing the Narmada we reached the great city of [Mandu], the former importance of which, in the days of its prosperity, is indicated by the huge circuit of its walls, the vastness of the buildings which remain standing, and the ruins of those which have fallen. The walls are still perfect in those places which are not defended by precipitous crags; their total circuit is nearly 24 miles. The city stands on the level top of a hill, and is everywhere defended by deep gorges and inaccessible cliffs. It has only one very narrow entrance. It can never lack water, as there are many tanks and springs in it, as well as never-failing wells of abundant and sweet water. In that quarter where the single entrance to the town is situated there are five walls placed one above the other at the head of a steep approach, so that the city is impregnable and can only be subdued by lack of food. No one can tell with any degree of certainty by whom and at what time this great city was founded; for the *Musalmans*, whose nature is indeed that of barbarians, take no interest in such things: their chronicles being scanty and unreliable, and full of old wives' tales. However, judging from the structure of the walls, one may venture a confident conjecture that the town is fairly modern and was built by *Musalmans*. I was told that its builders were *Mongols*, of a different tribe from that which has become so celebrated in our own time. For it is said that two hundred years ago, the *Mongols*, being in search of a fresh country to occupy, left their ancestral encampments, invaded India, and settled at Mandu, both because it is by nature very easily defended and also because it is the most fertile part of the district, and indeed of the whole province of Malwa. These *Mongols*, however, were afterwards crushed by the *Pathans* in a number of battles, were driven into the single stronghold of Mandu, were besieged there for seven years, and finally, having been compelled to submit, were destroyed. For the *Pathan* King, who was in command of the besieging army, after many vain attempts to storm the city, fully perceived that it could only be subdued by compelling it to surrender through hunger. He therefore summoned masons, smiths, contractors and workmen, and ordered them to build walls, defences and houses for the soldiers to live in—indeed a whole city—in the very place, close to the gate in the walls, where his camp was at that time pitched. He gave strict injunctions also that all provisions intended for the city should be intercepted by his cavalry, who occupied all roads to the town and especially one path which approached the city from behind and was so rough and precipitous that soldiers could scarcely climb it even on their hands and knees. Finally he captured the city and ordered it to be razed to the ground.

Inside the city is to be seen a fragment of a huge iron gun which for some superstitious reason or other the heathen revere and worship. It is smeared with oil and coloured red. There is also a great palace, the home of the ancient kings, in which the governor of the province now lives. There is an excellently fortified citadel, and a half-finished royal tomb, which I suppose will never be completed; but it is worth seeing for its architecture and huge size. It stands in the middle of a square platform, which is raised five cubits above the ground, is eighty feet wide at the top, and is everywhere surrounded below by arches and colonnades. The tomb itself, which is crowned by a dome, measures twenty feet across, forty feet from the floor-level to the base of the dome, and forty feet from that point to the top of the dome. At the four corners of the platform rise minarets, seven storeys high and octagonal in shape. Each storey of these minarets is five cubits high. They have windows directed towards the four winds, out of which the *Musalman* call to prayer is pronounced. Opposite this tomb is another great building of similar magnificence and costliness. In the tomb are buried three *Mongol* kings, and also the tutor of one of these kings. Each sepulchre is embellished with mosaics, bass-reliefs and inlaid work. In front of these sepulchres are preserved the gilded thrones of the three kings, these being regarded as the emblems of royal rank, just as we regard the crown and sceptre as such emblems.

There is also a temple built like a Christian Church. Beneath, one on each side of the building, are two shrines with arched roofs, in which altars might be placed. Above these are two rooms, also with arched roofs, opening into each other and thus forming a passage towards the sanctuary of the High Altar. Probably it will appear to many an incredible traveller's tale when I declare that outside the walls of the city is a graveyard six miles long. This may sound an exaggeration; but no one who knows with what magnificence and costliness the *Musalmans* are wont to build tombs will wonder at it. For, believing as they do that those whose life here is ended can only be admitted amongst the saints of Heaven through the name of Muhammad, they therefore honour their dead with elaborately built tombs, which, as they esteem, are worthy of those who are now holy saints in Heaven. Indeed in this respect—namely their belief that fitting honours should be paid to heavenly saints and seemly tombs made for the dead—these *Musalmans* are wiser and better than certain abandoned creatures of our own age.

The above is a description of Mandu. The party arrived at [Ujjain], near the river Machiwara, on the second day after leaving this vast city. The founder of Ujjain is said to have been Birbitcremas [Chandra Gupta II, Vikramaditya, 375-413, sic], who is venerated as a God, and as the inventor of all the mechanic arts, by the people of the whole of [Gujarat] and the neighbouring provinces. This superstition may probably be accounted for by Vikramaditya's interest and skill in such arts. For he was a very powerful and wealthy king, and the designer of many great works, which he left as a memorial of his glory, and which are still to be seen in the shape of numerous ancient temples. If one comes across an ancient temple of this type anywhere in this part of India and asks who was its builder, the reply is sure to be 'Vikramaditya'. And if a builder or carpenter is asked whom he honours and worships as his god, he will surely answer 'Vikramaditya'. The said Vikramaditya's style of architecture possesses a distinctive character of its own, and is not unpleasing to the eye, though it is infinitely inferior to the glories of the Roman workmanship.

While the party was at Ujjain, the Hindus carried to the pyre an old man who had died and whom they regarded as a god. The bier was gaily painted and gilded. The funeral procession took place at night, and was conducted with such exact observance that even tiny pieces of chaff and straw were removed from the path by which the bier was to be carried. Incense and sweet-smelling spices were placed in censers around the bier and there burnt. How extraordinary it is that the heathen should pay these honours to men whom they mistakenly regard as saintly, while wicked renegades from the Christian Faith refuse such honours to true saintliness!

Sarangpur was reached in two days from Ujjain. On the way a river was crossed flowing westward. This town is the seat and residence of the King's viceroy in that province. After three days' rest at Sarangpur; the river Paharbati was crossed and three days later the party passed through Pipaldar, which is situated on the tropic of Cancer.

Next [Sironj] was reached. This town suffers from a most unhealthy climate, as a consequence of which the cracks and dark corners of the houses are infested with all manner of poisonous vermin, which are found here in great quantities. At night also the beds are beset by scorpions whose sting brings on horrible agony. In the neighbouring marshes certain lizards are found (although indeed they are just as much at home in dry places as in marshes), whose bite is fatal. In bushes and thickets the many-coloured Regulus is found, which kills by the glance of its eye. The middle part of its body is red towards the head—a more brilliant red even than scarlet—but elsewhere it is orange-coloured, varying towards dark-brown. It attracts the eyes of all who see it by reason of the beauty of its colouring. However, the mercy of God has decreed that its nature shall be such that, if a man see it first, the Regulus—like the wolf, if one may believe the common tale—is compelled to retreat precipitately to some hiding-place, where it conceals itself. But if some unfortunate man who in ignorance of his danger is doing something else, is seen by the Regulus (which like other creatures of this class is very proud of its own beauty) some little time before he sees it, then he is bound to perish miserably, at least so the inhabitants of that region stoutly declare. One of the Fathers unwittingly ran a risk of perishing in this way; for seeing the little creature, and being attracted by its beauty, he tried to catch it and followed it till the Regulus hid itself in a thicket. When he returned to his quarters and asked the inhabitants of that place what sort of lizard it was that he had seen, they were no less surprised at his having escaped the glance of the Regulus than were the inhabitants of Malta at Saint Paul's remaining unharmed by the bite of the snake. This creature is roughly the size of a dormouse, and resembles the lizard called 'chamaeleon' which feeds on air and disguises itself with the colour of whatever object is nearest.

Many of the inferior classes in this town live in small round huts. Indeed nowhere else in that region are such miserable hovels to be seen. They live by agriculture, though the land which can be worked is scanty and poor. Their fields are everywhere surrounded by rocky hills, from which I suppose come the swarms of noxious beasts, and especially of scorpions.

Three days of difficult and even dangerous travelling brought the party from Sironj to [Narwar]; for after the town of [Sipri] is passed the country is uninhabited and mountainous, and many narrow defiles and streams are met with. This district is called after the neighbouring town; its savage inhabitants, knowing that they can commit robberies with impunity, are wont to attack travellers from ambush and to carry off their goods as plunder.

The town of Narwar is situated at the foot of a hill, the levelled top of which is occupied by a fort. Fierce storms and violent whirlwinds are so frequent there that not a house in the town would be able to retain its roof, had not God himself solved this difficult problem by supplying a natural abundance of marble slabs, which are used for roofing. Whilst the party was at this place, about the 15ᵗʰ day of the month of February the *Musalman* nine-days' [*Muharram*] festival began. At the same time the Hindus held their Idaean [Holi] festival. The former is held in honour of Asson and Hossen [Hasan and Hussein], grandsons of Muhammad by his daughter Fatima. Their father was Halis [Ali]. They are said to have been conquered by the Christians [sic] in a war which they had undertaken in order to establish and spread their grandfather's religious system. They were thereupon cruelly tortured by the unbelievers (as the *Musalmans* call us) and were compelled to walk with bare feet over hot coals. For this reason the *Musalmans* fast for nine days, only eating pulse; and on certain of these days some of them publicly recite the story of the sufferings of Asson and Hossen from a raised platform, and their words stir the whole assembly to lamentation and tears. On the last day of the festival funeral pyres are erected and burnt one after the other. The people jump over these, and afterwards scatter the glowing ashes with their feet. Meanwhile they shriek 'Asson Hossen' with wild and savage cries.

Nor is the Idaean festival of the Hindus less savage and degraded. For during a space of fifteen days they are at liberty freely to cast dust upon themselves and upon whoever passes by. They plaster with mud their own bodies and those of any persons they may meet. They also squirt a red dye out of hollow reeds. Having thus degraded themselves they come at length, on the fifteenth day, to the most abominable part of the whole festival. On this day they dedicate a tree, of a species somewhat similar to the palm, to that Mother of the Gods, who is called by many names (the ancient Romans knew her as Cybele and the Great Mother and 'Idaea'). Such superstition is indeed senseless and absurd. When the tree has been dedicated, they make offerings to it as though it were a god. At last, having vowed that they will dedicate another tree the following year, they build up huge piles of logs, as high as towers, in front of the houses, in places where three ways meet. When night comes they pace round these piles singing: and finally burn to ashes the consecrated (or rather most execrable) tree.

The party came to [Gwalior] in two days after leaving Narwar. This city is embellished by a very strong fortress on the top of a rocky hill, on which there is also a royal palace; the city itself stands at the foot of this hill. There is only one path up to the fortress, and that a rough and difficult one. In front of the gates is seen an immense statue of an elephant. In steep parts of the crag are underground temples and houses. The Fathers were astonished to see, carved in the wall of the vestibule of one temple, thirteen rude statues, of half length only; the middle one of these is (judging by the style and position) that of Christ: six are to the right and six to the of this, and appear to represent the Apostles. But it cannot definitely be proved whom the statues are intended to represent, since they lack the characteristic insignia of Christian sacred images. It is clear, however, that they were not placed there by *Musalmans*, as these show no reverence for such images, but ill-treat and break them. I am well aware of the fact that three hundred years ago this district was inhabited by Christians, who were, alas, defeated in various battles by the *Musalmans*, and so effectively crushed that all memory of Christianity has perished from the minds of men. The *Musalmans* might readily learn to expiate this sin (if only they were wise enough) from observing the fact that they are everywhere made fools of by the wiles, deceptions and lying tricks of worthless rascals. For a few years ago there lived in this very city a certain villain named Baba Capurius [Shaikh Kipur, d. 1571], a follower of Muhammad, who revived the fast disappearing habit of drinking intoxicating liquors, and discovered a certain new drink, made of poppy pods steeped in water. The damnable fellow believed that perfect happiness consists in the absence of all feeling and in insensibility towards the ills of the flesh and the troubles of the mind: though in reality one is more liable to be tortured by the incitements of the senses when in a state of semi-insensibility. He had noticed that his object could be effected by means of opium but that those who are addicted to this drug run an imminent risk of early death. So he devised his poppy-drink which is made in the following manner. The juice is first drained from the pods, which are split up for the purpose; these are then allowed to mature; then the seeds are removed, and the pods thrown into water, in which they are kept immersed until the liquid assumes the colour of wine. It is allowed to stand for a little longer, and is then passed off into another vessel through a strainer made of the finest linen. After impurities have been removed, the makers this drink themselves eagerly quaff it off in cupfuls. They eat no meat, onions, garlic or anything of that kind. They even abstain from fruit, and are particularly careful never to take any oil, which is fatal after opium or this drink. They eat only cooked pulse and any sweet food. Then they put their heads between their knees, and sleep as heavily as did Endymion.

One would have thought that Baba Kipur would have been heartily blamed for snoring his days away in this fashion, and for such disgraceful idleness. However he firmly believed that he would be honoured for his wonderful chastity, and held up to admiration rather than to blame. Nor was this hope ill-founded, as it proved, benighted though his mind truly was. For the nature of this drink is such that it numbs and freezes the impure desires of the flesh. Whence it has come about that this man has been so honoured for his sanctity as to be given a grand tomb and even a temple in this city. At least thirty of his followers are always on watch at this tomb, or rather are constantly asleep there, with no care for the morrow. This new leader of the Epicureans has countless admirers and followers, amongst whom are many princes and even the great king Zelaldinus [Jalal al-Din Akbar] himself. All these consider themselves to be honoured by the name Postinus, which is given to them from the drink, which is commonly known as post.

After leaving Gwalior the river [Chambal] was reached, which passes near [Dholpur]. This is the boundary between the province of Malwa and that of [Delhi], or rather of Indicum. The passage of the river has been excellently fortified both by nature and also by the careful labour of men. For in times gone by, before Malwa and Delhi were combined under one emperor, this river was the stoutest bulwark of Delhi, just as Gwalior was of Malwa. The nature of the place is such that cavalry can here achieve nothing worthy of warlike praise. For though the ground appears to those who look at it from a distance to be far-reaching, level and open, it is in reality so cut up and rugged, with such sudden defiles and deep gullies, that if anyone wanders from the path, he runs a grave risk either of only being able to return to it by a wide detour along rough and exceedingly narrow tracks, or of falling into the hands of the enemy or of brigands.

Dholpur will be the 'White City' in Latin. The Chambal is a large river and flows westwards towards the coast of Gujarat. It is equidistant (i.e., a two days' journey) from Agra, which is the capital of the empire, and from [Fatehpur] where the great King resides. The Fathers were conducted by the ambassador to the latter city.

In commenting on the journey that was thus brought to a conclusion, one may notice in the first place that the country from the coast northward rises, as it were, in a series of terraces, such as are seen in gardens placed on a slope. The mountain-ranges represent the walls of these terraces. Secondly it should be observed that the religious zeal of the *Musalmans* has destroyed all the idol temples, which used to be very numerous. But the carelessness of these same *Musalmans* has on the other hand allowed sacrifices to be publicly performed, incense to be offered, and perfumes to be poured out, the ground to be sprinkled with flowers, and wreaths to be hung up, wherever—either amongst the ruins of these old temples or elsewhere—any fragment of an idol is to be found. Thirdly, in place of the Hindu temples, countless tombs and little shrines of wicked and worthless *Musalmans* have been erected, in which these men are worshipped with vain superstition, as though they were saints. This moved the Fathers to deep pity, not unaccompanied by tears and heart-felt grief. For who would not deeply pity these who—to the destruction of their souls—give reverence to vices instead of virtues, to crimes instead of miracles, to abandoned wretches instead of holy saints?

When the Fathers perceived from afar the city of Fatehpur, they gave hearty thanks to the Eternal God who had brought them safe to their destination. They then began to gaze with the keenest delight upon the great size and magnificent appearance of the city. On entering the city they became the cynosure of all eyes on account of their strange attire. Everyone stopped and stared in great surprise and perplexity, wondering who these strange-looking, unarmed men might be, with their long black robes, their curious caps, their shaven faces, and their tonsured heads.

At length they were taken before the King, who having looked at them from his high dais, ordered them to come nearer to him, and asked them a few questions. Thereupon they presented to him an Atlas, which the Archbishop of Goa had sent as a present. This he graciously received. He was greatly pleased to see them, but was not too warm in his greeting, and shortly afterwards withdrew, partly in order to hide his true feelings and partly to preserve his dignity. Having retired for a short time into an inner apartment, he ordered them to be conducted to him there (i.e., to the hall which is known as [Kapur Talao, 'Peerless Pool']), in order that he might exhibit them to his wives. Then he took them to another courtyard called the *Dulatqhana*, where he seized the opportunity presented by a sudden rain-storm and put on Portuguese dress—a scarlet cloak with golden fastenings. He ordered his sons also to don the same dress, together with Portuguese hats. This he did in order to please his guests. He also ordered 800 pieces of gold to be presented to them; but the Fathers replied that they had not come there to get money. Nothing that he could say would persuade them to accept the present, whereupon he expressed admiration at their self-control, and ordering the money to be distributed to certain attendants of [Fr. Pietro] Tavarius, who had remained behind, he retired to the inner part of the palace.

The Fathers were delighted at the King's kindly reception and were conducted rejoicing to their quarters. For they were persuaded that these signs foretold the speedy conversion of the king to the true religion and the worship of Christ...

Fatehpur (that is the 'city of victory') had been recently built by the King on his return to his seat of government alter the successful termination of his Gujarat war. It is placed on a spur of the mountain range which in former times was called, I believe, Vindhya, and which stretches westwards for a hundred miles towards [Ajmer]. The site is rocky and not very beautiful, near to an old town which for this reason is called Purana Siquiris, (for Purana means 'old' in the vernacular, and [Sikri] is the name of the place). In the past nine years the city has been marvellously extended and beautified, at the expense both of the royal treasury and of the great nobles and courtiers, who eagerly follow the King's example and wishes.

The most noteworthy features of Fatehpur are, firstly, the King's audience chamber, which is of huge size and very beautiful in appearance, overlooking the whole city; secondly, a great building supported on arches, around which is a very spacious courtyard; thirdly, the Circus where elephants fight, gladiatorial displays take place, and a game is played, on horseback, with a wooden ball which is hit by hammers also of wood; fourthly, the baths; fifthly, the *bazaar*, which is more than half a mile long, and is filled with an astonishing quantity of every description of merchandise, and with countless people, who are always standing there in dense crowds.

To supply the city with water a tank has been carefully and laboriously constructed, two miles long and half a mile wide. The work was performed, by the King's directions, in the following manner. Across the end of a low-lying valley which was filled with water in the rains, (although the water afterwards drained away or dried up), a great dam was slowly built. By this means not only was a copious supply of water assured, but the discomfort of the climate was mitigated. For when the sun gets low in the sky, the heat, which in Fatehpur is very great, is tempered by a cool and pleasant breeze blowing over the tank. Besides this the King descends to the lake on holidays, and refreshes himself with its many beauties.

Passing over the other remarkable features of Fatehpur, I must mention that the citadel is two miles in circumference and embellished with towers at very frequent intervals, though it has only four gates. The Agra gate is to the east, the Ajmer to the west, that of the Circus to the north, and that of Delhi to the south. The most striking of these is the Circus gate, through which the King frequently descends to the Circus. For there stand in front of this gateway, which they seem to guard, two statues of elephants, with uplifted trunks, and of life-size. These statues are so majestic and so true to life, that one might judge them to be the work of Phidias. Close to the Circus rises a pyramid from which are measured the distances for the mile-stones (or rather half-mile-stones, for such they are), which have been placed after the Roman manner along the roads eastwards to Agra and westwards to Ajmer.

While Jalal al-Din was residing at Agra, he decided to remove his court to Sikri in accordance with the advice of a certain philosopher (member of a class professing both wisdom and piety [Shaykh Salim Chishti, d. 1571]) who was then living in a small hut on this hill.

Agra is a magnificent city, both for its size and for its antiquity. It stands on the river [Jumna]. In it Jalal al-Din the Great was born [sic] and brought up, and first proclaimed king upon the terrible death of his father. For while his father, whose name was Emaumus [Humayun] was walking upon the roof of his hall at Delhi leaning upon a stick, he came too near the edge; his stick slipped, and he was precipitated into the garden below. This sudden and terrible fall proved fatal. He was devoted to literary studies, and was a great patron of the learned, but was not keen and active in war. Jalal al-Din on the contrary, who is uneducated, has become famous for his war-like skill and courage. Hence Jalal al-Din on being acclaimed King changed the seat of government from Delhi, where it had been established since the time of the Christian kings, to Agra, where he himself had been born; and built there a palace and citadel which are in themselves as big as a great city; for he included in the confines of the citadel the mansions of his nobles, the magazines, the treasury, the arsenal, the stable of the cavalry, and the shops and huts of drug-sellers, barbers, and all manner of common workmen. The stones of these buildings are so cunningly fitted that the joints are scarcely visible, although no lime was used to fix them together. The beautiful colour of the stone, which is all red, also produces the same effect of uniform solidity. In front of the gateway are statues of two petty kings, whom Jalal al-Din himself shot with his own musket; these are seated on life-size statues of elephants on which the kings used to ride when alive. These statues serve both as trophies of the King's prowess, and as monuments of his military victories.

If all had happened as he wished, Agra would indeed have formed a fitting memorial of the King's wisdom. For it has the advantage over almost all other cities of that region in respect of its mild climate, of its fertile soil, of its great river, of its beautiful gardens, of its fame spread to the end of earth, and of its large size. For it is four miles long and two broad. All the necessaries and conveniences of human life can be obtained here, if desired. This is even true of articles which have to be imported from distant corners of Europe...

The army began to advance [against Mirza Muhammad Hakim, in Kabul] on February 8th, 1581. The next day the King devoted to hunting, as was his wont. Orders are always given that no one is to approach the line of march. The object of this is both to avoid crowds, to lessen the risk of treachery, and to prevent wild beasts being frightened away. These beasts are the same as those of Europe, with the exception of the blue cow, which is very similar to the red-deer, except as regards its size and the shape of its head. Jalal al-Din spends enormous sums on keeping countless hunting panthers; for hounds such as those of the Gallic and Alan breeds are unknown in this country. These panthers are drawn by horses, under the care of keepers, to the place where the game is feeding. They are blindfolded so that they may not attack anyone on the way. When they are freed, they dash ravenously upon the quarry; for they are kept in a state of starvation. The *Mongols* are not very fond of hawking. It is regarded however, as a mark of royal dignity for the King to be accompanied on the march by fowlers carrying many birds on their wrists. These birds are fed on crows to save expense.

The distance of each day's march is measured with a ten-foot rod by special officers, who are instructed to follow the King closely and to measure the distance from the moment he leaves his pavilion. These measurements are afterwards found very useful in computing the area of provinces and the distances of places apart, for purposes of sending envoys and royal edicts, and in emergencies. Two hundred lengths of the ten-foot rod make what is called in Persian a 'Coroo,' but in the Indian tongue a '*Kos*'. This is equal to two miles, and is the usual measure of distance.

After spending two days in camp near Fatehpur, the King judged his army to be sufficiently well-equipped to advance with safety and dignity. The signal for advance was accordingly given...

Four days after leaving Fatehpur, [Mathura] was reached, a city dating from the first appearance in these regions of the superstitious religion of the Brahman. The city is believed to have been founded by Crustnu [Krishna] who is also called Viznu [Vishnu]; at any rate there is no doubt that he was born in a small town near Mathura. Temples dedicated to Vishnu are to be found in many places in the neighbourhood, built in spots where the silly old-wives-fables (of the Hindus) declare that he performed some action. These fanes (or rather 'profanes') are elegantly built in the pyramidical style of India. Their doors face east, and the rising sun bathes the face of the idol with his light.

The Hindus throughout India worship Krishna as a god. They say that he was the son of Parabrama whom they call Paramaessuris [Parameshwar], that is 'immortal God' and that he had two brothers, Maessuris [Maheshwar] and Brama, and a sister Sethis, who was born from the forehead of Parameshwar without a mother, and married Maheshwar, just as Juno married Jupiter. For the Evil One, in order to avoid inconsistency, implanted in the minds of the men of ancient India the same ideas about the birth of the gods as he implanted in the minds of our own foolish ancestors. For the ancients used to say that Saturn was the father of Jupiter, Neptune, and Orcus, and that Minerva was born from his head. There is this difference, however, viz, that European poets used to give these names to the sky, to the elements and to things connected with the elements; whilst the Indians say that these are merely the ideas of vulgar people, and are due to faulty comprehension (just as the Athenians thought that the Resurrection was some new goddess, and that Saint Paul was preaching new gods of this kind; or as the Manichaeans declared that the gods were in reality the five elements mixing together by their own action; for they held that these elements were distilled one from the other, succeeding each other like the links of a chain; whence they were compelled to acknowledge that one was born from another; and this shows the folly of their notion that the elements are combined and united, as it were, in the bond of matrimony).

To pass on from Krishna's parentage and the stories about his brothers— the religious preceptors of the Indians and of the Brahman say that he was born nine times, first in the form of a sea-monster, in order that he might free his brother Brama from a sea-snail which was slaying him; secondly in the form of a tortoise, that he might support the world, which was being over-balanced by the weight of two giants; thirdly, in the form of a filthy hog, that he might purify the defiled world; fourthly in the form of a lion below his middle, and of a man above, that he might slay a giant by whom the world was being cruelly oppressed; fifthly in the form of a dwarf, who asked for alms as a beggar; sixthly in the form of a mighty warrior, who flew away to heaven as soon as he appeared on earth; seventhly he lay concealed in the belly of a shepherd who used to sell milk, and on being delivered from his belly he sold glass bangles and rings in order that he might secretly and wickedly assassinate his uncle, which he did; eighthly he became a king and reigned for 4673 years: ninthly he was born as a peasant, and slew unbelievers with the sword. He was a restless and unruly boy, a petty thief and a liar. He lived with a shepherd, and stole milk, ghi and cheese. He denied the theft when accused of it; and stole the clothes of some girls who were bathing in a river. He broke the pots and furniture of the neighbours, and let their calves out of the pens so that they might run away, thus giving trouble to the herdsmen. Beginning thus with childish mischief, he went on to steal eight wives from their husbands by force, and sixteen thousand by fraud and guile, as soon as he attained manhood (if indeed he be worthy of the name of man). The temples I have referred to preserve the memory of these wonderful deeds, lest they should be forgotten. Such is the shamelessness of the Brahmans, and the folly of the common people of India. How true was the saying of Cicero—the father of eloquence—'what land is more savage than India: what land more barbarous?' True indeed for the tales that old women tell over the fire in winter are more credible than such fables.

Since Vishnu is the most famous of the Indian false gods, it follows that Mathura has for long been the fountain-head of superstitions in India, just as Rome was in Europe. It used to be a great and well populated city, with splendid buildings and a great circuit of walls. The ruins plainly indicate how imposing its buildings were. For out of these forgotten ruins are dug up columns and very ancient statues, of skilful and cunning workmanship. Only one Hindu temple is left out of many, for the *Musalmans* have completely destroyed all except the pyramids. Huge crowds of pilgrims come from all over India to this temple, which is situated on the high bank of the Jumna. The Brahman do not allow these pilgrims to enter the temple till they have been to the river-side and shaved off their hair and beards in the case of men and their hair and eye-brows in the case of women; then they must dip themselves several times into the river, that the water may wash away their sins: for the Brahman promise forgiveness of all sins to those who have bathed in this water. It is an extraordinary sight; for there are more than three hundred barbers, who very swiftly shave a huge multitude both of men and women standing up to their waists in the river, on steps which have been built there. The sexes are mixed together; but all is done with perfect modesty. For the cunning of the Evil One is such that he has put a false idea of religion into their minds: so that they regard it as a heinous offence to do anything foul or immodest in such a sacred place (as they regard it). They may not even think for a moment of any evil action whilst they are engaged in these impious ceremonies. Moreover, once they have bathed, they take the greatest care for the rest of their lives to avoid what they regard as sins. Surely it is greatly to be desired that real sins should be avoided with equal zeal and care by those who have been trained not in a false but in the true religion, and have gained true pardon by a genuinely pious ceremony—the Sacrament of repentance.

About six miles from Mathura is a shrine of Anumantus [Hanuman], near to which three hundred or more monkeys are kept in a grove, at the public expense. These monkeys, on the ringing of a bell, take up arms and, dividing into two companies, fight like gladiators, ceasing again and laying down their arms at the sound of the same bell. At the same signal they come to lunch or dine, and return to their grove after their meal, greatly to the wonder of the poor folk, who imagine this to be achieved by a divine miracle; for they are miserably deceived by the Brahman, so that in their folly they not only believe in but are entranced by such tricks. For the monkeys are carefully and laboriously trained to perform these actions, following the example of the older monkeys who have already been trained. But the Brahman declare that the monkeys do all this of their own accord, paying honour and worship to their patron Hanuman.

The following is the story of this Hanuman. He is said to have been the brother of Maheshwar, Krishna, and Brama, and the son of Parameshwar, who had visited his mother by means of the wind, when she was praying alone on a mountain. She afterwards gave birth to Hanuman in the form of a monkey. When he asked his mother who his father had been, they say she replied 'The wind'. But the wind was unwilling that such a miracle should remain unknown: or perhaps was afraid that it would be compelled to support the child. It was also continually busy with causing storms and sending rain, and had no settled abiding place, except when it was shut up in the cave of Aeolus. Hence it was afraid that the child would be in danger, or else it was displeased by his monkey form. At any rate it suddenly declared that Maheshwar and not itself was the father of the monkey. Maheshwar then caused it to be proclaimed to all mankind that no evil spirit should enter the house of or do any harm to him or the sons of him who should worship that monkey. They say that monkeys dart from tree to tree because Hanuman was begotten by the help of the wind; and there is also a story that this Hanuman gave assistance to the gods when they were warring against the giants. Even Jalal al-Din has a credulous belief in these fables. For, by the advice of a certain sorcerer, he inscribed the name of Hanuman amongst the titles of God.

These tales which I have been writing down are indeed unworthy of the ears of wise and pious and clean-minded men. But I have recorded them in order that my readers may feel pity for the ignorance of these poor people, and pray to God that His light may illumine their minds. I purposely pass over the stories about Ganessus [Ganesh], who is called the door-keeper of the gods, has an elephant's face and trunk, and a protruding belly, and is said to have been born from the sweat of a goddess (if such expressions may be allowed). I also pass over Madaeus [Mahadev], and the huge hodgepodge of other deities who are worshipped by these miserable people, and whose statues and idols are placed in their temples. I return to my main subject.

Delhi…is a very great and very rich city, built near the Jumna, and has been the capital of India from the time of the Christian kings. After their fall it was the seat of the *Pathan* kings. Humayun, the father of Jalal al-Din, was very fond of it, residing here during his lifetime and meeting here his tragic death. He is buried in a tomb built by his son Jalal al-Din. This tomb is of great size, and is surrounded by beautiful gardens. One of his wives, the mother of Mirsachimus [Mirza Hakim], king of [Kabul], who was then fighting against Jalal al-Din, had loved Humayun so faithfully that she had had a small house built close by the tomb and had watched there till the day of her death. Throughout her widowhood she devoted herself to prayer and to alms-giving. Indeed she maintained five hundred poor people by her alms. Had she only been a Christian, hers would have been the life of a heroine. For, as some writer has wisely said, the *Musalmans* are the apes of the Christians. In many ways they imitate the piety of the Christians, though without gaining the reward of that piety; for they have wandered away from the true faith and the true charity.

Delhi is noteworthy for its public buildings, its remarkable fort (built by Humayun), its walls, and a number of mosques, especially the one said to have been built by king Peruzius [Firoz Shah Tughluq, r. 1351-88]. This mosque is constructed of wonderfully polished white marble, the exterior is covered with brilliant whitewash, made by mixing lime with milk, instead of water. It shines like a mirror; for this mixture of lime and milk is not only of such remarkable consistency that no cracks appear in it anywhere, but also when polished it shines most magnificently. Firoz, who was by race a *Pathan*, was much devoted to piety; for he gave orders that throughout his dominions, at intervals of every two miles, resting-places should be built, in which a shady tree should be planted, a well dug whence man and beast might get water, and a mosque built, where travellers might pray. He also planted trees in a long avenue on both sides of the roads, wherever there was room, in order that tired wayfarers might find shelter. He built bridges over torrents, rivers and ditches. He reduced the gradients on the roads, and paved them in soft and marshy places. In short he omitted nothing which might contribute to the public convenience and to his own magnificence. In a valley three miles from Delhi he built a wonderfully beautiful and very costly palace. On the terrace in front of it he set a solid marble column all in one piece, thirty feet high and about five feet thick. He also had a subterranean passage made to Old Delhi, where the Christian Kings are believed to have lived, (a distance of nearly forty *stadia*) in order that he might withdraw unattended from the Court and from state business, as often as he had leisure, and refresh himself in the solitude of his country-seat there. Many stories are told of his kindly actions, which—if they are true—would have exalted him to heaven, if only he had been a Christian.

Delhi is inhabited by substantial and wealthy Brahman, and of course by a *Mongol* garrison. Hence its many fine private mansions add considerably to the magnificence of the city. For the neighbourhood is rich in stone and lime, and the rich men construct for themselves well-built, lofty and handsomely decorated residences. Thanks to Humayun, who was devoted to architecture and loved fine buildings and broad roads, the streets of the city are more imposing and impressive than in other *Musalman* towns. They are planted down the middle with beautiful green trees which cast a grateful shade. Time fails me to describe the lovely parks and the many residential districts on both sides of the Jumna, which passes close by the city on the east. The parks and gardens are filled with a rich profusion of fruit and flowers; for the climate is mild, and the land around Delhi is very rich and fertile. The ruined towers and half-fallen walls of old Delhi may still be seen. They show it to have been a populous city. It is situated at a distance of about thirty-two *stades* from the new city, to the westward.

Two days later Sonepat was reached—a small town, but more famous than many a city on account of the swords, scimitars, daggers, poniards, and steel points for spears, pikes and javelins, which are skilfully manufactured here and exported to all parts of the empire. For there is in that region great store of iron and steel, the ore for which is mined in the neighbouring spurs of the Himalayas, and very many manufacturers of this kind of weapon live here…

The camp was next moved to Panipat, where the inhabitants, especially the women, filled the balconies and the roofs in their eagerness to see the King. Leaving Panipat and passing by the town of [Karnal], we came to a tributary of the Jumna. The infantry crossed this by a stone bridge, without any of the crowding or tumult which sometimes occurs in narrow places. The elephants, camels and cavalry, in accordance with the orders which had been given to them, crossed by a ford. Three days later [Thanesar] was reached—a town of Brahman and merchants…

About this time the army was compelled to halt for some time owing to a violent tempest, which rendered the roads impassable by reason of mud and sudden torrents. As soon as the weather cleared, the advance was resumed; and to the east the snow-covered Himalaya mountains were seen gleaming white. The inhabitants of that region call this range [Kumaun]. From the mountains blew a cold wind. The Hindus who inhabit Kumaun do not owe allegiance to Jalal al-Din, and are protected by exceedingly thick forests. The source of the Jumna is said by the inhabitants to be situated in this district on the side of the mountains which looks westward towards the district of Delhi. The source of the Ganges is however on the opposite, i.e., eastward, slope of the mountains. To adopt the language of geographers, it is in the same latitude (as the source of the Jumna) but is 280 1/2 miles eastward in longitude.

Next, Ambala was reached…[Sirhind] is two days' journey distant from Ambala. Camp was pitched in the eastern outskirts of the city, which is said to owe its name to the following circumstance. It is recounted that in this place a certain king fought with and vanquished a lion. The town is also called Sirhind, because it is situated on the frontier of the provinces of India and of Lahore. For Sarahat means frontier; and thus the name of the city signifies the frontier of India. The city is of great size and is divided into separate quarters, in which respect it resembles Memphis in Egypt, which is commonly called Cairo. At Sirhind is a very famous school of medicine, from which doctors are sent out all over the empire. Bows, quivers, shoes, greaves and made here and exported by traders to the empire. Sirhind is situated in a very broad plain, beautified by many groves of trees and pleasant gardens. This plain is dry; but the inhabitants have met the difficulty of lack of water of water by making a deep artificial lake on the southern side of the city. Care is taken to fill this lake during the rainy season by means of irrigation channels. In the middle of the lake stands a tower, which is open to the public for their enjoyment. From this tower there is a pleasant prospect over the lake and the surrounding parks and gardens. Setting out from Sirhind the army encamped at Pael, where the King was informed that Mirza Hakim had fled. The King was so pleased by this good news that he ordered it to be told to the priest who was in camp. On the following day the priest congratulated the King with the greatest delight and the King showed that he was pleased with the congratulations. Up till then the King had seemed to be constantly frowning with deep anxiety; but after receiving this good news his cheerful expression showed that he had laid aside all his care. Moreover he went on several pleasure excursions in his two-horse chariot.

Passing by Machiwara, that is, 'the village of fishes' the army encamped on the bank of the [Sutlej], which was called by the ancients the Zaradrus. A halt was necessary while a wooden bridge was being built... The King next ordered the army to be led towards the Himalayas, from which the Zaradrus flows towards the west, joining the Indus. This river contains crocodiles, or water-lizards, of the girth of a barrel. They are called 'cissares', that is 'three-headed'. They have six feet, on which they crawl; and they swallow men unawares from below when they are swimming in the water. They seize by the foot, and drag down under the water, oxen and buffaloes and sheep and other animals whilst drinking at the side of the river. The ignorant people call this same river 'Machivara' from the neighbouring village, or 'Ludhiana' from the town of Ludhiana. The latter place is about 26 miles downstream from Machivara along the direct road to Basilipolis (by which flows a stream whose water is a deadly poison), Govindivicus and Lahore. However, the army left this road on the left-hand; and after reaching the Zaradrus at Machivara followed the river up towards the mountains. Here the camp was pitched in a rough and very cold country.

On the fifth day after leaving the Zaradrus a certain stronghold of the *Pathan* was reached, which is called Dungarii, that is 'two hours'. Here the King ordered fifty pieces of gold, to be given to the Priest, in order that he might distribute them to the Christians. This was to signify the joy of Jalal al-Din at having on the previous day received express despatches from Mirza Hakim, in which he besought pardon for his treachery, prayed that the horrors of war might be averted, and begged that the King who enriched others with the grant of provinces would allow himself to remain in possession of his kingdom. He seemed, however, not so much to pray for forgiveness as to demand a gift; and therefore Jalal al-Din continued the advance. Fording a small river, the army marched for two days along the Bibasis, which is now called the Beas, searching for a ford which the elephants could cross and for a narrow place in the river, where a wooden bridge could be erected. When the scouts found a suitable place for their purposes, the camp was pitched there.

The King hastened with a few chosen cavalry to [Nagarkot] in order to help a certain petty king, who had been driven out by his son and had begged for assistance. When the usurper heard of the arrival of Jalal al-Din he hid himself, with his band of soldiers, in a fastness situated amongst precipitous and inaccessible mountains, and hence the King had to return to camp without fulfilling his errand. This district produces in abundance those fruits and crops which are characteristic of Spain and Italy, but which are not found elsewhere in India.

On the next day the army crossed the Bibasis by a wooden bridge, and advanced nearly ten miles… The next day's march brought the army to [Kalanaur]. Near this town Jalal al-Din had routed the *Pathan*, vanquished Beyramcanus [Bairam Khan], and been hailed king of Lahore. He had received the sceptre and other marks of royalty in a very large and beautiful park, which is near the city. In this park the former kings of Lahore had been wont to receive their title in the same way. Kalanaur stands on a small river which flows into the Bibasis. It is the stream which Strabo, as has been noted above, calls the Hypanis; and on its further bank he says that Alexander the Great stopped his march, not daring to advance beyond this point. The Roman authors say that Kalanaur is a large city: and indeed the ruins and fallen walls show clearly that it once was so; but in our time it seems absurd to call this paltry place Kalanaur…

[*After marching to Kabul and routing his rebellious half-brother, Akbar led his army back to Lahore.*]

I must now give some account of Lahore. This city is second to none, either in Asia or in Europe, with regard to size, population, and wealth. It is crowded with merchants, who foregather there from all over Asia. In all these respects it excels other cities, as also in the huge quantity of every kind of merchandise which is imported. Moreover there is no art or craft useful to human life which is not practised there. The population is so large that men jostle each other in the streets. The citadel alone, which is built of brickwork laid in cement, has a circumference of nearly three miles. Within this citadel is a *bazaar* which is protected against the sun in summer and the rain in winter by a high-pitched, wooden roof—a design whose clever execution and practical utility should call for imitation. Perfumes are sold in this *bazaar* and the scent in the early morning is most delicious. The remainder of the city (outside the citadel) is widely spread. Its buildings are of brick. Most of the citizens are wealthy Brahman and Hindus of every caste, especially [Kashmiris]. These Kashmiris are bakers, eating-house-keepers, and sellers of second-hand rubbish, a type of trade which well suits their Jewish descent...

At Lahore the King dismissed almost all his forces into winter quarters, and proceeded by a rapid march to Fatehpur, attended by only the guard, which he is accustomed to employ, for the sake of dignity, in the capital city. He was welcomed there by his mother with the greatest joy; and, as is the custom, public games were held in honour of his arrival.

Soon thereafter, Monserrate left Akbar's court for Goa in the company of Sayyid Muzaffar, ambassador-designate to King Philip II of Spain (the ambassador was to reach no further than the Deccan). Monserrate himself, after partly writing up his notes, was sent by his superiors to Abyssinia in 1588, where he was captured and imprisoned by a local ruler. Ransomed by the Portuguese in 1596, he returned to Goa where he died in 1600. His Latin text never reached Europe but was rediscovered in Calcutta by Reverend W. K. Firminger. Father H. Hosten, S. J,. edited and published it in *Memoirs of the Asiatic Society of Bengal,* vol. 3 (1914), pp. 513-704. It was then translated into English by John S. Hoyland and annotated by S. N. Banerjee as *The Commentary of Father Monserrate, S. J., on His Journey to the Court of Akbar* (London: Oxford University Press, 1922), from which this selection comes.

Chapter Four

William Hawkins

In 1608, after a sixteen-month sea voyage, the youthful but widely travelled English merchant, ambassador and explorer William Hawkins (c.1585-1613), reached Surat in Gujarat on the first East India Company fleet to India. King James I (r. England 1603-25) had delegated Hawkins to negotiate with Emperor Jahangir (r.1605-27) for trade concessions and a permanent English base ('factory') for its merchants ('factors'). To impress the Emperor, the Company instructed Hawkins to wear a violet and scarlet outfit with a taffeta-lined and silver lace-trimmed cloak and to present many 'toys' (curiosities and preciosities). Hawkins knew Turkish which enabled him to communicate directly with Mughal officials and the Emperor. He also regarded his embassy as an opportunity to profit personally from trade in Indian goods.

From the moment of Hawkins' arrival, the rival Portuguese resented and attempted to frustrate his mission. Hawkins recounted to his East India Company employers in his report (which is the basis of this selection) how the local Portuguese commander told Mughal officials that King James was 'King of Fishermen, and of an Island of no import[ance]'. To this Hawkins retorted that the Portuguese captain was 'a base villaine, and a traytor to his King', challenging him to a duel to the death. As part of their own internecine factional struggles, various Mughal officials maneuvered to thwart Hawkins' efforts in India, while their opponents openly or secretly supported him.

Hawkins recorded his dangerous journey from Surat to the imperial court at Agra and the rich life and honours he enjoyed there, as well as his triumphs over his political enemies. Jahangir appointed him a high official and empowered him to maintain 400 cavalrymen in the Emperor's service, with a promised grand annual salary of £3,200 (equivalent to £366,600 today)—although only some £300 was ever paid to him by the Mughal bureaucracy. Hawkins also revealed how he came to marry Mariam, a fatherless ward of the Mughal imperial family. He further described treacherous Jesuit, Portuguese royal and Mughal factional plots that ultimately drove him and his wife to flee India after four years there.

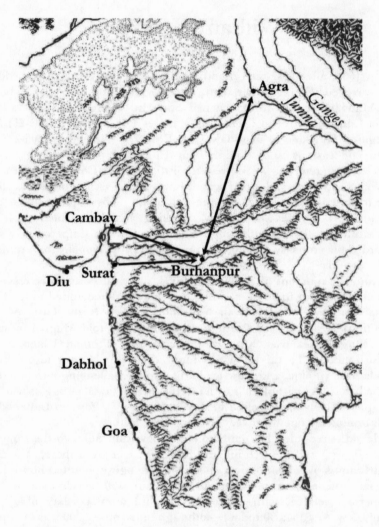

William Hawkins' travels by land in west and north India, 1608-13

~

[After seizing some of Hawkins' merchandise and men and threatening his life, but failing to persuade the Mughal Governor of Surat to deport Hawkins, Portuguese Jesuit Father Peniero felt] that it was not good to let me passe, for that I would complaine of him unto the King [Jahangir]. Thus he plotted with Mocreb-chan [Mukarrab Khan] to overthrow my journey, which he could not doe because I came from a king; but he said that he would not let me have any [escort] force to goe with me. And what else he would have him to doe, either with my truchman and coachman, to poyson or murther me, if one should faile, the other to doe it. This invention was put into Mukarrab Khan's head by the Father, but God for His mercie sake afterward discovered these plots, and the counsell of this Jesuite tooke not place. Before the plotting of this, the Jesuite and I fell out in the presence of Mukarrab Khan for vile speaches made by him of our king and nation to be vassals unto the King of Portugal; which words I could not brooke, in so much that, if I could have had my will, the Father had never spoken more, but I was prevented.

Now finding [Hawkins' assistant] William Finch in good health, newly recovered, I left all things touching the trade of merchandizing in his power, giving him my remembrance and order what he should doe in my absence. So I began to take up souldiers to conduct me, being denyed of Mukarrab Khan, besides shot and bow-men that I hired. For my better safety I went to one his captaines to let me have fortie or fiftie horsemen to conduct me to Chan-channa [Khan-i Khanan, Abdur Rahim], being then Vice-roy of *Deccan*, resident in [Burhanpur], who did to his power all that I demanded, giving me valiant horsemen, *Pathans*, a people very much feared in these parts; for if I had not done it, I had beene over-throwne. For the Portugals of Daman had wrought with an ancient friend of theirs, a Raja, who was absolute lord of a province (betweene Daman, Guzerat and *Deccan*) called Cruly, to be readie with two hundred horsemen to stay my passage; but I went so strong and well provided, that they durst not incounter with us; so likewise that time I escaped.

Then at [Dhaita], another province or princedome, my coachman being drunke with certaine of his kindred, discovered the treason that he was to worke against me, which was that he was hired to murther me; he being overheard by some of my souldiers, who at that present came and told me and how it should be done in the morning following, when we begin our travell (for we use to travell two houres before day); upon which notice I called the coachman unto me, examining him and his friends before the captaine of the horsemen I had with me; who could not deny; but he would never confesse who hired him, although he was very much beaten, cursing his fortune that he could not effect it, for he was to doe it the next morning. So I sent him prisoner unto the Governour of Surat. But afterward by my broker or truchman I understood that both he and the coachman were hired by Mukarrab Khan, but by the Fathers perswasion, the one to poyson me, and the other to murther me; but the truchman received nothing till he had done the deed, which he never meant to doe, for in that kind he was alwayes true unto me; thus God preserved me. This was five dayes after my departure from Surat, and my departure from Surat was the first of February, 1608 [sic, 1609]. So following on my travels for Burhanpur, some two dayes beyond Dhaita the *Pathans* left me, but to be conducted by another *Pathan* captaine, governour of that lordship, by whom I was most kindly entertained. His name was Sherchan [Sher Khan]. Beeing sometime a prisoner unto the Portugal and having the Portugal language perfect, he was glad to doe me any service, for that I was of the nation that was enemie unto the Portugal. Himself in person, with fortie horsemen, went two dayes journey with me till he had freed me from the dangerous places; at which time he met with a troupe of out-lawes and tooke some foure alive and slew and hurt eight; the rest escaped. This man very kindly writ his letter for me to have his house at Burhanpur, which was a great curtesie; otherwise I could not tell where to lodge myself, the towne being so full of souldiers, for then began the warres with the *Deccans*.

The eighteenth of the said moneth, thankes be to God, I came in safetie to Burhanpur, and the next day I went to the court to visit Khan-i Khanan, being then Lord Generall and Vice-roy of *Deccan*, giving him a present, who kindly tooke it; and after three houres conference with him, he made me a great feast, and being risen from the table, invested me with two clokes, one of fine woollen, and another of cloth of gold, giving me his most kind letter of favour to the King, which avayled much. That done, he imbraced me, and so we departed. The language that we spoke was Turkish, which he spake very well. I remayned in Burhanpur unto the second of March; till then I could not end my businesses of monies that I brought by exchange, staying likewise for a caravan. Having taken new souldiers, I followed my voyage or journey to Agra, where after much labour, toyle, and many dangers I arrived in safety the sixteenth of Aprill, 1609.

Being in the citie, and seeking out for an house in a very secret manner, notice was given the King that I was come, but not to be found. He presently charged both horsemen and footmen in many troupes not to leave before I was found, commanding his Knight Marshall to accompany me with great state to the court, as an embassador of a king ought to be; which he did with a great traine, making such extraordinary haste that I admired much, for I could scarce obtayne time to apparell myself in my best attyre. In fine, I was brought before the King. I came with a slight present, having nothing but cloth, and that not I esteemed; for what I had for the King, Mukarrab Khan tooke from me, wherewith I acquainted His Majestie. After salutation done, with a most kinde and smiling countenance he bade me most heartily welcome; upon which speech I did my obeysance and dutie againe. Having His Majestie's letter in my hand, he called me to come neere unto him, stretching downe his hand from the seate royall, where he sate in great majestie something high for to be seene of the people; receiving very kindly the letter of me. Viewing the letter a prettie while, both the seale and the manner of the making of it up, he called for an old Jesuite that was there present to read it. In the meane space, while the Jesuite was reading it, he spake unto me in the kindest manner that could be, demanding of me the contents of the letter, which I told him; upon which notice presently granting and promising me by God that all what the King had there written he would grant and allow with all his heart, and more if His Majestie would require it. The Jesuite likewise told him the effect of the letter, but discommending the stile, saying it was basely penned, writing Vestra without Majestad. My answere was unto the King: and if it shall please Your Majestie, these people are our enemies; how can this letter be ill written, when my king demandeth favour of Your Majestie? He said it was true.

Perceiving I had the Turkish tongue, which himself well understood, he commanded me to follow him unto his chamber of presence, being then risen from that place of open audience, desiring, to have further conference with me; in which place I stayed some two houres, till the King came forth from his women. Then calling me unto him, the first thing that he spake was that he understood that Mukarrab Khan had not dealt well with me; bidding me be of good cheere, for he would remedie all. It should seeme that Mukarrab Khan's enemies had acquainted the King with all his proceedings, for indeed the King hath spies upon every nobleman. I answered most humbly that I was certaine all matters would goe well on my side so long as His Majestie protected me; upon which speech he presently sent away a post for Surat, with his command to Mukarrab Khan, writing unto him very earnestly in our behalfes, conjuring him to be none of his friend if he did not deale well with the English in that kind as their desire was. This being dispatched and sent, by the same messenger I sent my letter to William Finch, wishing him to goe with this command to Mukarrab Khan; at the receit of which he wondred that I came safe to Agra and was not murthered or poysoned by the way, of which speech William Finch advertised me afterward.

It grew late, and having had some small conference with the King at that time, he commanded that I should daily be brought into his presence, and gave a captaine named Hous-haber-chan [Khush Khabar Khan] charge that I should lodge at his house till a house were found convenient for me, and when I needed anything of the King, that he should be my solicitor. According to command I resorted to the court, where I had daily conference with the King. Both night and day his delight was very much to talke with me, both of the affaires of England and other countries, as also many demands of the West Indies, whereof he had notice long before, being in doubt if there were any such place till he had spoken with me, who had beene in the countrey.

Many dayes and weekes being past and I now in great favour with the King, to the griefe of all mine enemies, espying my time, I demanded for his commandment or commission with capitulations for the establishing of our factory to be in mine owne power. His answere was whether I would remayne with him in his court. I replyed, till shipping came; then my desire was to goe home with the answere of His Majestie's letter. He replyed againe that his meaning was a longer time, for he meant to send an embassador to the King of England at the coming of the next shipping, and that I should stay with him untill some other be sent from my king to remayne in my place, saying this: Thy staying would be highly for the benefit of thy nation; and that he would give me good maintenance, and my being heere in his presence would be the cause to right all wrongs that should be offered unto my nation; and further, what I should see beneficiall for them, upon my petition made, he would grant; swearing by his father's soule that, if I would remayne with him, he would grant me articles for out factorie to my hearts desire, and would never goe from his word. I replyed againe, that I would consider of it. Thus daily inticing me to stay with him, alleaging as is above written, and that I should doe service both to my naturall king and to him, and likewise he would allow me by the yeare three thousand and two hundred pounds sterling for my first, and so yeerely he promised me to augment my living till I came to a thousand horse. So my first should be foure hundred horse; for the nobilitie of India have their titles by the number of their horses, that is to say, from fortie to twelve thousand, which pay belongeth to princes and his sonnes. I trusting upon his promise, and seeing it was beneficiall both to my nation and myself, beeing dispossessed of that benefit which I should have reaped if I had gone to Bantam, and that after halfe a dozen yeeres, Your Worships would send another man of sort in my place, in the meane time I should feather my neast, and doe you service; and further perceiving great injuries offered us, by reason the King is so farre from the ports; for all which causes above specified, I did not thinke it amisse to yeeld unto his request. Then, because my name was something hard for his pronuntiation, he called me by the name of English Chan, that is to say, English Lord, but in Persian is the title for a Duke; and this went currant throughout the countrey.

Now your Worships shall understand that I being now in the highest of my favours, the Jesuites and Portugals slept not, but by all meanes sought my overthrow; and, to say the truth, the principall Mahumetans neere the King envyed much that a Christian should be so nigh unto him. The Jesuite Peniero being with Mukarrab Khan, and the Jesuites here, I thinke did little regard their masses and church matters for studying how to overthrow my affaires; advice being gone to Goa by the Jesuites here, I meane in Agra, and to Padre Peniero at Surat or Cambay, he working with Mukarrab Khan to be the Portugals assistance, and the Vice-roy sending him a great present, together with many toyes unto the King with his letter. These presents and many more promises wrought so much with Mukarrab Khan that he writeth his petition…

Now here I meane to speake a little of manners and customes in the court. First, in the morning about the breake of day [Jahangir] is at his beades, with his face turned to the west-ward. The manner of his praying, when he is in Agra, is in a private faire roome, upon a goodly jet stone, having only a Persian lamb-skinne under him; having also some eight chaines of beads, everyone of them containing foure hundred. The beads are of rich pearle, ballace rubyes, diamonds, rubyes, emeralds, lignum aloes, eshem, and corall. At the upper end of this jet stone the pictures of Our Lady and Christ are placed graven in stone; so he turneth over his beads, and saith three thousand two hundred words, according to the number of his beads, and then his prayer is ended. After he hath done, he sheweth himself to the people, receiving their salames or good morrowes; unto whom multitudes resort every morning for this purpose. This done, he sleepeth two houres more, and then dineth and passeth his time with his women, and at noone he sheweth himself to the people againe sitting till three of the clocke, viewing and seeing his pastimes and sports made by men, and fighting of many sorts of beasts, every day sundry kinds of pastimes. Then at three of the clocke, all the nobles in generall (that be in Agra and are well) resort unto the court, the King coming forth in open audience, sitting in his seat-royall, and every man standing in his degree before him, his chiefest sort of the nobles standing within a red rayle, and the rest without. They are all placed by his Lieutenant-Generall. This red rayle is three steppes higher than the place where the rest stand; and within this red rayle I was placed, amongst the chiefest of all. The rest are placed by officers, and they likewise be within another very spacious place rayled; and without that rayle stand all sorts of horsemen and souldiers that belong unto his captaines, and all other comers. At these rayles there are many doores kept by many porters, who have white rods to keepe men in order. In the middest of the place, right before the King, standeth one of his sheriffes, together with his master hangman, who is accompanied with forty hangmen wearing on their heads a certaine quilted cap, different from all others, with an hatchet on their shoulders; and others with all sorts of whips being there, readie to doe what the King commandeth. The King heareth all causes in this place, and stayeth some two houres every day (these Kings of India sit daily in justice every day, and on the Tuesdayes doe their executions). Then he departeth towards his private place of prayer. His prayer beeing ended, foure or five sorts of very well dressed and roasted meats are brought him, of which, as he pleaseth, he eateth a bit to stay his stomacke, drinking once of his strong drinke. Then he cometh forth into a private roome, where none can come but such as himself nominateth (for two yeeres together I was one of his attendants here). In this place he drinketh other five cupfuls, which is the portion that the physicians alot him. This done, he eateth opium, and then he ariseth; and being in the height of his drinke he layeth him downe to sleepe, every man departing to his owne home. And after he hath slept two houres, they awake him and bring his supper to him; at which time he is not able to feed himself, but it is thrust into his mouth by others; and this is about one of the clocke, and then he sleepeth the rest of the night.

Now in the space of these five cups he doth many idle things; and whatsoever he doth, either without or within, drunken or sober, he hath writers who by turnes set downe everything in writing which he doth, so that there is nothing passeth in his lifetime which is not noted, no, not so much as his going to the necessary, and how often he lieth with his women, and with whom; and all this is done unto this end, that when he dieth these writings of all his actions and speeches which are worthy to be set downe might be recorded in the chronicles. At my being with him, he made his brother's children Christians; the doing whereof was not for any zeale he had to Christianitie, as the Fathers and all Christians thought, but upon the prophecie of certain learned *Gentiles*, who told him that the sonnes of his body should be disinherited and the children of his brother should raigne; and therefore he did it to make these children hatefull to all *Moores*, as Christians are odious in their sight, and that they beeing once Christians, when any such matter should happen, they should find no subjects. But God is omnipotent and can turne the making of these Christians unto a good ende, if it be His pleasure.

This King amongst his children hath one called Sultan Shariar, of seven yeeres of age; and his father on a day, being to goe somewhere to solace himself, demanded of him whether he would goe with him. The child answered that if it pleased His Highnesse he would either goe or stay, as the pleasure of his father was. But because his answer was not that with all his heart he would waite upon His Majestie, he was very well buffeted by the King, and that in such sort that no child in the world but would have cryed, which this child did not. Wherefore his father demanded why he cryed not. He answered that his nurses told him that it was the greatest shame in the world for princes to cry when they were beaten; and ever since they nurtured me in this kind, saith he, I never cryed, and nothing shall make me cry to the death. Upon which speech his father, being more vexed, stroke him againe, and caused a bodkin to be brought him, which he thrust through his cheeke; but all this would not make him cry , although he bled very much; which was admired of all that the father should doe this unto his child, and that he was so stout that he would not crie. There is great hope of this child to exceed all the rest...

The custome of the Indians is to burne their dead, as you have read in other authors, and at their burning many of their wives will burne with them, because they will be registred in their bookes for famous and most modest and loving wives, who, leaving all worldly affaires, content themselves to live no longer then their husbands. I have seene many proper women brought before the King, whom (by his commandment) none may burne without his leave and sight of them; I meane those of Agra. When any of these cometh, he doth perswade them with many promises of gifts and living if they will live, but in my time no perswasion could prevaile, but burne they would. The King, seeing that all would not serve, giveth his leave for her to be carried to the fire, where she burneth herself alive with her dead husband.

Likewise his custome is, when any great noble-man hath been absent from him two or three yeeres, if they come in favour and have performed well, he receiveth them in manner and forme following. First, the noble-man stayeth at the gate of the pallace till the Vizir and Lieutenant-Generall and Knight Martiall come to accompany him unto the King. Then he is brought to the gate of the outermost rayles, whereof I have spoken before, where he standeth in the view of the King, in the middest betweene these two nobles. Then he toucheth the ground with his hand and also with his head, very gravely, and doth thus three times. This done, he kneeleth downe touching the ground with his forehead; which being once done, he is carried forward towards the King, and in the midway he is made to doe this reverence againe. Then he cometh to the doore of the red rayles, doing the like reverence the third time; and having thus done, he cometh within the red rayles and doth it once more upon the carpets. Then the King commandeth him to come up the staires or ladder of seaven steppes that he may embrace him; where the King most lovingly embraceth him before all the people, whereby they shall take notice that he is in the Kings favour. The King having done this, he then cometh downe, and is placed by the Lieutenant-Generall according to his degree. Now if he come in disgrace, through exclamations made against him, he hath none of these honours from the King, but is placed in his place till he come to his tryall. This King is very much adored of the heathen commonalty, insomuch that they will spread their bodies all upon the ground, rubbing the earth with their faces on both sides. They use many other fopperies and superstitions, which I omit, leaving them for other travellers which shall come from thence hereafter.

After I had written this, there came into my memory another feast, solemnized at his fathers funerall, which is kept at his sepulchre, where likewise himself, with all his posterity, meane to be buried. Upon this day there is great store of victuals dressed, and much money given to the poore. This sepulchre may be counted one of the rarest monuments of the world. It hath beene this fourteene yeares a building, and it is thought it will not be finished these seaven yeares more, in ending gates and walls and other needfull things for the beautifying and setting of it forth. The least that worke there daily are three thousand people; but thus much I will say, that one of our worke-men will dispatch more than three of them. The sepulchre is some three-quarters of a mile about, made square. It hath seaven heights built, every height narrower then the other, till you come to the top where his herse is. At the outermost gate before you come to the sepulchre there is a most stately palace building. The compasse of the wall joyning to this gate of the sepulchre and garding, being within, may be at the least three miles. This sepulchre is some foure miles distant from the citie of Agra.

...the King was very earnest with me to take a white Mayden out of his Palace, who would give me all things necessary, with slaves, and he would promise me she should turne Christian; and by this means my meates and drinkes would be looked unto by them, and I should live without feare. In regard she was a *Moore*, I refused, but if so be there could be a Christian found, I would accept it. At which my speech, I little thought a Christian's Daughter could be found. So the King called to memorie on Mubarique Sha [Mubarak Shah] his daughter, who was a Christian Armenian, and of the race of the most ancient Christians, who was a captaine and in great favour with Ekber Padasha, this king's father. This captaine dyed suddenly and without will, worth a masse of money, and all robbed by his brothers and kindred, and debts that cannot be recovered, leaving the child but only a few jewels. I, seeing she was of so honest a descent, having passed my word to the King, could not withstand my fortunes; wherefore I tooke her and, for want of a minister, before Christian witnesses I married her. The priest was my man Nicholas [Ufflet], which I thought had beene lawfull, till I met with a preacher that came with Sir Henry Middleton and, he shewing me the error, I was new marryed againe. So ever after I lived content and without feare, she being willing to goe where I went, and live as I lived.

After these matters ended, newes came hither that the [English ship] Ascension was to come, by the men of her pinnasse, that was cast away neere Surat; upon which newes I presently went to the King and told him, craving his licence, together with his commission for the settling of our trade; which the King was willing to doe, limiting me a time to returne and be with him againe. But the King's chiefe Vizir, Abdal Hassan, a man envious to all Christians, told the King that my going would be the occasion of warre, and thus harme might happen unto a great man who was sent for Goa to buy toyes for the King. Upon which speach the Kings pleasure was I should stay, and send away his commission to my chiefe factor at Surat; and presently gave order that it should be most effectually written. In fine, under his great seale with golden letters his commission was written, so firmely for our good and so free as heart can wish. This I obtained presently and sent it to William Finch. Before it came there, newes came that the Ascension was cast away and her men saved, but not suffered to come into the citie of Surat. Of that likewise I told the King, who seemed to be very much discontented with that great captaine Mukarrab Khan, my enemy, and gave me another commandment for their good usage and meanes to be wrought to save the goods, if it were possible. These two commandments came almost together, to the great joy of William Finch and the rest, admiring much at these things.

And now continuing these great favours with the King, being continually in his sight, for the one halfe of foure and twentie houres serving him day and night, I wanted not the greater part of his nobles that were Mahumetans to be mine enemies, for it went against their hearts that a Christian should be so great and neere the King; and the more, because the King had promised to make his brother's children Christians, which two yeares after my coming he performed, commanding them to be made Christians. A while after came some of the Ascension's company unto me (whom I could have wished of better behaviour, a thing pryed into by the King). In all this time I could not get my debts of Mukarrab Khan, till at length he was sent for up to the King to answere for many faults and tyrannicall injustice which he did to all people in those parts, many a man being undone by him, who petitioned to the King for justice. Now this dogge to make his peace sent many bribes to the King's sonnes and noblemen that were neere the King, who laboured in his behalfe.

After newes came that Mukarrab Khan was approached neere, the King presently sent to attach all his goods, which were in that abundance that the King was two moneths in viewing of them, every day allotting a certaine quantitie to be brought before me; and what he thought fitting for his owne turne he kept, and the rest delivered againe to Mukarrab Khan. In the viewing of these goods there came those peeces and costlet and head-peece, with other presents that he tooke from me for the King of mine owne, not suffering me to bring them myself; at the sight whereof I was so bold to tell the King what was mine. After the King had viewed these goods, a very great complaint was made by a *Banian*, how that Mukarrab Khan had taken his daughter, saying she was for the King; which was his excuse, deflowring her himself, and afterwards gave her to a Brahman belonging to Mukarrab Khan. The man who gave notice of this child protested her to passe all that ever he saw for beautie. The matter being examined, and the offence done by Mukarrab Khan found to be true, he was committed to prison in the power of a great nobleman, and commandment was given that the Brahman his privy members should be cut off.

Before this happened to Mukarrab Khan, I went to visite him divers times, who made me verie faire promises that he would deale very kindly with me and be my friend, and that I should have my right. Now being in this disgrace, his friends daily solliciting for him, at length got him cleere, with commandment that he pay every man his right, and that no more complaints be made of him if he loved his life. So Mukarrab Khan by the King's command paid everyone his due excepting me, whom he would not pay but deliver me my cloath, whereof I was desirous and to make (if it were possible) by faire meanes an end with him; but he put me off the more, delaying time till his departure, which was shortly after. For the King had restored him his old place againe, and he was to goe for Goa about a faire ballace ruby and other rare things promised the King.

All my going and sending to Mukarrab Khan for my money or cloath was in vaine, I being abused so basely by him that I was forced to demaund justice of the King, who commanded that the money be brought before him; but for all the Kings command he did as he listed, and, doe what I could, he cut me off twelve thousand and five hundred *mamadies*. For the greatest man in this kingdome was his friend, and many others holding on his side, murmuring to the King the suffering of English to come into his countrey, for that we were a nation that, if we once set foot, we would take his countrey from him. The King called me to make answere to that they said. I answered His Majestie that, if any such matter were, I would answer it with my life, and that we were not so base a nation as these mine enemies reported; all this was because I demaunded my due and yet cannot get it. At this time those that were neere favourites and neerest unto the King, whom I daily visited and kept in withall, spake in my behalfe; and the King, holding on my side, commanded that no more such wrongs be offred me. So I thinking to use my best in the recovery of this, intreting the head Vizir that he would be meanes that I receive not so great a losse, he answered me in a threatning manner, that if I did open my mouth anymore he would make me to pay an hundred thousand *mamadies*, which the King had lost in his customes by entertaining me, and no man durst adventure by reason of the Portugal. So by this meanes I was forced to hold my tongue, for I know this money was swallowed by both these dogges. Now Mukarrab Khan being commanded in publicke that by such a day he be ready to depart for Guzerat, and so for Goa, and then come and take his leave, as the custome is; in this meane time three of the principallest merchants of Surat were sent for by the Kings commandment and come to the court about affaires wherein the King or his Vizir had imployed them, being then present there when Mukarrab Khan was taking his leave, this being a plot laid both by the Portugals, Mukarrab Khan, and the Vizir, for some six daies before a letter came unto the King from the Portugal Vice-roy, with a present of many rare things. The contents of this letter were, how highly the King of Portugal tooke in ill part the entertaining of the English, he being of an ancient amitie, with other complements; and withall, how that a merchant was there arrived with a very faire ballace ruby, weighing three hundred and fiftie *rotties*, of which stone the pattern was sent. Upon this newes Mukarrab Khan was to be hastened away; at whose coming to take his leave, together with Padre Pineiro that was to goe with him, the above named merchants of Surat being then there present, Mukarrab Khan began to make his speech to the King, saying that this and many other things he hoped to obtaine of the Portugal, so that the English were disanulled; saying more, that it would redound to great losse unto His Majestie and subjects if he did further suffer the English to come into his parts. Upon which speech he called the merchants before the King to declare what losse it would be, for that they best knew. They affirmed that they were like to be all undone because of the English, nor hereafter any toy could come into this countrey, because the Portugal was so strong at sea and would not suffer them to goe in or out of their ports, and all their excuse was for suffering the English. These speeches now and formerly, and lucre of this stone, and promises by the Fathers of rare things were the causes the King overthrew my affaires, saying: Let the English come no more; presently giving Mukarrab Khan his commandment to deliver the Vice-roy to that effect, that he would never suffer the English to come any more into his ports. I now saw that it booted me not to meddle upon a sudden, or to make any petition unto the King till a pretty while after the departure of Mukarrab Khan; and seeing my enemies were so many, although they had eaten of me many presents. When I saw my time, I made petition unto the King. In this space I found a toy to give, as the order is, for there is no man that cometh to make petition who cometh emptie-handed. Upon which petition made him, he presently granted my request, commanding his Vizir to make me another commandment in as ample manner as my former, and commanded that no man should open his mouth to the contrary, for it was his pleasure that the English should come into his ports.

So this time againe I was afloate. Of this alteration at that instant the Jesuite had notice; for there is no matter passeth in the *Mogol's* court in secret, but it is knowne halfe an houre after, giving a small matter to the writer of that day, for there is nothing that passeth but it is written, and writers appointed by turnes, so that the Father nor I could passe any businesse, but when we would we had notice. So the Jesuite presently sent away the most speedy messenger that could be gotten, with his letter to Padre Pineiro and Mukarrab Khan, advertising them of all that had passed. At the receit of which they consulted amongst themselves not to goe forward on their voyage for Goa till I were overthrown againe. Wherefore Mukarrab Khan wrote his petition unto the King, and letters unto his friend the head Vizir, how it stood not with the King's honour to send him, if he performed not what he promised the Portugal, and that his voyage would be overthrowne, if he did not call in the commandment he had given the Englishman. Upon the receiving and reading of this, the King went againe from his word, esteeming a few toyes which the Fathers had promised him more then his honour.

Now beeing desirous to see the full issue of this, I went to Hogio Jahan [? Mir Miran, Sadr Jahan, d. 1611/2] Lord General of the Kings Palace (the second man in place in the kingdome), intreating him that he would stand my friend. He very kindly presently went unto the King, telling him that I was very heavy and discontent that Abdal Hassan would not deliver me my commandment, which His Majestie had granted me. The King answered him (I being present and very neere him), saying, it was true that the commandment is sealed, and ready to be delivered him: But upon letters received from Mukarrab Khan and better consideration by me had on these my affaires in my ports in Guzerat, I thought it fitting not to let him have it. Thus was I tossed and tumbled in the kind of a rich merchant adventuring all he had in one bottome, and by casualtie of stormes or pirates lost it all at once. So that on the other side, concerning my living, I was so crossed that many times this Abdal Hassan his answere would be unto me: I knowe well enough you stand not in such need, for your master beareth your charges, and the King knew not what he did in giving to you, from whom he should receive. My answer was that it was the King's pleasure and none of my request, and seeing it is His Majestie's gift, I had no reason to lose it. So that from time to time he bade me have patience and he would find out a good living for me. Thus was I dallied withall by this mine enemie, in so much that in all the time I served in court I could not get a living that would yeeld any thing, giving me my living still in places where out-lawes raigned. Only once at Lahore, by an especiall commandment from the King; but I was soon deprived of it, and all that I received from the beginning was not fully three hundred pounds, a great part whereof was spent upon charges of men sent to the lordships. When that I saw that the living which the King absolutely gave me was taken from me, I was then past all hopes; for before, at the newes of the arrivall of shipping, I had great hope that the King would performe former grants, in hope of rare things that should come from England. But when I made arze or petition unto the King concerning my living, he turned me over to Abdal Hassan, who not only denied me my living, but also gave order that I be suffered no more to enter within the red rayles, which is a place of honour where all my time I was placed very neere unto the King, in which place there were but five men in the kingdome before me.

Now perceiving that all my affaires were overthrowne, I determined with the councell of those that were neere me to resolve whereto to trust, either to be well in or well out. Upon this resolution I had my petition made ready, by which I made known unto the King how Abdal Hassan had dealt with me, having himself eaten what His Majestie gave me; and how that my charges of so long time (being by His Majestie desired to stay in his court, upon the faithfull promises he made me) were so much that it would be my utter overthrow; therefore I besought His Majestie that he would consider my cause, either to establish me as formerly, or give me leave to depart. His answere was that he gave me leave, commanding his safe conduct to be made me to passe freely without molestation throughout his kingdomes. When this commandment was made, as the custome is, I came to doe my obeysance and to take my leave, intreating for an answere of my king's letter. Abdal Hassan, coming unto me from the King, in a disdainfull manner utterly denied me, saying that it was not the custome of so great a monarch to write in the kind of a letter unto a pettie prince or governour. I answered him that the King knew more of the mightinesse of the King of England then to be a petty governour. Well, this was mine answere, together with my leave taken. I went home to my house, studying with all my endeavours to get all my goods and debts together, and to buy commodities with those monies that were remayning, using all the speed I could to cleere myself of the countrey, staying only for Nicholas Ufflet to come from Lahore with a remainder of indigo that was in William Finch's power, who determined to goe overland, being past all hopes for ever imbarking ourselves at Surat; which course I also would willingly have taken, but that (as it is well knowne) for some causes I could not travell thorow Turkie, and especially with a woman [Mariam]; so I was forced to currie favour with the Jesuites to get me a safe conduct or seguro from the Vice-roy to goe for Goa, and so to Portugal, and from thence to England, thinking (as the opinion of others was) that, the Vice-roy giving his secure royall, there would be no danger for me. But when my wife's mother and kindred saw that I was to carry her away, suspecting that they should never see her any more, they did so distaste me in these my travels that I was forced to yeeld unto them that my wife go no further then Goa, because it was India, and that they could goe and come and visit her, and that, if at any time I meant to goe for Portugal, or any otherwhere, that I leave her that portion that the custome of Portugal is to leave to their wives when they dye; unto which I was forced to yeeld, to give them content to prevent all mischiefes. But knowing that, if my wife would goe with me, all would be of no effect, I effected with the Jesuite to send for two secures, the one concerning my quiet being and free libertie of conscience in Goa, and to be as a Portugal in all tradings and commerce in Goa (this was to shew my wife's parents), the other was an absolute grant for free passage into Portugal, and so for England, with my wife and goods, without any disturbances of any of my wife's friends: And what agreements I made with them to be void and of none effect, but I should stay or goe when I pleased, with free libertie of conscience for myself. This last securo I should receive at Cambay, which at my departure for our shippes was not yet come, but was to come with the caravan of frigates. This and much more the Fathers would have done for me, only to rid me out of the country; for being cleere of me, they should much more quietly sleepe. About this time I had notice of the coming of three English shipps, that were arrived at Mocha, and without faile their determination was to come for Surat at the time of the yeare; having this advertisement by Nicholas Bangham from Burhanpur, who departed from me some six weekes before, both for the recovery of certaine debts, as also with my letter to our shipping (if it were possible to send it) advertising them of my proceedings. In this time of my dispatching, newes came of Mukarrab Khan's returne from Goa with many gallant and rare things, which he brought for the King. But that ballace ruby was not for his turne, saying it was false, or at the least made his excuse, for feare that if he should give the Portugal his price and when it came into the King's power it should be valued much lesse (which overplus he should be forced to pay, as he had done in former times for other things), he left it behind him. And besides I understood that Mukarrab Khan had not his full content as he expected of the Portugals. And likewise at this instant the Vizir, my enemy, was thrust out of his place for many complaints made of him by noblemen that were at great charges and in debt, and could not receive their livings in places that were good, but in barren and rebellious places, and that he made a benefit of the good places himself and robbed them all. For these complaints and others he had much ado to escape with life, being put out of his place and sent to the wars of *Deccan*. Now one Gaih-beig [Ghias Beg, d. 1620/1], being the King's chiefe treasurer (a man that in outward shew made much of me and was alwayes willing to pleasure me when I had occasion to use him), was made chiefe Vizir, and his daughter marryed with the King, being his chiefe queene or paramour. This Vizir's sonne and myself were great friends, he having beene often at my house, and was now exalted to high dignities by the King. Perceiving this alteration, and being certified of the coming of shipping by certaine advise sundry wayes, knowing the custome of these *Moores* that without gifts and bribes nothing would either goe forward or be accomplished, I sent my broker to seeke out for jewels fitting for the King's sister and new paramour, and likewise for this new Vizir and his sonne.

Now after they had my gifts, they beganne on all sides to solicit my cause; at which time newes came to Agra by *Banians* of Diu how that of Diu three English ships were seene, and three dayes after other newes came that they were at the barre of Surat. Upon which newes the Great Vizir asked me what toy I had for the King, I shewed him a ruby ring that I had gotten, at the sight of which he bade me make readie to goe with him at court time and he would make my petition to the King, and told me that the King was alreadie won. So once more coming before His Greatness, and my petition being read, he presently granted me the establishing of our factorie, and that the English come and freely trade for Surat; willing the Vizir that with all expedition my commandment be made; upon which grant the Vizir made signe unto me to make obeysance, which I did according to the custome. But now what followed? A great nobleman and neerest favourite of the King, being the dearest friend that Mukarrab Khan and likewise Abdal Hassan had, brought up together from their childhood, and pages together unto the King, began to make a speech unto the King, saying that the granting of this would be the utter overthrow of his sea coasts and people, as His Majestie had beene informed by petition from divers of his subjects: And besides, that it stood not with His Majestie's honour to contradict that which he had granted to his ancient friends the Portugals, and whosoever laboured for the English knew not what he did; if knowing, he was not His Majestie's friend. Upon the speech of this nobleman my businesse once againe was quite overthrowne, and all my time and presents lost; the King answering that, for my nation, he would not grant trade at the sea ports, for the inconvenience that divers times had beene scanned upon; but, for myself, if I would remayne in his service, he would command that what he had allowed me should be given me to my content; which I denyed, unlesse the English should come unto his ports according to promise, and, as for my particular maintenance, my King would not see me want. Then desiring againe answere of the King's letter, he consulted awhile with his Vizirs and then sent me his denyall. So I tooke my leave, and departed from Agra the second of November, 1611, being of a thousand thoughts what course I were best to take; for I still had a doubt of the Portugals that for lucre of my goods they would poyson me. Againe, on the other side, it was dangerous by reason of the warres to travell thorow *Deccan* unto Masulipatan. By land, by reason of the Turkes, I could not goe; and to stay I would not amongst these faithlesse infidels.

I arrived at Cambay the last of December, 1611, where I had certaine newes of the English ships that were at Surat. Immediately I sent a footman unto the ships with my letter, with certaine advice, affirmed for a truth by the Fathers of Cambay unto me, that the Vice-roy had in a readinesse prepared to depart from Goa foure great ships, with certaine gallies and frigates, for to come upon them, and treasons plotted against Sir Henry Middleton's person; of which newes I was wished by the Fathers to advise Sir Henry; which I found afterward to be but their policie to put him in feare, and so to depart; and withall I wished them to be well advised. And as for me, my shifts were to goe home by the way of the Portugals, for so I had promised my wife and her brother, who at that present was with me, and to delude him and the Fathers till I had notice for certaine that I might freely get aboard without feare, which I was assured to know at the returne of my letter. In the meane time I did all that I could to dispatch her brother away; who within two dayes after departed for Agra, not suspecting that I had any intent for the ships. Nicholas Ufflet now departing from me to survey the way, beeing two dayes journey on his way, met with Captaine William Sharpeigh, Master Fraine and Hugh Greete, sent by Sir Henry to Cambay unto me, which was no small joy unto me. So understanding of the place (which was miraculously found out by Sir Henry Middleton, and never knowne to any of the countrey), I admired and gave God thankes: for if this place had not beene found, it had beene impossible for me to have gotten aboard with my goods. Wherefore making all the haste that I could in dispatching myself away, I departed from Cambay the eighteenth of January, 1611 [sic, 1612] and came unto the ships the six and twentieth of the said moneth, where I was most kindly received by Sir Henry Middleton.

From this place we departed the eleventh of February, 1611 [sic, 1612] and arrived at Dabhol the sixteenth of the same; in which place we tooke a Portugal ship and frigate, out of which we tooke some quantitie of goods. And from thence we departed the fifth of March, 1611 [sic, 1612] for the Red Sea, with an intent to revenge us of the wrongs offered us, both by Turkes and *Mogols*...

Hawkins and Mariam sailed first to Sumatra and then via South Africa toward England. After he finished his report for the East India Company, adverse winds blew the small fleet to Ireland. Before they reached land, Hawkins died from the rigours of the voyage. His widow buried him and travelled on to London with the captain of another ship in the fleet, Gabriel Towerson, eventually marrying him there in 1614. This selection comes from Sir Clements R. Markham, ed., *The Hawkins' Voyages during the Reigns of Henry VIII, Queen Elizabeth, and James I* (London: Hakluyt Society, 1878).

Chapter Five

Peter Mundy

Peter Mundy (1596-c.1667), the son of a Cornwall pilchard merchant, spent much of his youth travelling in various capacities, including as a cabin-boy and merchant, through France, Spain and the Mediterranean. In 1627, at the age of 33, he gained employment from the East India Company. After serving in Surat, he was promoted to junior merchant ('under factor') and stationed as a buyer in Agra. Mundy's perspective as an employee of the already established and expanding East India Company differed considerably from that of his fellow Englishman, William Hawkins (Chapter Four), who had first petitioned the emperor for permission for the Company to begin trading just two decades earlier.

This selection integrates two complementary accounts (Mundy's diary and his report) of his journey from Agra to Surat at the end of his first visit to India. During the cool season (when the rains he encountered were unseasonable and also unwelcome), he led a caphila (caravan) consisting of 170 Indian attendants and soldiers, 268 camels and 109 carts, transporting fardles [bundles, each weighing about 312 English pounds] of indigo dye and of saltpetre for gunpowder and food preservation, to be exported to England. His frustrations as commander of the beleaguered caravan were legion, which he attributed to quarrelling Muslim Balloach camel-drivers and Hindu Jat-caste bullock-carters, imperious Mughal noblemen, hostile villagers and exacting local rulers—all combined with the inhospitable weather, wretched roads, inferior equipment, awkward cargo and unsympathetic and unsupportive supervisors. In an effort to gain protection and avoid exploitation by customs-tax collectors along the way, Mundy's employers arranged for him to travel alongside the lashkar (military convoy) of Bakir Khan, former Governor of Orissa and newly-appointed Governor of Gujarat.

Even before he set out on this particularly fraught journey, Mundy felt hard used. He had recently returned from a difficult and fruitless four-month expedition of more than 1,000 miles when his employers had by 'mistake' sent him from Agra to Patna when they 'in Errour' wrote the wrong city name in his letter of instructions and meant only to send him to nearby Punjab. His five year contract of employment was up and he

Peter Mundy's travels by land in north and west India, 1632-33

was anxious to return home. Nonetheless, his fascination with the people and prospects around him never flagged, even when his curiosity led to deadly encounters.

✑

25 February 1632. I departed from Agra in the morning; that night I came to [Fatehpur]…

In our way were certaine Minars, or small Towers made Taperwise, built by king Ecbar [Akbar] on this occasion. Hee having never a Sonne to succeede him, hee was perswaded by a Fackeere that if hee went barefoot to [Ajmer] to visit, and to offer to the Tombe of Qfuaz Mondeene [Khwaja Mu'inu'd-din Chishti] (a reputed Saint among the *Moores*) hee should obtaine his desire, which hee accordingly performed (…there being 150 *Course* from Agra to Ajmer) and at every *Course* end hee caused those Minars to bee built; hee had after this three Sonnes. It is said hee went on carpets all the way, but on this manner, there being a good space first spread, as fast as hee went on, the hindermost carpets were taken away, and ready spread in his way before hee came to them: half a mile out of Agra was a little Tank lay by the wayside, of one entire massie peece of white Marble, fowre square, each square conteyning at least 2 1/2 yards, brought for the king, yet unpollished, of about a foot thick.

Within 3 *Course* of Fatehpur there is a ruinated building, named Gonga *Mohol*, that is the 'house of the dumb', built by King Akbar of purpose, where hee caused little children to be brought up by dumb Nurses to know what language they would naturally speak, but it is sayd that in a long time they spake nothing at all.

The Citie of Fatehpur was also built by King Akbar aforesaid at his return from the Conquest of Gujarat, naming it the 'Town of Victorie'. It is encompassed with a faire high wall of bigg square redd stone. In my opinion it was the only place that might any way resemble our Europe Cities, for conformitie of stately buildings; now it lyes in a manner of a heap (the ruynes to bee seen of broken Arches, galleries, pillars, etc) excepting the King's house, the great *Mossit*, and one *Bazare*.

The king's house or *Mohol* stands on the highest hill, within which are aboundance of Courts, Conveyances, galleries, *Chowtrees*, Arches, pillars, Tanks, *Chaboothares*, private rooms, all verie rich, curious, and full of invention of paintings, carvings, etc, also a little garden. The water to water it is also to fill the Tanks aloft and for their use is drawn from the valley, first into one Tank, and then from that into another higher, and so into 4 or 5 untill it come aloft, by that which wee in Spain call Noraies. The *Mossit* is the fairest I have yet seen in India, standing verie high, built by a Fackeere much reputed of. So that a certaine *Amrawe* being bound for the wars, and having no sonne, left his meanes with this Fackeere, with condition that if hee returned not, it should bee all his. The *Amrawe* was slayne, and hee remayned with all his riches, wherewith hee built this *Mossit*, as also his own tombe. It is a verie curious building; a faire arched entrance full of Copulaes round about on the walls, very large, paved with Marble. It hath many Fackeers, etc to attend it, who at certain tymes in the day, and night beat on great drums, and sound with Trumpetts, which is usually done at all great men's tombes, according as they are of abillitie. As the Turks at Constantinople, so do the *Moores* in this Countrie make their Sepulchers without the Cities for the most part (Greate men in Gardens of their own, or eminent places, as on the Tops of some hills, by great Tanks etc). The Common sort have a common place, and over every one they build a form of a herse or Coffin, with some invention, according as their means will stretch.

Under the Citie is a lake of 10 or 12 mile long, having store of Fish. By it is a curious Minar, or tower of a great height, to bee ascended within side, having on the outside, peeces of white Marble made in form of Elephant's Teeth built into it, and sticking out about three quarters of a yard, and so much distance between one and another, having on the top a fine *Chowtree* and a Copulae supported with pillars, to bee ascended within side with steps. It is commonly called the Tower of Elephant's teeth, many thinking them to bee real.

There is also a conceipoted Stable standing on the side of the hill towards the lake, which is made into severall flats, or degrees, like steps one above another with pillars, and arches to support a Covering to it; on each of those degrees stood a rank of horses, the entrance at one end.

Likewise a Park or Meadow walled in, wherein were severall beasts, among the rest *Nilgaues*, a kind of deere as high as a good Colt, or Mule with short hornes.

Within the kings house was a great Jarre made of playster and lyme like a Tynaja in Spain. It might conteyne 3 or 4 butts, wherein was put water of Ganges for the kings own drinking; for it is a Custom that the kings of India drink no other water but of that river, bee they never so far off, which is brought on Cammells' backs in brasse or Copper vessells. About 3 *Course* off lies Rupbas where are the quarries of those redd stones; which supplye all their parts for the principall buildings, as the Castle of Agra, this place, great men's houses, tombes, etc...

26 February. ...to [Khanua] where I found Mr Fremlen, who had already dispeeded the Carts to [Nibnira]; the Cammells being to follow that night. About Noon wee had much thunder with a Terrible gust of wynde, and so much dust that wee could hardly see one another; after which followed aboundance of rayne, which lasted all the afternoon. Wee departed thence about one a clock afternoon (the rayne continuing) and came to Nibnira aforesaid. The Cammells not being able to lade by reason of the fowle weather, 1/3 part of the Carts being without covers, and 3/4 of the Cammells' goods lyeing open in the fields, but wee hoped it took no hurt. There wee

found Backur Chaun [Bakir Khan] with a small *Laskarre* bound for Ahmedabad appointed *Sehebsooba* of Gujarat.

27 February. We made one *Moccame*, or daily stay, by reason of the rain, which about noon poured down in such manner, that the like hath seldom been seen for the tyme; it came with very great hail and such a gust of wind, that our tent or field covering did little availe to keep ourselves dry. This morning the Cammells arrived, the goods enduring this terrible shower with the rest in the open fields; the rain still continueing but not so violent...

28 February. Wee came to Bayana in Company of Bakir Khan, who promised to protect and free us from paying Customes on the way. Mr Fremlen had formerly agreed with *Adowyaes* (I would it had held) for rupees 45 per Cart and rupees 9 1/2 per Cammell, to pay the Customs of the goods from Agra to Ahmedabad, but on confidence of this occasion they were dismissed. About 1 1/2 *Course* this side of Bayana, one of our Carts brake in two, and another lay in the river (occasioned by rains) hard by the town, where the goods lay under water neere 1 1/2 hour without being able to remedy it. The cart was so sunk in a pitt of sand; so wee were faine to take the *fardles* of Indico ashoare on men's shoulders, and much ado wee had to gett so much help amongst 170 hired servants; the night being dark and foule weather, every man shifted himself out of the way. Divers other of the carts came through very deep water, but by reason of their little stay, there cannot bee so much dammage thought as on the former, which was left at Bayana, there opened, and put to dry, being very much damnifyed; and had it not been the sooner prevented, the whole cart loading (being seven *fardles*) had been utterly spoyled. To the broken cart they sent two empty ones to fetch away the goods. Thus puzling, it was neere midnight before our Carts came together. By this beginning Mr Fremlen might judge of the future, and farther proceed of this *Caphila*; for here himself was present, the House broker, the house servants, Cart Brokers, Cammell Brokers, etc to assist him, the oxen unwrought, and the *Monsull* but 5 or 6 *Course*, and yet all the former trouble, dammage, and hindrance befell. How could hee then think I could strive all alone with weary oxen, broken carts, long *Monsulls*, a tedious journey, and to keep Company with a *Laskarre*, besides other inconveniencies?

29 February, 1-2 March. Wee stayed 1 day in Bayana, and the next day set forward... Wee pitched neere the Town ([Hindaun], 5 *course*) on the further side from hence. Bakir Khan sent his sonne Mirza Facur before to Ahmedabad to take possession of the Government there in his name, with order to proceede 16 *Course* a day.

3 March. This Town ([Sop ka sarai], 9 *course*) was dispeopled through sickness... whether Mr Fremlen accompanied us, and having ended Accompts

with the Cammellers, Carter *Balloaches*, etc (a very troublesome peece of busines), hee returned to Agra leaving mee to my Charge...

5 March. There is a little Castle overlookes this Town ([Lalsot], 7 *course*), which lyes on the side of a hill as do many others; most part rebels. Here is some base Indico made.

6 March. (Jampda, 5 *course*). Wee travelled under the Hill, not encountring any thing worthie of notice.

7 March. Some 3 *course* short of this place (Chatsu), wee passed by a Town, out of which came 3 or 4 fellowes, who carried away an Oxe out of our *Caphila* belonging to some of our *Balloaches*, who had bought him and laden him with graine to carrie to Gujarat to relieve their necessetie with it in tyme of that great dearth (which...yet continued in some parts), upon Complaint to the Khan wee took 3 of the Townspeople along with us to use them at our pleasure till they returned the Oxe, which stayed not long, for at our *Monsull*, it was brought us, with provision, and all. This town stands on a little rising, reasonable big, with an old pair of Castle walles, and close to it is a faire Tank by which Bakir Khan pitched.

8 March. Wee made a *Moccame*, there being set up an extraordinarie great and high pavillion close to the water, and Masons set on worke to make a *Chowtree*, where Bakir Khan meant the next day to sitt his *Nouroze*.

9 March. Wee made another *Moccame* by reason the Khan did solemnize his *Nouroze* aforesaid with all the Magnificence the way could afford, as by shooting off his shutternal (or 'Cammell peeces', because they are fitted on Cammell's backs), in number 16, beating of Drumms, whereof hee hath with him 6 or 7 paire, to bee carried on Elephant's backs, of which one paire weigh 16 *Maund* Jehangueere, which is neere 1000 [lb.] weight English, sounding of his trumpetts, (having by report when hee came from [Orissa], drums of silver, and trumpetts of gold, which now the King is possessed of, as also jewels, and 9 great Elephants). But to return to our *Nouroze*, there was also the fighting of furious Cammells, called Bagdadees. The afternoon hee feasted all his chief Favourites and followers; at night all the Tank was set round about with 3 Rowes of lights; they keep this Feast as their New Yeares tide...

10 March. Wee set out before day and came hither ([Pipalgam], 6 *course*) about 10 a clock in the morning, meeting by the way 4 or 5 who carried Faggotts of rodds like switches. I asked what they meant; it was told mee that by the Holyness of Khwaja Mu'inu'd-din, whosoever had a rodd of those in his hands should not bee bit by any venomous things, as Snake, Scorpion, etc; and they

carried them to Agra where they sold them for 5 or 6 pice each, bringing them from Ajmer where they grow, and where also is the tombe of their said Saint.

11 March. Having removed at midnight, wee came hither ([Mozamabad], 11 *course*) about 9 in the forenoon. The way from Lalsot plaine with some little hills here and there, which appeared in the plaine like Islands in the Sea; many theeves, water scarce, and wood. Wee pitched hard by [Jogi ka Talao], in which were a number of wilde ducks which (because they are not suffered to bee hurt), come close aboard the shore without shew of feare. This priviledge they have from the Raja of this place. Bakir Khan sent his *peshconna* before. To give you to understand what it is, I will relate the manner of great men's travelling through the Countrie: First (as before), they send away their *peshconna*, which is a suite of Tents, *cannatts*, etc, as accommodation, to the place where they mean next to rest (hee in the mean tyme remaining in another suite of tents, etc). The which, when hee begins to set forth, is carryed 2 dayes Journey forward, vizt., where hee intends to stay the morrow, when himself is on the way. There first certain Elephants goe before him, about 1/4 mile distance with flaggs, then the measurer of the way, then troops of horses, and among them other Elephants with drums on their backs continually beating a kind of march, and now and then the Trumpets sound; Then a great number of flaggs carried by footmen; Then cometh himself, either in a *palanqueene*, if it bee dark, with Caracks or great lights before him; or hott, or dirtye weather, else on horseback, or upon an elephant; severall servants about him, some to beat away flys, others carry fans to keep away the sunne, others with his coole water, with divers others; Then come his favourites, then the Cohouree or maine bodie of horse and foot; then, after all, his lumberment and people of service, as Cookes, Horsekeepers, Frosts or Tent setters, water bearers, *Cahares*, etc; there coming of these afore gone with the former *peshconna*, it being now the turne of this to goe two dayes forward, having also drummes with them on Cammells. It being the Custom of *Caphilaes*, *Banjares*, etc to have them when travelling the Countrie.

In this Town is made yearly 4 or 500 *Maunds* of base Indico. 7 *Course* Northward lyes Sambar, the *Jaggueere* of Mirza Zilkurne [Mirza Alexander] of 1000 horse pay, each horse 25 rupees per month, who is now putt out [from his governorship in Bengal] and himself wife, children and servants in prison because the King is informed hee hath store of money and demands of him 60 *Lack*, having sent Pioneers to search, and digg his house; before I came away [from Agra] hee offers 5 *Lack*, which will not bee accepted, so remains still prisoner. Hee is a Christian, and the Chiefest in all India, formerly in favour. At Sambar is a myne of excellent white salt much esteemed of, and serves for great men's uses, being carried to all parts...

12 March. From hence Bakir Khan and his *Laskarre* past through to Ajmer, being 13 *course*, but then neither our Cammells nor Carts Could keep him

Company. The former stayed halfe the way but the latter proceeded three *Course* farther. I stayed with the Cammells, as being hindermost and neerest daunger, where one of our Cammellers was carried to [Kishanghar], a Castle hard by, demaunding 100 rupees for hurt done by the Cammells in their Corne (being no such matter)…

13 March. At 4 in the morning wee stayed here amonge the [Aravalli] Hills, (Sethila, 6 *course*), our Cammells and Oxen not being able to follow Bakir Khan, who went to Ajmer…where the Khan made another *Moccame* for his own occasions, else had wee been already left behinde. By his letter wee got our Cammeller free with the expence of about 20 rupees to the plaintiff's Horsemen etc, the Khan's Officers. It was 3 a clock afternoon next day before our Carts came, So wee made no *Moccame* at all. Here my servant overtook mee with whom I expected Abdull Careeme, an auntient and trustie Servitor of the Companies, whom, after much importunitie of my self, Dongee and others, Mr Fremlen promised to send after mee, but deteyned him. Never had *Caphila* more need of Assistance then this, considering the greatness of the charge, length of the way, multitude and diversitie of the worst sort of people in India to deale withall, baddness of the tyme, but, last and worst, bound to keep Company with a *Laskarre* with such a number of base Cattle and Carts that all that saw them held it impossible they should long hold out. Yet with all these hard Conditions am I thrust out alone, with little language, having no body that I can trust or cares to take any paines to ease mee to look after the Companies goods, to helpe to compound the unreasonable demaunds of Carters, Cammellers, etc, to decide their quarrells, differences etc, to perswade them to reason, they being most comonlye obstinately bent to do what they liste, although to the Companies losse, which I am afraid will be no small matter…

14 March. The way hither (Ajmer, 7 *course*) plaine, till wee came within 2 *Course* of it, and then it proved hilly and stony. The Citie it self stands under a high Mountaine, whereon is a Castle, with many other [hills] on every side, high, steepie, and ragged, especially one, where is the tombe of Shaw Madare, a reputed Saint amongst them. At the foot of the adjoyning hills are many ruinated buildings, formerly belonging to the *Amrawes* in Jehangueer's tyme, who resided here about 3 yeares, by whose *Mohol* or Pallace wee rested, which now lyes to ruine. Shaw Jehan hath also his, hard by a faire tank, named Anasawgur, with a garden wherein are many Cipresse trees. Wee ascended the Castle hill; wee found it 1 1/2 mile up, and steepie, with wyndings and turnings so that Elephants may goe up, but there is a neerer way, to be only ascended and descended by men, and that with difficultie. On the topp is a plaine of 1 1/2 mile in circuit, taken in with a strong wall, within which are about 100 dwellers, and a prettie *Mossit* wherein is interred Scied Miran Ching [Sayyid Miran Chang], a *Suare*, who won this part of the Countrie from the *Rashpootes*, and reputed a Sainte, of whom they faine some Miracles. Within the said

Castle or plaine is a naturall rockie concavity, which receives so much rain water as serves their necesseties. There are also little gardens and fresh greene trees, and flowers.

After my coming downe, I went for curiositie to see the tombe of Qfauz Mondeene standing at one end of the town. This is the saint to whom King Akbar came barefoot on pilgrimage to have children... Wee coming by way of Lalsot saw not the Minars, but at our setting out, for 20 or 30 *Course*. Hither also (as report went) Shaw Jehan would have sent his 2 elder Sonnes, 2 monthes since, to take their oathes to be true, and obedient to him, and never to undertake any thing against him, fearing (as hee might justly) that they would do to him as hee did to his father, and elder brother.

The going in is through a great gate, the floore paved with marble white, and black, kept verie pollisht with the bare feete of those that enter in, for all must leave their shoes without; having passed 2 Courts, you come to the place of his tombe; there sitting at the entrie on either side are divers old *Mullahs*, or Churchmen. The place is a *Chowtree*, some 1 1/2 yards high, and 2 yards square every waie, on the which was a raile, and within that his Monument or Herse, in form like those ordinarie ones, but covered all over with flowers; Right over it hung divers lights, globes of steele, Estridge eggs, shells, etc. When I came forth, one presents mee with a rodd, another with seedes, another with Sandall, another with water, etc, all belonging to their Saint, for which they must have your goodwill (some pice). Great resort of people contynuallie from all parts thronging in and out. Of him also are reported a world of false miracles...

16 March. Coming from [Badhwara] to [Rian], about 50 of our Carts lost their way. I being then with our Cammells; and coming at our *Monsull*, I found but 11 Carts in all, some out of the way as aforesaid, and others hindred by Sands, so that they were faine to put 8, 10 and 12 Oxen to one Cart to gett them over 1/4 mile of the said deepe sand; so that wee wrought about them till 9 a clock that night, yet came they not to the rest for that night, neither the other 50, after whom I sent 8 men severall wayes to bring newes, [which] wee had about 3 a clock morning, that they were gone towards Merta another way; that night also another Cart broke in the middle.

The next day wee came all to Merta, vizt., 50 by the high way, 48 I came along withall, and the rest came after, for whose safer passage I desired a Horseman of Bakir Khan to goe along with them. The Carts were sore tottered, and shaken with the sand that they were scarce repaired and fitted in 3 dayes *Moccames* the *Amrawe* made there. And had hee not made the said *Moccames*, as well here, as at the places aforementioned (although for his own ends), it had been impossible for us to have kept Company with him hither. Here the Carters required 50 rupees per Cart to supply themselves with oxen etc. I never thought of this; but Mr Fremlen knew it, unto whom they had made the same demand, who bidd them rest satisfied; for that I carried wherewith to content them all, which was but rupees 2000, untill by Dongee's perswasion I had 1000 more, in all rupees 3000. Of this the Cammellers had 1000 to provide themselves with other Cammells in lieu of those that should die or faile.

In former tymes, as I am informed, they used to carry spare Cammells for that purpose in the *Caphila*, but now there are none, or if there be any, they are laden with graine for their provision to and in Gujarat. Such is the feare they have of the famine, which now, by report, is much deminished (God be praised). To the Carters I paid all that was left, being rupees 1650, only reserving 50 or 60 for expence of dyett. Cutwall Chaun [Kotwal Khan] of whom Mr Fremlen took rupees 21000 by exchange (remitting it on Ahmedabad), promised before our coming out to lend us 4 or 5000 rupees if wee wanted on the way. Upon which proffer I addressed mee to him; but his answer was that Bakir Khan, standing in great neede of money to pay his soldiers, had taken of him all hee had, and faine besides to pawne his Jewells and plate to procure more in Merta (all this I believed). Howsoever, hee promised that within 3 or 4 dayes hee would furnish mee. I do think the Carters had not soo much neede of money as they complained, only to make provision of meat etc, by which meanes their poore weake Carts were the more laden, and wee consequently the more hindred by their slowe proceed, besides breaking of them, and tyring their oxen etc. As for the most part of the Carts, they were the unfittest, and weakest that ever were sent out of Agra in one *Caphila*; and the greatest part of their oxen suitable [matching], so that every day wee were afraid wee should not hold out the next; nor never a day, night, nor scarce an hour but that one or other tells mee that there is such a Carte broken, and would know what I would enorder about it. Another comes after him, and sayes that such a Cart's wheel is in peeces. Another after him that the Oxen of such a Cart are tired and can goe no farther; and that 1 Cart is gone another way; and that another Cart is 2 or 3 *Course* behinde the rest. And thus much of the Carts. With the Cammells there is not 1/2 so much trouble, although they dye and tire, and many tymes their goods lye by the high way, but they fetch it againe; so that they are somewhat tollerable.

A *Caphila* of the best Cammells in the best tyme with good assistance is troublesome enough. A *Caphila* of Carts of the best, with the former conditions, is worse. Cammells and Carts together, although of the best sort, worse than that. But a *Caphila* of the worst sort of Carts and Cammells in a badd tyme, without Assistants, and to keep way with a *Laskarre*, is as badd as may bee trouble and hazard. For with a *Laskarre* those that can keep Company must proceede on, and not stay for those that are behinde which are not fewe nor seldome. How many tymes have some of our Carts arrived 24 hours after the *Laskarre*, others 12, and others 7 or 8; but the places that wee have past hitherto have not been verie dangerous, which if it should happen hereafter, the cost and danger is most apparent for theeves, and Custom, making that 1 or more to pay for all the rest; so that by no meanes must wee leave any behinde (cost what it will) for wee have every day newes of Cammells and goods taken out of *Caphilaes*, vizt., from under [Abugarh] out of the Dutch *Caphila*, and out of this *Laskarre* severall tymes, and otherwaies. I say if wee went by ourselves wee might stay one for another, but with a Laskar wee cannot, which will stay for none...

17 March. From Rian hither (Merta, 7 *course*) the way plaine, little wood and water, but better peopled and manured then former dayes Journys. This Town was auntiently the head of this province called Marwar; It stands on a little rising, faire to see too. About the middle of it are 6 or 7 *Dewraes*, or Hindooe Churches, in a cluster, of verie curious workemanshipp for matter of building, especially the inside of the Copulaes (whereof they most consist), but their Imagery is not proportionable. One of the said *Dewraes* is of white Marble. This lyes in the *Jaggueere* of Raja Gutzing [Gaj Singh] as farr as [Jalor], which by him is kept in good order, so that people passe without molestation. These Inhabitants are *Rashpootes* which goe after a more free and Souldier like manner, then other Hindooes, rather like Masters then Subjects. Hereabout instead of horses, they ryde on high Cammells, commonly 2 and 2 in a long saddle, which goe a great pace. This Town is reasonable bigg, verie well peopled, although of no great traffique and commerce. Here wee spake with a Puttamare or 'foot post', who told us that under Abugarh there were certaine Cammells laden with Indico violently taken out of the Dutch *Caphila* by theeves, and [who had] slaine one of their *Balloaches*. Also that beyond [Sidhpur] 11 Cammells were carried away as they were feeding. Also at Rian wee were told of 12 more carried away feeding, all belonging to ditto *Caphila*.

18, 19 and 20 March. Wee made *Moccames* by reason Bakir Khan had occasion to take up money to pay his Soldiers...

22 March. Wee came to [Pipar], to which place some of our Carts were not arrived by 3 *Course* the next day, while the *Laskarre*, *Peshconna* and all, were by Computation at [Talab Jogi], one Journey before us. So that I rode back and hired 3 Carts out of the neerest Town to ease the rest, That if it were possible wee might attaine the *Laskarre* by night. On each of which Carts there was 3 *Maunds* graine at least; And how to remedie it I know not, they alleadging it is the sustent of their lives and the lives of their Cattell. Coming within 2 *Course* of our *Monsull* I overtook 18 Carts going on. It being somewhat late, I left them to come after, and past forward to look for more. These latter Carts arrived but 2 hours before the *Laskarre* set away for the next *Monsull*...

The way stony as it is in some places of Cornwall, being of the same kinde of Stone, which wee call *Moore* stone. Good hunting, for 5 hares were chased by the people to and againe just before my face, besides one that was killed by one of the Carters in another place.

I think this Companie vizt., *Laskarre*, *Peshconna*, *Caphila*, *Zungs* returning etc, merchants took up 7 miles at length at the least, So that some are at their

Journies end before others set out. The water in our 2 former Journies 14 or 15 Fathome deepe, and here not above 2 or 3. In our way hither was a fruitefull valley of corne, as wheat, barley, etc, which lay along by a channell of a River, of which sort wee passed many from Agra hitherto, but no running water in any of them at this tyme. Only in the raynes, or little after, they are supplyed and run like rivers.

There were also many fields of Poppie of which they make opium, called here aphim by this Countrie people, much used for many purposes. The seede thereof they put on their bread, I mean of white poppy. Of the huskes they make a kinde of beveredge called Post, steeping them in water a while, and squeezeing, and strayning out the liquor, they drink it, which doth enebriate. In the like manner they use a certaine [cannabis plant] called Bang working the same effect; so that most commonly they will call a drunken fellowe either 'Aphimee', 'Postee', or 'Banggee', although 'Muttwallee' is the right name of a drunkard. Here is a little old Castle with a faire entrance.

23 March. It was morning before some of the Carts arrived. The *Laskarre* being already departed. The Countrie a little better refreshed with water. This is called [Talab Jogi] by the reason of the residence of a Jooguee or Faqueere by it. This night a horse was stolen out of the *Laskarre* and a man hurt in divers places. The Countrie plaine, only here and there a little hill very farr distant one from an other...

This morning there were 4 Carts stayed behind all the rest, mending their wheeles, as also wanting Oxen; These wee supplyed from the Town, and sent them away. Passing onwards wee should find 15 Carts at a stand, in another place 20, and their Oxen a grazeing as though they had nothing else to do, nor by their goodwills would they stirr, not caring what became of the goods so they might refresh their Oxen. All these wee hastened forward, who arrived about Sunset. Then had wee newes of 2 Carts that were out of their way, whom wee sent presently to look after...

24 March. Within 4 *Course* of our *Monsull*, ([Kakani], 9 *course*) was a wood of Thorne trees of about 1 1/2 *Course* longe; Trees of any sort scarce all the way. A few poore Townes environed with hedges of thornes 8 or 9 foot high, heaped together to keep out pilfring Theeves. The Inhabitants generallie *Rashpootes*; this from Ajmer hither. One *Course* farther wee past by [Garha], a Town not ruinated through the late famine that raged in Gujarat, and it seemes reacheth hitherto, there being to be seene aboundaunce of Skulls and bones of men and beasts...

26 March. Wee began to ingulfe our selves among the [Aravalli] Hills, being on either side of us, but as yet some distance of, very stony, ragged and inhabitable to see to, not any water in 7 *Course*; a poore Countrie...

The Carters importuning mee for money, and I not having the oppertunity to sollicit Kotwal Khan for his promise (because most commonly I came up late in the night with the latter Carts), I desired one of the *Chowdrees* to take care of the Carts that day, that I would goe before and procure money for them, being all other tymes putt off that it was too late. Hee promised mee hee would. Kotwal Khan, notwithstanding his faire promises and our urgent necessity, put us off yet 2 or 3 days longer, so was faine to borrowe 20 rupees in one place and 30 in another to supply our want, only to hire Oxen and Carts to ease the rest untill then. The *Chowdree* aforementioned came away that day and left 11 Carts behinde, whereof some came 2 hours in the night and some at 12 a clock. And by 2 a clock in the morning, when wee were makeing ready to bee going, there were 3 Carts wanting, whom I was faine to goe seeke my self, our people being all wearie, unwilling, and fearefull to goe back. With much ado I gott 4 oxen of the other Carters and carried them with mee to bring up the said Carts, who were about 2 miles behinde, not able to proceede any farther. Wee came back with them just as the *Laskarre* was setting out; so that without giveing meat or drink to the poore cattle (who tasted neither in 24 hours before), they were forced forward. About 1 1/2 miles further wee hired 4 oxen more. Those 12 that belonged to the 3 Carts became altogether unserviceable and appertained to Jessa, the Companies Debtor.

This was our continuall life, by reason of the weakness of our Cattell, badness of the Carts, weight of their Lading, and length of the *Monsulls*, commonly 8, 9, 10 *Course* a day, whereas good strong Carts with easie Charge goe not above 5, 6 or 7 *Course* voluntarily at most. Besides that being a tyme of scarcitie, they had put into each Cart 2 or 3 *Maunds* of graine etc provision, when as they were scarce able to stirr with what they had before. Oxen died and failed dayly, the labour and vexation continuall and extraordinarie; but nothing troubled mee more then the feare to leave some Cart or other behinde, of which there was never hope it would ever overtake us more, but run hazard to bee robd—great costs for its bringing forward. Besides, there is no question but the Rebells would make those latter Carts to pay for all the rest that were escaped without Custom as before sayd; my self all day riding forth and back in the Sunne, scarce suffered to eate, or rest at any tyme, through seeking after lingring Carts, who most commonly would arrive about midnight, and to bee dispeeded againe within 2 or 3 hours after. How many mornings have I found 2 or 3 Carts remaining, not able to stirr (when all the rest were gone) through some default or other, whom I must supply in all haste with Oxen, wheels, etc, as I could bee furnished from the next Town, and then set them forward after the rest. The unsufficiency of these Carts and Oxen was apparent enough in Bayana to all that saw them, who made it a difficult matter they should hold out longe (as is before said).

It were not amisse for the avoyding of such inconveniences hereafter that in such a case as this there were a sufficient man entertained for Majorall over all the Carts in general; One of the same profession that knows how to deal with them, to allow them what is fitting, to appoynt their tymes of setting out, and place of rest, to compound their differences, to see them fitted, and that they perform their task. In fine, to command over them. Whereas now they do and demand what they list, goe, come, set out and remain when and where they please. The like I say for the Cammellers; Also a trusty man or two to assist him that hath the charge of the *Caphila*, to ease him of his Care and labour, to stand by him on all occasions, to councell him in compounding of differences and quarrells, which have not been a few in this *Caphila*, consisting of such diversity of people and professions, as Cammellers, Carters, *Balloaches*, *Jatts*, often tymes fighting among themselves to mortall wounds, pillageing one another like deadly enemies. I myself alone not being able to reconcile them.

27 March. At [Bharwani], the Carters supplyed themselves with above 250 Oxen, what bought and changed, among the rest Jessa aforementioned, who of 20 hee brought from Agra, had now but one lefte, the rest dead, and changed; so by the tyme God shall send us to Surat, hee will be twice more indebted to the Companie then hee was before his setting forth of Agra, although hee sell Oxen and Carts, and all.

28 March. When wee were at Bharwani, the *Laskarre* was at Jalor but by reason it made a *Moccame*, wee overtook it once againe. The next appointed *Monsull* by report was 12 *Course*; the tyme of lading being come, no bodie would stirr, all strucken into a feare of impossibillitie of holding out, as also of their means, and lives by certain reports that the Rebells would meete with us, who would not lose their due for the *Laskarre*, nor for the King himself, and that if they could not have their right by faire meanes, they would spoyle us as wee past through the woods; and although wee might escape this tyme, the next shall pay for all; neither would the Cammellers stirr for the reasons aforesaid, as also that they should have their Cammells stolen as they did put them to feed in the woods.

29 March. Nevertheless, with much ado, wee perswaded them to put out, but it was noon before any of our Carts were gotten 1/2 *Course* further, so that finally wee were left in a desperate case, many of our Carts stopped, and some of them lying broken in the Sand, no hope now left to hold out, having hitherto kept Company with the *Laskarre* with extraordinarie labour, hazard and vexation, loss of Cattle, tiring of men etc. I, for my own particular, will take my oath that, to my remembrance, I never took more care and paynes, nor suffered more disquietnes and discontent in all my life (for the tyme), then I have done in this business, scarce eating my meat in peace, some dayes without tasting any thing at all nor taking any rest, men now growing unwilling to do what I bidd them, wearied with extraordinary labour, and watching, and many tymes in danger of their lives attending on Carts at all tymes of the night in woods, and perrilous places.

Seeing the business overthrowne, and that the Carts could not proceed with the *Laskarre* for all our uttermost endeavour, and earnest desire, and the Carters' contract, I concluded to send the Cammells with the *Laskarre* and my self to come after with the Carts, and leaving them in Jalor, I went with the *Moccadames* of the Cammells to Modra by way of [Dantwada], with intent to recommend them to Kotwal Khan untill they came to Ahmedabad. Wee were no sooner arrived, but they fell a Consulting, as is their manner, and after 3 hours resolved againe not to go (having first given their consents thereto) alledging that their Cammells would neither hold out, that they had tired 6 that day, which left their Lading in the midway, which they sent for afterward.

30 March. Bakir Khan (upon his own occasion going now in haste extraordinary), of whom having taken my leave this morning as they did set out, as also of Kotwal Khan (they being both upon Elephants), I returned to the Carts with purpose to bring them that way, and so to go altogether; by the way back I mett many of the Khan's Carts, who were not able to attaine to Modra till next day; not only leaving these behind him but all the rest of his Carts also, himself proceeding with all expedition with some of his best and biggest Cammells in manner halfe Laden. His hasty march hath been the death, tyreing and spoyling of neere 350 Oxen, besides Cammells, and all to keep Company with his *Laskarre*; so that there is none that heare of this Consortshipp but say it was not the best course to joyne such an ill accommodated *Caphila* with a *Laskarre* that went with more then ordinary haste (but it was on their then faire now false promises). When wee came to Jalor wee found more of our Carts, the rest not arrived, being hindered by much sand, and want of water.

31 March. These being also come, wee made a *Moccame* for them that they might repair and mend their tottered and broken Carts. The Cammells in the mean tyme staying at Modra expecting our coming (which they might long enough have done) for notwithstanding all the reasons wee could alledge to persuade them (which were many), they flatly denyed to go that way; that they would rather lose their heads, as they sayd, for it would break all their Carts, and kill all their Oxen. The occasion of this was one Gunna, a *Chowdree*, a perverse fellow, who had the very worst Carts, and Oxen, and conditions that were in all the *Caphila* besides.

So once more concluded to goe by way of [Sherohi] although the more tedious and Costly by 5 dayes Journey, and 1000 rupees by computation.

1 Aprill. Wee made one day more to amend their Carts, or rather to marre them by putting graine into them, bought (as I conceive) with the money they took at Imprest, for which purpose I was faine to take up in Jalor 7000 rupees by exchange, remitting it to bee payd in Ahmedabad, whereof 2000, after many dayes importunity to Kotwal Khan, I received of Bakir Khan, whose Treasurer

gave mee a Bill for 160 *Mohers*, to him was allowed 2 per Centum to a *Sharaffe* (to pay the gold there, it being payable in Ahmedabad), I gave 5 per Centum; the *Mohers* were sold at 12 1/2 rupees each, the money to be repayed in *Mohers* at Ahmedabad, on which I feare there will not bee less then 6 or 7 per Centum loss more, besides 1 1/2 per Cent to severall officers, in all about 15 or 16 per Centum loss. This is the effect of Kotwal Khan's proffer. Of Bakir Khan you have already heard in leaving us behind; the rest of the money I took at 8 and 10 per Centum. Money I must have perforce, and thus I must give or goe without it. I acquainted Mr Fremlen hereof by word of mouth and letters, desyring to have letters of Creditt on Merta, Jalor, etc on all occasions that might befall, but it was not regarded by relying on Kotwal Khan's faire promises. Being thus left to try at the very point of danger and Cost, wee had recourse to the first thought of, and safest way of proceeding, vizt., [by] *Adowyaes*, whom also these are two sorts of Contracts, one to give him so much for his pains to goe along with us to compound the *Jaggatt*, and wee to pay it on our own heads. Another to give him so much per Cart or Cammell, and hee to pay the said customes to his profit, or loss. This latter I made choyce of, in regard that the gaine or loss concerning themselves, they will be the more wary; sundrey *Adowyaes* proffered themselves; some demaunding 29, others 28, and others 27 rupees per Cart between this and Ahmedabad; 26 1/2 I offered, which was not accepted by any stranger, only our own Carters undertook it at that rate for the Carts. The Cammellers demanding 6 rupees per Cammell, I refused that proffer also, and would defray their charge myself.

2 Aprill. The first day after our arrivall at Jalor wee departed thence, having first sent word to the Cammellers to meete us at [Sena]; but in 2 dayes wee had no answer. This day wee came to Bagra, 3 *Course* short of Sena; from thence I sent 2 severall men, 1 to Modra and 1 to Sena; within a while after came 3 Cammellers and George the Christian. These I dispeeded back againe with order to meete us at Sena aforesaid, where wee would make one *Moccame* to stay for them; having againe vehemently urged the point to the Carters to goe by way of Dantwada, but labour in vaine

3 Aprill. The Cammells came not according to expectation, so sent againe to know the occasion of their stay; they sent us word one of their Cammells was lost, so made another *Moccame* for them, neither did they come that day but stayd 3 *Course* short of us...

This (Sena, 3 *course*), is a great Town of Hindooes, who not only refraine from killing any living Creature, but (as they say) also from cutting downe trees.

This day, in an unluckie hour, my curiositie carried mee to see one of those craggy hills (on whose topp there appeared the very forme of a high Towre), immagining it to bee somewhat neere, but found it to bee twice as farr; passing over rocks, clefts, etc dangerous places, here was the true patterne of a fearefull barren desert; Men I saw none, only owles out of the Clefts, wilde peacocks, foxes, hares, wilde catts, great Snakes, etc, and not a dropp of water to bee found. In fine, I gott up with much labour (leaveing behind mee fragments of my torne apparrell on thornes, and bushes as I passed). On the verie topp of this round peaked hill stood a huge stone, upright, appearing afarr off like a mighty high tower; being by my Computation neere 25 yards from the topp of it to the foot, and some 15 yards about, the strangest worke of Nature that I have seene (another is the Porto de Sainte Adrian in Biscay). The head of this is bigger then the foot of it, lessening from the topp.

I brought 4 men out with mee, first Mohabutt Chiefe, who having come 1/4 of the way, lingred behind and returned; then Peero that carried my launce, hee came 1/2 way, and stayed behind. Only the other two, whom I accounted less able, they kept mee company, but ascended not the hill. Being come on the other side with great difficulty, and danger, over great steepie rocks, between deep Clefts etc, I found my two fellowes that stayed for mee; so took our way towards the tent (it being late), wee went to and againe listning, fearing to happen on some theevish Cottagers that are thereabouts; as wee passed on, wee heard whooping and calling, and although wee were assured they were our own people seeking for us, yet answered not for fear of the worst. When wee were come to the tent, it was told us there were about sixty of our men abroad seeking of mee.

A little after wee heard an outcry about 1/4 of a mile off, which after wee learned to bee this. 5 or 6 of those mountainous theeves mett our people in the dark, and shooting amongst them, hitt Peero aforementioned through the neck, that hee fell downe. The rest seeing that, and imagining them to bee a great many, took to their heeles, and left their shoes behind them for haste, following their leader Mohabutt (who promised more in his presence and words), 2 or 3 excepting, who lurking among the bushes, shott among the rogues, crying, and calling after their fellows to return for shame; that there were but 4 or 5 of them; but all would not serve, for they durst scarce look behind them for fear. Next morning they went to look for their consort, who they found dead and stripped of all hee had. They brought him home, and buried him under a tree hard by our tent; they [the thieves] also took another of them that was not so nimble as the rest, and took from him his arms and clothes: vizt., sword and buckler, *Shash*, Coat, *Doopata*, girdle, breeches, and shoes, unto whom I made some satisfaction.

Wee complained to the Raja of the place, who brought with him the chiefest of the next town, whom was suspected, but it being a night business, and no evidence of the Delinquents. It was concluded that those whom wee thought culpable should thrust their arms into hott boyling oyle, where, if they were guiltless, the oyle would not hurt them, but if faulty, it would burn and scald them. This belike is the country tryall in doubtfull matters, but it was not then put in execution…

6 Aprill. At last our Cammells came to us after nine dayes being asunder, and not in my power to bring them together, as you have heard... At Sena there overtook us 40 Carts, whereof 7 of the Dutch laden with Saltpetre, who came with us as farr as Hindaun; having gotten off them in the way 8 dayes beforehand, besides 5 *Moccames* which wee all lost againe through the crossness of the Cammellers and Carters... About Noon wee arrived here (Ud, 7 *course*), the countrie well tilled and inhabited, but water scarce.

Towards night came Bazigharres, (men that use dauncing, tumbling, etc, feats) and this among the rest; one takes a pole of about 3 yards long, which hee setteth upright upon his head, holding it with his hands, while a boy clambers up to the topp of it (where is fastned a board halfe a foot broad) and with his foot stands upon it, when the other daunceth with him as aforesaid, not once touching the pole with his hands.

Another tyme I saw one sitting on the ground with his leggs a crosse after this Countrie manner, then poizing himself on his hands, hee brought up his body backward very leasurely by degrees without touching the ground till it came over his head, his leggs remaining in the same posture. These two tricks mee thought were somewhat strange; Your best in this kinde are the *Deccanees*, which goe up and downe the Countrie, do the rest. Their daunceing is full of antick gestures, faces, and postures, flinging out their leggs and bestirring themselves as fast as ever they can; others playing, and singing the while. But the daunceing wenches do it with kinde of grace, turning, traceing and wyndeing their bodies, and with it head, armes, and hands, also many wanton, womanish, and some lascivious gestures; themselves, as all the rest, keep on singing, and playing, without any pause, or intermission untill the daunce is ended

7 Aprill. At our setting out towards this place ([Sirohi], 4 *course*), our Cammells overtook us. This Town lyes under the hills, plenty of all things; one only *Beawly*, which serves both the Inhabitants, and strangers. At night the Raja thereof came from some 7 *course* off (hearing of the *Caphila*), and within 12 hours after departed againe on swifte Cammells...

At Sirohi there were 3 Carts of Gunna's not come with the rest, the place very dangerous, for now were wee come among the hills of robbers, and Rebells. Men exclaymed on him, and the badness of his Carts, refuseing to come with them; daily hindrance do wee suffer through his meanes; hee hath the Charge of 36 of those rotten Carts, neither had hee a good Oxe when hee came forth from Bayana, being now furnished with our meanes; this cannot bee remedied, being forced to give him money, and faire words to goe on with all expedition; otherwise wee might have been endangered to be stopped by the rains before our arrivall at Surat. Between Ud and Sirohi the Carts came in among the Cammells, and caused some hindrance in their way, belike so that the Camellers, and Carters were allmost by the eares about it, but were pacified for that tyme. Here wee found 2 *Balloaches* that were left by Signior Salomon to recover what was taken from them by theeves under Abugarh... Wee made 2 *Moccames* here, the Raja staying for us to receive his *Jaggatt.*

I also payd the Carters, Cammellers, Peones, Servants, etc their Chanderaat, a gratification which they expect every new moon, as duely as their wages; to the Cammellers I proferred 60 rupees (having order from Mr Fremlen to give but 20). Those men were so farr from accepting it, that they presently arose, and without further advice, fell to weighing the goods, nobody dareing to come neere to mediate; with such madness (or rather drunkennes) were they possessed that they had not been long about it, but they left off, fell a daunceing, and clapping their hands after their manner, which lasted an hour, or two. Then they brought divers leane and sick Cammells and tyed them to my Tent door, one saying, here are 3 left of 14, do you make use of the rest; another that there was 1 left him of 7, and bade mee take him; so others in like manner, that their Cammells were killed by over weight, and themselves undone; that they would have all the goods weighed presently, and satisfaction for the overplus; the next morning I was faine to quiet them with 120 rupees *ename*, promising them also to have the goods weighed at Ahmedabad, the overplus to be given them, and if it wanted, to allow so much to the Company, to which they condescended. I asked them why they did it not before they came from Agra; they said they would, but Mr Fremlen told them, in regard the ropes and skynnes were wett, they could not have the true weight, that therefore they might do it on the way where and when they listed.

The Cammellers pacified and our Custom paid at Sirohi, as also provided a Cart to Carry 6 Cammells lading that dyed and fayled, also bespoken about 100 men to conduct us through the straights [passes] of the hills, wee intended to bee gone by 3 clock morning. By 10 the same night the Carts were a going without order, nor would they stay, do, or say what wee could, but drove on in a tumult. The Cammellers they would not stirr till morning. Here were wee divided againe, when it concerned us most to keep together; neither did our Convoy come by the tyme appointed, so went our way without them, leaveing 3 men to bring them after us...

8-9 April. Wee made *Moccames* to agree and pay the *Jaggatt* or Custom, which at this place is extorted for all Merchandize passing this way. Upon report of 600 or 700 *Coolees* said to lye in waite for this *Caphila*, wee hired 8 horsemen and 115 Footmen to goe with us to the place of Suspected daunger...

11 Aprill. Wee set forward by morning, accompanied with our aforementioned Convoy, and entred the straghts of the [Mt. Abu] hills; in many places but one way to passe, there being banks and thick woods on each side. About the middle of this passage is a plain, the place where the Dutch *Caphila* was assaulted, being alone without people [escort]. Signior Salomon with the Chiefe of the Cammellers etc, about some occasion stayed behind at Sirohi, so that 60 theeves, or thereabouts, issued out upon that part of the *Caphila* that

was nearest, and scattered many Cammells laden with goods, of whom they carryed away 8 with 11 *Fardles* Indico; the rest of the Cammells and *fardles* [the Dutch] found in the wood. 1 *Balloach* was slaine, and buried by the highway side. Signior Salomon left 2 servants to demand and recover the goods, whereof they had gotten in parcells about 3 *fardles* Indico; the rest, with the Cammells irrecoverable, being carryed away by the people of Rana, a great Raja hereabouts; God bee praised, wee escaped from forraiging violence, but our own disorder and dissention among ourselves had like to have wrought us more hurt; for the Cammellers and Carters fell out about the way, the Carts breaking into the fyles of the Cammells; so that from words they fell to blows, and wounds. The *Jatts*, who had charge of the Carts, having hurt one of the *Balloaches* on the brest very dangerously... , another shott in the Arme, another dyed next day of the blows hee then received; divers of the one side robbed by the other, all sides complayning. In conclusion, the quarrell was taken up for the present to be afterwards tryed in Ahmedabad by their King's lawes, although they have made proffers to assaile each other since, and live upon their guard, pitching [tents] severally, and never a man to mediate the matter but my self with my little language...

At our arrivall to our *Monsull* ([Nitura], 4 *course*), the *Balloaches* and Cammellers would have revenged themselves, but the *Jatts* came to meete them, with the Carters, with their weapons and peeces charged, these being both Hindooes, and the *Balloaches* and Cammellers *Mussellmen*, there being upwards of 220 of each side. With much ado the matter was pacified for that tyme, but had they gone by the eares, it might have endangered much of the Companys estate; this is the effect of joyning Cartes with Cammells, and *Jatts* with *Balloaches* in one *Caphila*.

This day wee travelled under Abugarh, a very great and large mountain, the outerside exceeding high, steepie, stony and ragged, but aloft within those craggs is all plaine, where are 12 Townes, having water, graine, etc maintenaunce sufficient of themselves. Next the place where wee pitched is the highest hill that I have yet seene in India, having 4 ridges, each of them higher then other, one within another, all very ragged, but the farthest at the Topp appeared just like a Sawe, or teeth of some wilde beasts all alongst; wee were now inclosed with the aforesaid hills. From [Jalor] hither wee payed for our water, and from hence wee dismissed our convoy...

12 Aprill. ([Amthara], 7 *course*). Wee still continued our way under the high and ragged hills of Abu, manie Townes, much Tillage; No water from all those hills. Lyons there bee, also Porcupines. On the sides of the aforesaid hills growe many bambooes, which, with the winde waved too and againe, and so rubb each other they kindle and burne all that is neere them, so that in the night wee might see severall great fires burning at once...

13 Aprill. By Sunne rising wee came hither ([Mungthala], 5 *course*), through woods of great Trees, especially *Burres*, from whose branches fall downe certaine threds, which, coming to ground, take roote and become a great body, so that there bee some of those trees seem like a little grove...

14 Aprill. Wee made one *Moccame* to pay our Custom to Chanda, the Raja of this place, who stands in feare of the Raja of Sirohi, so comes not neere himself, but sends his people some 1 1/2 mile out of Town amidds the woods, and, standing by the high way, told our Cammels and cars as they past on, and after carreing use behinde a hill hard by, wee then payed our *Jaggatt*. He acknowledgeth not any duetie at all to the King, but lives upon his guarde, and on the least rumours, flies to the mountaines...

16 Aprill. Comming to [Sarotra], the Cammellers demanded more money to buy Cammells in lieu of those that were dead and tired, for now their Cammells also began to fail dayly, having been beholding to the Carters to carry many of their *Fardles*. The Cammellers I say being so farr indebted to the Company alreadie, I made a doubt to lend them any more money, and having advised with Boola and Ismaell Chaun, Cammell Brokers, it was thought fit by them they should have no more.

17 Aprill. By three a clock morning the Carts were stirring and going out. Myself found the Cammellers all asleepe; neither would they stirr untill they had money; so was faine to let them have so much as to pay for certaine Cammells they had agreed for last evening. Having set them going, I by chance went to the place where the Carts had pitched (for most commonly they kept asunder) and found they were all gone; but had thrown down 2 *fardles* belonging to the Cammellers, not leaving any to look to them; only poore people that were gathering strawe told us where they lay. There leaving people to look to them, I rode two *Course* after the Cammellers to gett them to bring the said *Fardles* away, for which they sent a Cammell they had newly bought, and loaded them on her. It was ten to one they had not been lost, the people in generall being such Theeves...

  ([Ghod], 5 *course*). Some 1 1/2 *Course* from the Town in the passage, which is somewhat deepe and straight, are divers pairs of posts with holes to put long barrs across to hinder the said passage on all occasions, these [people] being also no better then Rebells. About 3 *course* farther I saw that which I much longed for, vizt., a Spring, which, issueing out of a little bank with a full and clear stream, ran into a little brook adjoyning, whose green and pleasant banks represented unto my memory England's flourishing and fruitefull soil, abounding in these kinds. The side towards Agra belonging to the Raja of Sarotra, and that of Surat side to the King, who hath a Governour in Sidhpur. All the people in generall goe halfe naked with bowes and arrowes, swords and daggers, having commonly two strings and sometymes three to their bow, both bow and strings made of Bamboo.

To day some sand. In most of the Townes where wee payed *Jaggatt*, the Raja himself, or his Sonnes will come to visitt and sitt with you in very friendly manner, sending you a present of refreshing, etc; but you must pay your Custom, if not, look to your self and stand upon your guard...

19 Aprill. Setting out from [Magarwada] to Sidhpur, wee were informed the way was very dangerous, so took a Convoy of 3 horsemen and 22 Footmen; and as it happened under Abugarh between the Carters and Cammellers, so here between the *Jatts* and Carters; in the place of most perrill they fell together by the eares, to drawing their swords, and wounding each other. Some may ask why I did not cause the offenders to bee punished by beating or otherwise. I answer, were the quarrell between two private parties it might bee so, but it is between 2 Companies in which the Chiefes are included, each alleadging the like reasons; for, if one side say they are robbed, the other say so too; if they produce a man that is hurt, the other doth the like, and you cannot favour the one but you must discontent the other. Also in matters of pilfering, thefts, etc (all of them being little better then theeves), they never produce the parties nor witnesses; but say such a thing was stolen from them when hee was a sleep, or from such a Cart, stealing one from another as fast as they can, especially eateable Commodities.

From Ahmedabad, according to my request, Mr Wyche sent a couple to assist me, but they were too honest, soft, and quiet to deal with such a Company. Setting out from Sidhpur there is very deepe sand; so that 2 of our Carts brake, and many others stuck fast; after 2 or 3 hours labour wee gott them all away...

20 Aprill. Not so good ground as yesterday, more woods... Here is a Hindooe *Dewra* ruinated, it seemes by *Moores* envying its beautie, adorned on the outside with the best carved worke that I have seene in India, verie spacious and high, yet not a handbreadth from the foot to the topp was [not] curiously wrought with the figures of men and weomen etc...

21 Aprill. Wee made a *Moccame* by reason there went a way a *Banjara* that night of 2000 Oxen, and there being but one Well, not able to suffice both. For avoyding of quarrells wee stayed here 1 day; they [the *banjaras*] had neere 100 small Shott and 6 paire of Drummes with a multitude of other people...

23 Aprill. Our Cammells set out at 3 a clock in the morning (Mehsana, 8 *course*), but the Carts not till breake of day, by whom I stayed; the place very daungerous for Theeves. Close by us lay a poor fellow, to whom came a *Coolee*, and, snatching at what hee had, ran away with it; the other running after him to recover his Clothes. There were 3 *Coolees* more that looked on, bidd him not to

trouble himself for that was gone, and with that word shott him in the shoulder; the Arrowe head stuck so fast in the bone, that with much ado, it was gotten out. Thus they raigne without controll.

4 *Course* in our way is Bandu, a Town of Rebells, where some of the Inhabitants standing by the way to tell our Cammells (because they also here exact Custom), our people Immagining them to bee pilferring theeves, took one of them, who after they had misused him, he was lett goe; the rest ran into the town and raised more Company; out of one of whose hands the partie misused takes a bowe, and ayming at him that wronged him, hits him in the bottom of the belly, so that hee dyed presently after (this was an Armenian, a Christian named George; his body was layed on a Cammell, and brought hither where it was buried).

Upon this came sundry horsemen armed in Coates of male, and a number of foot standing on their guard and demanding *Jaggatt*, who me having satisfied, wee past 1 *Course* farther to Dau, where wee must pay as much more; finding here a farr greater number of foot and horse, whom wee also contented. From Agra itself hither, and as I understand, to the Gates of Ahmedabad is a desert, barren and theevish Countrie, no *Saraes*, meat nor drink to bee had, except graine and water, the latter very scarce. Our Carts being gone before, and not having money to paye our Custom, wee left 9 of our men in pledge at Dau and Bandu untill they had notice, the money was paid in Mehsana to whom they should appoint. This is a bigg stragling town with a tank by it. Here Bakir Khan [impailed] 4 men on Stakes.

24 Aprill. This day wee made a *Moccame*, by reason our men came not yesterday as expected; but they came this morning about 9 a clock, and then [it was] too late to set out. At evening there were theeves fell on our Cammells, as they were feeding, so sent presently to their rescue, and took one of them, the rest ran away, being in all 15. Hee that was taken defended himself as long as hee had any Arrowes left; having hurt one of the *Balloaches*; wee brought him before the Deputie of Sheriare [Shahriyar], the Governour, who wee plainely saw took his part (and good reason for it, may bee hee should have part of the purchase). So, leaving the theife to his disposure, wee returned to our goods.

25 Aprill. Between this ([Jarnang], 7 *course*) and Mehsana, the way very daungerous for Theeves; woods and Champion mingled. Under a tree were 10 tombes in a rank, all of a bigness and likeness called [Sayidganj] being of 10 soldiers that were *scieds* slayne by the *Coolees*. 2 or 3 townes in our way, heaps of deadmen's bones and multitudes of them scattered here and there, the sad trophees of the late mortall famine not yet extinguished...

At Jarnang there fell some rain, so caused the *Palls* to bee set up. The Cammellers, *Balloaches*, etc, immagining they were provided for them, gott under, till I was faine to drive them out; then could not I persuade them to gett the goods out of the wett, shifting out of the way from *Pall* to *Pall*, none to speake to them but myself; the Cammellers alleadgeing that they had set their particular markes on the *Fardles*, and that next day no man should knowe his own burden, and that there would bee great strife about it. With much ado I gott them to bring under [cover] 150 *Fardles* or thereabouts; had it not pleased God to cease the rayne, the goods had layen at the mercy of the water. This is the manner of these Countrie people in tyme of neede. As Mr Fremlen, or any man else, might well perceave at Bayana, when the goods lay so long in the water. And if perchance they do any service extraordinary, they expect a particular reward, thinking themselves wronged if they have it not.

Setting out from thence, very much sand, although somewhat settled by rain; here the Carters left divers Oxen behinde them, some dead, some tyred. It had been a difficult Journey for the Carts had not the raine hardned the sand. All the fresh Oxen wee had at [Bharwani], etc, now growne leane and fainte; so that it will bee as much as they can do to reach to Ahmedabad without supply, having had already almost as much as I think their Oxen and Carts bee worth; and the Cammellers more then I can value their Cammells at, having had rupees 2800 in debts before they came out of Agra...

26 Aprill. ([Pansar], 7 *course*). Aboundaunce of *Kheernee* trees, which are very large, spreading, and fair to see too. Also Peelooe trees, resembling the willowe; good ground, store of Partridges. Men staked by the high way by Bakir Khan. This Town is in the *Jaggueere* of Mir Shemisha, who was Governour of Surat when I came to the Country, removed thence by Complaint of the English to the King; wee had a great gust of winde, dust, raine and hail, as wee had also yesterday.

27-28 Aprill. Our Carts set out before day; but the Cammells not untill towards night, by reason their Packsaddles were wett, which would spoile there Cammells' backs. That night wee came to [Adalaj], 7 *course*, where wee found the Carts. The Cammells past forward to [Chandkhera] (10 *course*) with order there to stopp. The Carts followed next morning where our *Caphila* was entire. There came from Ahmedabad to meete us Mr Nathaniell Wyche and Mr Edward Knype.

29 Aprill. Wee came to the Citie Ahmedabad (3 *course*), the Metrapolitan of Gujarat and the Auntient seate of their King; incompassed with a faire Compleat wall, 10 *Course* about (although Commonly accompted 12), and with the Suburbs, 16 *course*. The *Bazares* and streets very large, faire and conformable, now halfe ruynated and dispeopled by the last famine. A prettie River runs by it. A very faire Artificiall Tank of 32 squares with stepps to descend, as that in Surat, in the middle whereof stands a faire building with a pretty garden with a little tank in it. Also an Arched bridge, to come to it from the mayne. To the said Garden every evening there resort an Infinite number of parratts that roost in the Cocotrees (as at Surat the staires [starlings] do to

the little Island by the English house). By the said Tank is the Tombe of Captaine Browne, an English man, and once Principall in Ahmedabad. It is well kept and repaired. The Tank is in compasse at the least 1 1/4 mile English. It is the biggest of this kinde that I have seene in India...

After Mundy arrived with his caravan in Ahmedabad, Bakir Khan, the new Governor of Gujarat, demanded a gift of 20,000 rupees as compensation for his escort. After much tense negotiation, the East India Company finally and grudgingly persuaded him to accept only 4,000. Peter Mundy went on to Surat, where he remained until his departure for England in January 1634.

Despite the frustrations leading this caravan, Mundy returned to India twice more (1636-38, 1655-56). Between these trips, he also toured Japan, China, Russia, Europe and southeast Asia. On his trips back to London and Cornwall, he collated his notes into a travel narrative. He calculated his travels as 100,833 5/8 miles and 1,000 dangers for the 1611-47 period alone.

This selection comes from Mundy's manuscript (Harley 2286 in the British Library). A later published version is: Sir Richard Carnac Temple, ed., *The Travels of Peter Mundy, in Europe and Asia, 1608-1667*, 5 vols (Cambridge: Hakluyt Society, 1907).

Chapter Six

Friar Sebastien Manrique

Friar Sebastien Manrique (c.1585-1669), a Portuguese Catholic priest of the Augustinian Order went to India as a young man and took holy orders at the Portuguese colony of Goa in 1604. In July 1640, after a dozen years of missionary work in Southeast Asia, he found himself stranded on India's eastern Orissa coast. He took the bold decision to journey across Bengal and up the Ganges River, in order eventually to reach Rome. Over the weeks following his landing, his encounters with monsoon floods, voracious mosquitoes, appetizing peacocks, violent fever and affronted villagers—as well as threatening Mughal officials, challenged his resourcefulness and health. His high-flown language (originally written in Spanish) colourfully recounts this overland adventure, which would consume three years of his life and tells us much about everyday life on the road in Mughal India.

As soon as we landed...the *Xabandar* of that port came to see if we had brought any merchandise with us. As he saw that no duty was leviable on the clothes I had brought, he left us. Next day, when the Englishman [John Yard] proposed revisiting the Ship, we found she had gone, and heard, later on, that as the wind was favourable for entering the *Muana* of Piple, she had sailed there. He then told me that he was obliged to stay another three or four days to finish some business, but that after that was completed we should start for the City of [Harishpur], where he would arrange about my route. During this time we got news from Piple that the Danish ship when entering the *Muana* had encountered a sudden change of weather, a beam wind starting to blow accompanied by a fierce storm of rain, thunder, and lightning, so that although they put out all the anchors they had the force of the storm was such as to drive the vessel on to some rocks, breaking it into a thousand pieces. Twenty-seven people were drowned, including the Captain and skipper of the Ship. I was no little taken aback by this news, thinking how grateful I should be to God's infinite mercy to me in saving me from this and other great dangers.

When the Englishman had finished his business we went on to the City of Harishpur. This lay eight leagues inland, up a river covered over by great, pleasant, shady trees, whose thick branches here and there interlaced so as to

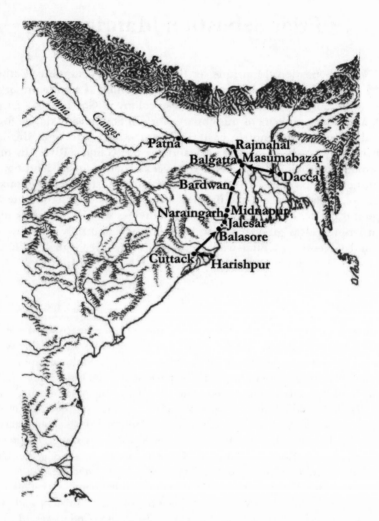

Friar Sebastien Manrique's travels by land in east India, 1640

look like an artificial avenue. This was full of most beautiful peacocks, of green screaming parrots, pure shy doves, simple wood-loving pigeons, in quantities which would satisfy the desire of anyone addicted to the pursuit of the lovely and chaste Ephesian Goddess, the sister of that false god adored at Delphos by the heathen.

The Englishman was addicted to this pursuit and carried his handy glittering implements for the volatile chase. On this he spent most of the time during our journey, and ended the day loaded with the rewards of his toil. On reaching the City of Harishpur we proceeded to examine the best route for me to pursue. After numerous discussions we rejected the route via Goa to Portugal as it involved many inconveniences for the business I had in hand, as well as the length and devious nature of that road as entailing a second journey into India. We settled that it would be best, as I had already gone so far, to continue my journey by land, and crossing through the twelve Kingdoms of Bengal enter Industan by the city and Province of Patna and from there pick up the direct route.

Having decided on taking this course I was obliged to change my dress and adopt *Mogor* costume. The proper clothes were therefore sent for, and I purchased a horse and engaged footmen or attendants and the necessary retinue for travelling in the guise of a Sodagor or merchant. On the fourth of August in the year 1640 I started—it being winter in those parts. I thus left Harishpur, a City in the Kingdom of [Orissa] under the Governorship of the *Nababo* or Viceroy of [Cuttack], and arrived at Balasore City, in a district of the same Province, on the eighth day exactly. We arrived tired out and exhausted both by the heavy rain and also by the constant crossing and recrossing of the rivers we met. In most cases there were no boats or bridges, and we crossed with water up to our knees, our waists, or even our breasts, and one day we crossed eleven streams at great risk, their currents being swollen and rapid. We were soaked to the skin all the time, and were consequently obliged to stop five days in that City and prepare some felt coats to protect us from the waters of heaven. On learning our route we steered for Balgatta, a City one hundred and thirty-seven leagues away, which stood on one of the fertile banks of the Ganges. From that point we were to proceed to Patna.

With this intention, therefore, we left the City of Balasore and, crossing the river, spent that night in the town of [Ramachandrapur], a small place of no great account. Leaving this place at dawn next day, we went on eight leagues, reaching at nightfall the City of Jalesar, an important populous trade centre. The chief articles of merchandise are cotton cloth, silk, herbs, much opium and poppy-seed... This city has an excellent *Caramossora* of moderate size, containing thirty-three rooms. Here we stayed, as these places are rest-houses designed for travellers not only in those parts of Bengal, but also in Industan and throughout the *Mogol* Empire, as well as in [Khorassan] and Persia. They are the refuge and shelter for travellers, weary and exhausted, travelling heated by ague or by the heat which the titanic and glowing Planet causes; or else, when maddened by the deluge which the dense moist clouds, saturated with moisture from the salt and bitter Ocean, after converting it into sweet soft waters, shower down, fertilizing the uncultivated earth. So after encountering all these troubles does he arrive panting at the longed-for inn. In order to fulfil my debt to the curious Reader I shall not continue my narrative until I have given a detailed description of their appearance and control, as well as of the arrangements made in them.

Most of these *Caramossoras* are located on high roads frequented by travellers. They are sometimes erected at the expense of neighbouring villages, sometimes at the cost of Princes or rich and powerful men, who erect them in order to keep their memory green or to satisfy their consciences, and large sums are left for such works, which in their opinion are works of piety and acceptable to God.

They are usually built in a square, like cloisters in a Monastery, and are divided up into dwelling rooms and chambers, with a male or female Regent: for women can also carry on this occupation. These attendants are called respectively Metres and Meteranis. Their business is to keep these rooms free from rubbish and clean and provided with cots, but without bedding, which travellers in these regions almost all carry with them.

The bedsteads are constructed with strips of woven material two or three inches wide called webbing, or sometimes with ropes of various materials. This makes them so pliant that they far surpass those heaps of over-soft mattresses we use in Europe. People carry a Godorim or mattress of cotton, which is light and not bulky. Those servants are also entrusted with the preparation of the food for guests, as well as doing all the other duties essential to comfort within the house, even to providing hot water for washing the feet. Hence on reaching a *Caramossora* all that one has to do is to send out and purchase food in the *Bazar* or market and leave other matters to these attentive servants. Besides these duties, if the Guests have horses, they are required also to cook mung or chick-pea, which is given instead of the barley we feed such animals on in Europe. Throughout the greater part of the *Mogol* Empire, especially in Bengal and Industan, they feed the horses on a kind of vegetable which is very sustaining and good: this, which they call mung, is much superior to lentils. Although lentils are very plentiful, the mung is so good and health-giving that it is also given to the sick. It is carefully cooked, allowed to cool down, collected and rolled into pellets, and placed in the mouth. Horses of value, and those especially hard worked, are usually given this food mixed with ghi and jagra, that is sugar well boiled down. This food is not given to them because barley is unprocurable in these parts, but in order to make them very fat and sleek, though it leaves them flabby. This is done because these people are particularly devoted to domestic animals, alleging that they are God's creatures and so we are bound to exercise kindness towards those who serve us and obey our behests. There are some who go to such lengths in showing this consideration that they give dogs wadded cotton coats in winter. In the

Kingdom of Gujarat, I saw cows and calves clothed in fine coats of this kind, buttoned and tied over their chests and round their bellies.

To return to the Metres and Meteranis, who, as I have remarked, are the stewards of these inns or *Caramossoras*. They are so obliging that they are content with one *debua*, or at the most two, which is so small a coin that a half real of eight contains fifty-six *debuas*, or *paisas*. Thus, uncivilized and Heathens though they are, they surpass our stable-men and innkeepers of Europe, who, being Christians, are under some obligation to be most moderate in all things, outwardly and inwardly. But many of them do exactly the reverse, so that one can only gather that they do not consider that they would be efficiently carrying out the duties of their position unless they were wicked and robbed of their substance the wretched travellers who fall into their hands...

After leaving the City of Jalesar, we made our way with considerable difficulty, owing to the heavy mud and the swamps we met with on the road, so that, though it was only seven leagues from Jalesar, we were unable to reach the City or [Naraingarh] that evening, and had to pass the night in a small Heathen village a little off our direct route. Moreover, as we were people of a different faith, who eat fowls, as well as cow's and pig's flesh, they were unable to admit us to their houses, since according to their Pagan religion they would then have become *ipso facto* unclean and impure. We were therefore obliged to seek refuge in a cowshed, which was by no means overclean, though this was not our worst complaint, since multitudes of mosquitoes gave us no chance of resting our weary, way-worn bodies: still, in spite of these drawbacks, we were plentifully supplied with rice, ghi, and other food made with milk, at a very low price. Each of us, however, before he could increase his supply of fresh blood through this food, was obliged to let these importunate insects extract with their delicate lancets the old blood which was perhaps present in excess. This, together with their harsh, unmelodious harmony, forced us to pass the whole night without our much-wished-for slumber; so, perforce keeping watch, we eagerly awaited the arrival of Aurora. She arrived at last, but only to increase our woes, as she appeared with a salvo of thunder and lightning accompanied by such heavy rain that this very flat country was, as we saw, covered with water in a few hours. We were therefore obliged to arm ourselves with patience and wait there till the next day, when we should find some one to lead us by a drier road. Meanwhile, as our enemies of the night had retired before the light of day into their obscure retreats, we all of us had an opportunity of giving rein to the sleep we so badly wanted, and thus pay the accustomed tribute to our frail nature. But to our misfortune, fate decided that we should pay for these few hours of ease by twice as many of restlessness. Now, as the bovine palace we inhabited was little, or indeed not at all, in good repair as regarded its doors and windows, peacocks, doves, and pigeons used to enter and take every advantage of the ample privileges accorded by that Heathen sect to wild animals, which thus become tame and enter into their houses. These

Barbarians thus prove, by the security with which these animals enter, how observant and punctilious they are in adhering to their false dogmas.

But these animals had made a mistake on this occasion, since they found the stable occupied by very different people; on the one hand by those who follow the true Gospel, and on the other by believers in the false doctrines of the Alcoran. But we both were at one in the opinion that we could without sin slay such animals and eat their flesh. The first man to wake up, who was a follower of the false *Hagarene Lycurgus*, cast his eyes and then his hands on the largest of the peacocks. The bird was doubtless accustomed to being petted on other occasions by those simple Heathen, and so let himself be caught quite easily; but to his own ill, as instead of gentle hands he met with those of another kind, which twisted his neck. So that he paid for his overweening confidence by perpetual silence. When this voluntary murder and one other had been committed, the man wished to pursue the chase, and the noise woke up several of the company and myself among them. Seeing the two bodies I was taken aback and nervous. I went out by the different doors and saw that there was no one about who could see us, and so was somewhat relieved. But I took the aggressor to task, and told him of the danger he ran in acting in this way in such a country, as he must indeed know. We gave orders that the peacocks should be concealed. On consultation, the best plan seemed to be that when all was quiet at night we should have them for dinner. After the meal we set to work to hide feathers and bones in the ground, so that no trace of the dead should remain, so important was it for us to keep the secret. But our evil fate and our carelessness, aided by the darkness of the night, ordained that a few of the smallest feathers should have been left uncovered. Next day, when the owners came to clear out the byre, they found the feathers, and so obtaining a clue discovered what had happened. Roused by the atrocity of so serious a crime and sin they raised the usual 'Babare', which…is the method they have of demanding justice. On this, all the inhabitants of the village came running up, and the sacrilege and crime we had committed being obvious to them, they at once took steps to be revenged on the offenders. They rapidly collected, some with bows and arrows and others with pointed sticks. They then set out to find us, in a great fury. They moved more rapidly and easily than we did and so caught us up in a few hours. As this took place in an open plain we sighted them, as they came on, from some distance. Recollecting the incident of the now long-forgotten peacocks, we gathered that this crowd was coming to make us pay for our fault. Since it is natural for people, whatever their rank or state, to defend themselves, we at once proceeded to make two muskets ready, placing those which were already loaded in front, without saying anything to the Guide we had with us; and so continued our march until these wild men came up with us. On getting within bowshot range they fired a volley of arrows, accompanied with most insulting exclamations, but God, in His infinite mercy, ordained that none of us should receive any injury. As soon as our Land-Pilot heard the tale, he abandoned us as people without the religious pale.

We had replied at once to the shower of arrows by a musket-shot in order to frighten them and keep them from advancing on us.

Though the shot had only been fired to scare them, our Guide was nevertheless so terrified by it, as he was rushing off towards his own people, that he fell down as if dead. This made his comrades suppose that he was in fact dead, which frightened them to such an extent that all they could do was to turn and fly, and that to some distance. When they found themselves some way off they halted, I think with the intention of following those of us who had gone to look after the man whom they thought was dead. When we saw that the enemy had retired we once more started on our way, but in order to do so we went to look for our Guide, whose wits were still obscured by the shadow of his terror. We took him by the hand and by kindly words encouraged him to continue to lead us until he brought us safely to the city of Naraingarh. He did this under the stimulus of fear rather than from hope of gain or his own wish.

We went on, from the spot where the heathen attacked us with arrows, to the City of Naraingarh. We reached it at nightfall, and our Guide took us to the *Caramossora*, where he provided us with good clean rooms. After seeing us settled in he came up to take leave of me, concealing his ill will towards us with a smiling face and pleased expression, to receive the pay owing for his duties, and moreover, besides giving him something over and above this amount, I ordered him to be presented with some pepper, an article which these Heathen esteem highly as a flavouring for their food, as I believed it might cause him to forget the dead peacocks.

But the villain did just the opposite, going at once to the house of the *Siguidar* or Governor of the City. He was out, and so he waited for his return. Meanwhile the other Heathen who had shot at us arrived, and he told them where he had left us.

As soon as the *Siguidar*, or Governor of the City, got back they threw themselves on their knees, and begged him with loud cries to grant them justice against certain foreigners, saying that after receiving them into their village with great kindness, they had violated their religion and scruples. This complaint they expanded by saying we were robbers who carried fire-arms, and were, moreover, men of violence, adding everything they could think of which would prejudice the *Siguidar* against us. On receiving this information and learning where we were, the *Siguidar* sent twelve Sipahis, or soldiers, to arrest us and bring us before him in the morning. On the receipt of this order, although it was already nearly midnight, these zealous officers came to the *Caramossora*. They were taken to where we were lying fast asleep, wholly unsuspicious of any such event as this. When the noise and the lights they were carrying awoke us all, some of us already had our hands tightly tied behind our backs, and this although I called out '*Doay Padcha*' and asked why we were being arrested, seeing that I was a merchant journeying to the Court of the Emperor, whose territory was free to the passage of all foreigners. To this one of them, who seemed to be the officer commanding the party, replied that if I was what I stated I was, I had nothing to fear. I then asked why they were pinioning us in this way, as we were ready to come voluntarily.

On this they abstained from binding me as they had bound the others. They then examined my stock of cloth, locking up the main entrance to the rooms and placing a seal on the lock. They then took us to the Governor's house, where they avoided the trouble of guarding us by confining us in a dungeon below ground, which was so deep that we had to descend many stairs to it. Here they left us, buried in darkness and plunged in a sea of racking and unfortunate speculation, after securing the doors with strong padlocks.

The wretched *chacores* and footmen who accompanied me were suffering severely from the tightness of the bonds which bound their arms, and also, as being naturally timid people, devoid of courage, were so down-hearted as to imagine that they would never emerge alive from those dark cells. For not all their tears, nor the promises I made, induced our captors to free their arms. But when the soldiers had left I was driven by their groans, each of which pierced me to the heart, to remember the proverb 'In for a penny, in for a pound', [literally, 'Arrested for 1000, same as for 1500'] and taking a small knife I possessed I cut all their bonds, in spite of the darkness, guided by the sound of their voices and the touch of my hand. This relieved them of their external pain, though their internal agitation necessarily remained, and with it ill feeling for the originator of our trouble, whose bonds they all besought me not to cut. But since this could in no way set right what had already taken place and was beyond remedy, this man enjoyed the same privilege as the rest.

We remained in this dungeon till the succeeding night, without these Barbarians remembering to bring us any food all day, this involuntary fast thus atoning for the voluntary and sudden greed displayed in eating the peacocks. It was about one in the morning when we heard the doors open, and a different set of officials to those who had brought us there came in, who took no notice of the fact that my companions were free. Without saying a word they took us out of the dungeon and into the presence of the Judge. He was seated in his tribunal and asked me in a severe tone what I was. I told him I was a Portuguese from Ugulim, as this fact as well as that of my voyage would be supported by the *Nabobo* of Cuttack's *formon*, which I then presented to him. He made one of his officials read it. After hearing what the passport said he salaamed, and requested me to go nearer to him. He told me of the Heathens' complaint, in reply to which I gave him the true story of the occurrence. He then asked which of my attendants had committed the outrage on the peacocks; and while I hesitated in my reply, pretending not to understand, so as not to condemn the offender, one of his companions, with greater assiduity, at once named him. The *Siguidar* then turned to the offender and said, 'Art thou not, as it seems, a Bengali and *Musalman* (that is, a *Moor* and follower of the true law)? How then didst thou dare in a Hindu district (which means of Heathens) to kill a living thing?'

As the wretched man was more dead than alive with fear, and unable to reply, I was obliged to take his hand and, after the usual salaam, exclaim, 'Sahib (that is "Sir")! as a good *Musalman* and follower of your Prophet Mahomet's tenets he pays no heed to the ridiculous precepts of the Hindus; as you yourself would not. This, principally because God in His final, sacred, and true faith has nowhere prohibited the slaying of such animals; for His Divine Majesty created all of them for man's use. And, if we accept this dictum, this man has committed no fault against God or against His precepts or those of your Alcoran: so you can easily pardon him.' The *Siguidar* and several other venerable *Moors* who were with him listened to me carefully and with great attention. They looked at each other in great surprise, and in approval of what I stated the *Siguidar* said to them, 'Allah, the sacred, has bestowed much wisdom on the Franguis (for such is the name with which they, the Portuguese, are baptized in these parts).'

He then turned to me and said that he had nothing to say in reply to me, as these were all truths in our sacred Anzir (for so they name our blessed Gospel), but the Emperor [Akbar] who had conquered these lands from the Heathen had given his word, taking an oath in the *Mossaffo* of his holy Prophet, that he and his successors would let them live under their own laws and customs: he therefore allowed no breach of them. He promised me, however, that the punishment would be far less severe than that demanded by his accusers. He therefore ordered them to remove the offender to the bundicana or public prison, and set the rest of us free and at liberty. On this we returned to the *Caramossora* well pleased at what had taken place, and then, although it was three o'clock in the morning, since we were more anxious to fill our empty stomachs than go to sleep, we first took steps to remedy that, and afterwards paid sleep its dues. So when the brilliant planet arose, seeing that both needs were satisfied, we went to the Droua or audience held by the *Siguidar*. Before he appeared I tried to intervene on behalf of our imprisoned comrade through a great confidant of the Governor's lady or *Siguidareza* about whom I had obtained information. After mollifying him by the usual inducements on such occasions, I sent, through him, a piece of green flowered Chinese taffeta, worked with white, pink, and yellow flowers, to this lady. It was a sufficiently rich and pleasing gift, and being such the lady gave as good a return, to show her gratitude, and did her best with her husband to get him to send me secretly to set the prisoner free, on the pretence that he had escaped.

But since the complainants voiced a whole village, though a small one, the *Siguidar* did not dare to offend them. The case, moreover, was simplified because according; to custom the offence had to be atoned for by a whipping and the amputation of the right hand. This the prisoner, with good reason, felt deeply, and would not even listen to the encouragement his companions gave him in explaining all the endeavours that I was making to get him set free. In fact he did nothing but weep, and refused to take any food or say a word except that they must go and call the Father. On learning this, though I was very much depressed, I decided to go to the prison and console him, I besought God most earnestly to free that poor boy, in the flower of his youth, from the execution of so severe a sentence, but I forgot, negligent minister of our Lord that I was, to also beseech His Divine Majesty to liberate him from that final and irremediable penalty of damnation to which he was sentenced unless he liberated himself from the errors of the false and wicked faith under which he was living. But the pitying Father of Mercies had decided to show that lost sheep the straight road to those fertile and living pastures of the soul. So in His divine Mercy He allowed me, while I only thought of freeing him from bodily and transitory ills, to inspire him to seek escape from the eternal pains which threatened his soul. As soon as I entered the cell the prisoner, directly he saw me, threw himself on his knees and embraced me closely, weeping copiously and unable to utter a word.

Pity reacting on me made me also mingle my tears with his, adding such comforting words as I could think of at the moment and an exhortation to him to beseech God not only to save him from this danger but from the other greater ill he suffered under in being a *Moor* and a follower of the perverse and false tenets of the Alcoran, precepts so at variance with God's true faith. Moreover I added that the divine Grace might well have caused him to suffer these trials in order that the eyes of his understanding might be opened by their influence so that he should perceive how he was wandering off the way to salvation. These outward softnesses, together with the Divine Softener's influence within his soul, which I had hitherto found so hard, affected him, so that he answered me with a most serene and peaceful look, saying that he wished to become a Christian, and that this once accomplished God could do as He wished with him. But I reflected on how vigorously he had so far rejected what he now asked for, and that it might be only Mahometan guile to deceive me and get me to urge his liberation more vigorously. I therefore praised his decision, but told him that he must persevere in it and prove that he was not abandoning his own faith for any other reason than that he had now recognized that it was false and that so long as he lived in it he could never please God. He replied that it was quite true that he had never desired to become a Christian; but until he had entered that prison, he had not known his own innermost thoughts, which had been urging him to become one, and for many days he had now wished for nothing else. I urged him to be firm in this good resolve, and pointed out to him, as clearly as I could, the errors he was living in. Seeing that he was much consoled I made him eat some food. I then left him and went to find the eunuch who was acting as my mediator, in order to learn what our kind intercessor had done. She, by importuning her husband, cajoling him, and pretending to be annoyed with him, at length accomplished what we so ardently desired, that no mutilation of any of the prisoner's members should take place; for, although the Governor had decided to forgo the punishment of the amputation of a hand, it did not follow that they would not cut off the fingers from it.

But such is the power of a lovely face, strengthened by the seal of matrimony, that even the remission of the fingers was acceded to, and in the end it resolved itself into no more than the carrying out of the whipping. For when the complainants insisted on the carrying out of the rest of the punishment, believing the prisoner to be still in the gaol, they contrived so that he should leave it one night, I being given a definite order to go and await him in the City of [Bardwan], through which I had anyhow to pass.

Together with the news that the prisoner had been set free that lady also induced me to stop three days longer, on the grounds that I had no need to start at once, and that I should thus the more effectually conceal my object. I did as she asked me, even professing to do so with great pleasure, whereas in truth it was of vital importance to me to lose no time. Still, as I was under so great an obligation, it was necessary to show that unsophisticated but kindly lady that there is nothing which the divine virtue of gratitude cannot vanquish or satisfy. On the third day, the last to which I had been asked to stay, I took leave of the Governor and his lady, as well as of the eunuch through whom I had carried out the affair. Then, just as the dawn of the following day was arousing the sleeping birds in their nests, I set out for the City of Bardwan, thirty-four leagues away. I arrived there on the fourth day and found my fugitive prisoner at the City gates. As soon as he had reached the town he made it a practice to come and watch for me at that point. The moment he saw me arriving he rushed to meet me with such obvious joy that I knew he had not changed his intention of becoming a Christian. For this I gave many secret thanks to God and thought how easy this task, so difficult to me, was to His Divine Majesty. We continued our way and halted that night at the usual travellers' resting-place, which, as I have said, are the *Caramossoras*. Here, finding a suitable opportunity, I confirmed the opinion formed when he had told me that the time had come to carry out his promise to God, who had freed him from so great a danger, adding that he had no doubts as to what he had said, having said it with all his heart; had it not been so he could have gone off to his own country, which, however, as well as his mother and brothers, he had erased from his memory, as he had decided that when once he had become a Christian he would never again leave me, and, if I was not prepared to agree to baptize him, he desired that I should at any rate take him to the nearest Christian country. In reply to this very fair request I said that I was ready to do what he asked me, but that since no danger could come from some delay it would be best and even necessary that he should first learn the rudiments of the faith he was going to profess, and that I would proceed to teach him these when we should, with God's help, reach Balgatta, where, as he knew, I had to leave his companions behind. Moreover, if they learnt that he intended becoming a Christian they would also gather that he meant to follow me and would be easily able to prevent his doing this. He was perfectly content and satisfied with this answer.

We then continued our journey through flat, highly populated, fertile country, which was, however, troublesome and difficult to cross owing to the amount of water and marshes in it. Yet God our Lord ordained that we should reach the City of Masumabazar, standing on the banks of the swift Ganges, which separated it from the City of Balgatta, but in such a way that these two towns, varying in name, equally enjoyed its fertile and pleasant banks.

The first of these is of the greatest importance and is, on account of its size, called by the people Masumabazar, which means in our tongue '*The place of mighty marts and markets*'.

Here we stayed three days, as we were obliged to register all we brought with us at the *choquidar* or customs-post there, before crossing the river. I took advantage of this halt to view and ponder on all that was good and worthy of admiration. Among the things which I saw there I was by no means the least struck by the abundance I noticed of everything in those marts, especially of eatables and household necessaries, as corn, rice, vegetables, sugar-cane, ghi, and many kinds of oil; from each of these articles several vessels could have been loaded.

Besides this, many kinds of cotton goods, drugs, tobacco, opium, and numerous other articles of various sorts attracted the eye and also led one to ponder; for the eyes were attracted by the sight of such superabundance of many things in one City, and secondly one's thoughts were awakened by remembering the great lack of these things in so many parts of our Europe.

When we were at length free of the *choquidars* or customs officials we crossed the Ganges, which at this point is about three-quarters of a league wide. On reaching Balgatta, I made up my accounts and, paying off the *chacores* who had accompanied me, dismissed them and took immediate steps to embark for Patna. Just as I had secured a vessel for Patna I was attacked with such a violent fever, that by the third day I was reduced to a condition which made me believe that it was essential that I should take steps to secure a very different and more trustworthy vessel to the life beyond, through the Sacraments of Penitence and the Eucharist. I knew that missionary Brethren of my sacred Order resided in the Cities of Daack or Dacca and Seripur and so went to find them, although this meant losing seven days on my journey, while in order to regain them it would take more than fourteen, as I should be obliged to make my way against the swift current of the Ganges. But as the fever did not leave me, and with it the inevitable and natural fear of death, that rock, on which the vessel of our life on earth is broken to pieces, grew stronger, I paid no heed to the obstacles which due consideration raised before my eyes and started for Dacca, where, by God our Lord's grace, I arrived somewhat in better case. Here I found Father Fray Juan de la Trinidad, a most zealous and kindly priest, who was held in high esteem by those Infidels. I at once arranged with him to myself receive spiritual treatment, and also for the baptizing of the youth whom I had freed from the justice of Naraingarh. Later, God our Lord willed that within a dozen days, aided by certain simples and antidotes, I should be freed from my fever. Thereupon, I once more arranged to proceed on my way. But no one was allowed to leave the City just then, for I had traversed the borders and passed the customs outposts as a merchant, and the City itself and the frontiers of the province were now under arms owing to the receipt of the news that the *Magh* king was advancing on the town with a strong fleet. Every obstacle was thus placed in the way to hinder my departure, the greatest of these being the absence at that time of the Portuguese Captain Francisco Ribero and most of the Christians; and though I besought the assistance of his son-in-law, Luis Gomez, also a man much respected in that region, who did his very utmost to get me permission to leave, I had nevertheless to wait some days until the Captain came back and obtained a passport from the *Nababo's* lieutenant. The *Nababo* at that time was the second son of the Padcha or Emperor [Shah Jahan], Sultan Shah Shuja [defeated then assassinated in 1660 by his brother Aurangzeb], who was then residing in the town of [Rajmahal].

I was twenty-seven days in the City of Daack, or as the Lusitanian idiom has it, Dacca. When I entered it I had but slight hopes of ever leaving it, owing to the continuous fever, which declined to leave me. However, through our Lord's pity, it at length departed. This delay would have been excusable, but for the other obstacle I have noted. As soon as this was overcome I at once proceeded to continue on my journey up the Ganges. In order to shorten the journey, in accordance with the opinions I had heard from men familiar with those routes, I decided to hire a boat as far as the City of Patna. Though at once prepared and manned by first-rate *paiques* or rowers, yet (although I had a *formon* or passport issued from the chautera or chief customs office) all my timely diligence was useless, as the whole of that day we were I unable to clear the vessel at the other stations and lesser customs offices. As soon as we had received all the documents we needed for presentation during the seven stages between Dacca and the City of Azarati, the route which all leaving this part for Patna were obliged to follow, we started off very early the next day. We only made a short journey because the heavy current and the floods on the river at that time were against us. The first day, therefore, we were obliged, when it was already late, to anchor in a tiny pagan village called Amadampur. Our fate ordained that these Barbarians should, on that very day, be there carrying out a service to the wretched memory of a Bramene or Priest to their idols, who had been reputed a saint. Death had, in the preceding year, put an end to the sinful course of his life, and sent him to the abodes of Tartary, there to suffer the penalties due to his idolatry.

On reaching the shore the vessel was moored fore and aft with strong cables, owing to the violence, rapidity, and force of the current. We then all went ashore, as is usual in the case of vessels of this kind. Now before we reached the shore, we had, on noticing the concourse of people and hearing the noise, suspected more or less, from previous experience, what was afoot. So we took the precaution to moor our vessel more than a musket-shot's length from the Pagoda or idol temple, around which the crowd was collected, as we supposed that the ridiculous superstitions of the Heathen would not be roused at that distance and aloofness; but we were mistaken. For as soon as we landed some of them came to ask us to go away from that spot, or re-embark. To the second proposition we replied courteously, that as soon as our *paiques* had taken their meal we would at once put off. They departed on receiving this answer, and imagining that they were satisfied, each of us went on doing whatever he was at. But, meanwhile, night advanced with slow steps, bringing her shadowy curtains of concealment with her, that cloak for the carrying out of ideas, whether good or evil. Now the ideas of those Idolators centred on the purity of their rites and ceremonies, which, by our presence even at a distance, were rendered imperfect and impure, and so they decided to turn us out. Then, since no remedy appeared more rapid or convenient of execution than the use of violence, they took advantage of the night and the high cotton crop then growing in the fields thereabouts, as a screen for their evil ends, and sent out men who secretly severed the cords which held the vessel. In one moment it left the shore and gave no chance to those sailors who swam out to rescue the boat and to secure it. God so willed it that at this moment I should be on board with one servant. We seized two oars and brought the vessel's head up to her course, as she was drifting away at great speed and, owing to the force of the water, was in danger of striking abeam on a sand-bank, and, if uncontrolled, would fill, with the loss of all there was within her. The river carried the vessel away with such great rapidity that, although we did our utmost by rowing to keep her prow to the force of the stream, the impetuous current, aided by a breeze from the north-east which had begun to blow and increase in power as the moon rose, was too much for our weary and weakened arms, which were wholly incapable of resisting the fury of those powerful elements. So we recognized our weakness and, giving up the struggle, turned her stern to the wind and waves, and admitting the weakness of human nature, surrendered ourselves up to the mercy of the waters, unable as we were to make either one bank or the other. At last we grounded on a small island of reeds, where we contrived to secure the vessel to the best of our ability with what remained to us of the cables, and settled down to await the coming day. With it our sailors appeared. They had not dared to follow us by swimming, so they had come along by the bank of the river. As soon as they saw us, one of them entered the river on a large water-pot, and by hauling on a piece of cable he brought the vessel's head round and we thus reached the shore easily. We continued to make way by being towed till we reached the place from which we had been cut loose. We here picked up our cooking utensils and the man guarding them, and set off, sufficiently wearied and disgusted at the trick played on us by those Barbarians of Amadampur.

When this matter was ended we continued on our way, constantly tacking on the wide, and here unfrequented, Ganges, without seeing in the space of five days anything but various species of caimanes or crocodiles, some of

114

which were so enormous in size that their appearance astonished us. We could scarcely believe our eyes, so that it seems to me best to leave the description of their size to the arithmetic and computation of the meticulous; for were I to describe them as they appeared to me, I should make statements that, owing to their strangeness, might make people disbelieve whatever I said on this point.

As soon as we reached the City and customs outpost of Azarati we produced the *formon* or passport we had obtained in the Capital of Dacca, at the head customs office, on which they allowed us to pass through without question. We continued our voyage up the same river for another nine days. We met with villages and country towns all along its fertile banks; every bit of the land along that river which we saw was cultivated, bearing fruit trees, wheat, rice, and vegetables; when these things were not met with large areas of pasture existed, covered with immense herds of cows, tame buffaloes, sheep, and goats; but not pig, as they do not use them...

Friar Sebastien Manrique continued his journey across north India, eventually reaching Rome in 1643. He wrote his *Itinerario de las missiones orientales* in Castilian Spanish, publishing it in Rome in 1649. This selection comes from the translation by C. Eckford Luard supported by Father H. Hosten, *Travels of Fray Sebastien Manrique, 1629-1643* (London: Hakluyt Society, 1927).

Chapter Seven

Niccolao Manucci

Niccolao Manucci (1639-1717) ran away from his native Venice at age fourteen. He soon joined as a servant the entourage of Englishman Henry Bard (1615-56), Viscount Bellomont in the Irish peerage. Bard had converted to Roman Catholicism and journeyed as ambassador to the Persian emperor, representing the exiled fellow Catholic King Charles II. When that mission failed, Bard advanced to India as self-proclaimed 'English Ambassador to the Mughals'. His ambiguous position explains the rough reception Bard received from anti-Jacobite East India Company officials in India.

After what Manucci suggests was Bard's assassination by his English rivals, the eighteen year old struggled to recover his property and make a place for himself at the Mughal imperial court. As a European, he prospered by his own wits in the service of the eldest but ill-fated Mughal imperial prince, Dara Shukoh (1615-59). Dara was hospitable to Europeans and sympathetic to Hindus but he lost the succession war for the Mughal throne to his brother Aurangzeb, who subsequently executed him. In this selection, Manucci describes his arrival and first months in India, but retrospectively contextualizes them within his many later decades and adventures there.

Setting sail [from Hormuz], we arrived in twelve days [on 27 December 1655], having favourable winds, at a port in the Great *Mogul's* territory called Sind. There the vessel anchored, and we travelled upstream by the river for a whole night to an inhabited place, which stood twelve hours' journey from the sea. This [Indus] river is a very large one, it being formed of seven rivers which flow down from the interior of the country... Here we saw many Arabian and Persian vessels which import great quantities of dates, horses, seed-pearls, pearls, incense, gummastic, senna-leaves, and Jew's stones, which come from Mecca. In return they load up with white and black sugar, butter, olive oil, and cocos, which medical men call 'nos Indica'... They also export many kinds of white linen [sic, cotton] and printed goods, which are manufactured in the same region.

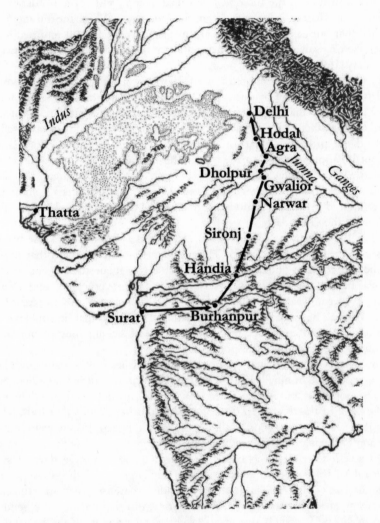

Niccolao Manucci's travels by land in west and north India, 1655-56

In the town were three small factories, one English, another Dutch, and another Portuguese. A barefooted Carmelite father also dwelt there in his little hermitage, but nowadays [1699] there are none of these Europeans there. The principal city of the country of Sind was at a distance of twelve leagues from this town, further in the interior; it is called Thatta, and is the residence of a governor or viceroy, who rules over this country. When the business was finished that our captain had to do at this place, we left it, and returned to the vessel. Setting sail, we arrived in a few days at the port of Surat on the twelfth of January [1656].

As soon as we had anchored milord [Bard] went ashore secretly, following the advice given to him by our captain and by a private trader to seek a refuge in the town. For the English were going to seize him and put him by force on board one or other of the English vessels, then in harbour and about to sail for England. It produced great astonishment in me to see how milord landed without breathing a word to me. But I heard the reason afterwards when I reached Surat, bringing all the baggage which was in my charge. There we found Mestre Jonh [Master Henry Young], who had left Persia a short time before us; and my master announced that he had come as an ambassador from the king to the Great *Mogul*.

When the governor of Surat heard of the ambassador's arrival, he ordered his secretary to pay him a visit. The message thus brought was that rumour said he had come as ambassador, therefore ne was requested to state whether this was true or not. It was necessary for him [the governor] to send a report to the emperor Xaajahan [Shah Jahan], then ruling over the empire of the Great *Mogul*. The ambassador replied that it was correct, that he could write in all confidence and announce his arrival. Before I say anything of our stay, I will state something about this port.

Three times have I visited the port of Surat. It lies on the banks of a large river at a distance of nine leagues from the sea. The first time I was there Surat was very populous, but not encircled by walls, its only defence being then a fort on the bank of the river. On the second and third occasions that I visited the port the town had a good wall, made by Orangzeb [Aurangzeb] on the occasion of the war with Xevagi [Shivaji]…

On my first arrival I was much pleased to see such a large river of sweet water full of ships. These latter were not very large, for such only as were of moderate size could come up it unless unloaded; therefore, they send the cargo in boats as far as the sea and load there, and from the sea they also send the cargo inland by boats. It is a great delight to take a seat on the bank of the river and behold the numerous boats which shoot to and fro like arrows. It is the largest port in India and the best river. Thus, it is resorted to by a great number of ships from different parts of Europe, Persia, Arabia, Mecca, Bassora, the coasts of Malabar and Choramandal, Massulapatao, Bengal, Siam, Acheen, Queddah, the Maldives, Malacca, Batavia, Manila, China and many other parts of the world.

Whenever a loaded vessel arrives, the Hindu traders go aboard, and ask if the captain wishes to sell the whole cargo of the ship. If so, they pay for it in money, or furnish goods for the return cargo, whichever is preferred. This is all done without delays, and merchants can thus acquire whatever merchandise they are in search of, and for which they have left home. On this river are built very fine lofty ships in a very short time, everything necessary being found, principally excellent timber; for which reason these ships last much longer than those made in Europe.

On my first visit to the port I found there no more than two factories, one English, and one Dutch, and a little church belonging to the French Capuchin fathers, whose superior was the famous priest Brother Ambrozio. Afterwards the French came and built a handsome factory. Thus Surat, which was inhabited by rich traders, Mohamedan, Hindu, English, Dutch, became still more populous by the arrival of the French. Upon the sea-shore, on the other side of the river, the Europeans have their gardens, to which they can retire should at any time the Mahomedans attempt to attack them. For there, with the assistance of the ships, they would be able to defend themselves.

I was much amused when I landed to see the greater number of the inhabitants dressed in white clothes, also the many different kinds of people, as well men as women. The latter, mostly Hindus, do not conceal the face as in Persia and Turkey, where women go about with their faces hidden. It is true that the Mahomedan women do not allow their faces to be seen by anyone, it being contrary to their law to allow themselves to be seen with an uncovered face.

But among other things I was much surprised to see that almost everybody was spitting something red as blood. I imagined it must be due to some complaint of the country, or that their teeth had become broken. I asked an English lady what was the matter, and whether it was the practice in this country for the inhabitants to have their teeth extracted. When she understood my question, she answered that it was not any disease, but a certain aromatic leaf called in the language of the country *pan*, or in Portuguese *betel*. She ordered some leaves to be brought, ate some herself, and gave me some to eat. Having taken them, my head swam to such an extent that I feared I was dying. It caused me to fall down; I lost my colour, and endured agonies; but she poured into my mouth a little salt, and brought me to my senses. The lady assured me that everyone who ate it for the first time felt the same effects.

Betel, or *pan*, is a leaf similar to the ivy-leaf, but the *betel* leaf is longer; it is very medicinal, and eaten by everybody in India. They chew it along with 'arrecas', which physicians call *Avelans Indicas*, and a little *kath*, which is the dried juice of a certain plant that grows in India. Smearing the *betel* leaf with a little of the *kath*, they chew them together, which makes the lips scarlet and gives a pleasant scent. It happens with the eaters of *betel*, as to those accustomed to take tobacco, that they are unable to refrain from taking it many times a day.

Thus the women of India, whose principal business it is to tell stories and eat *betel*, are unable to remain many minutes without having it in their mouths.

It is an exceedingly common practice in India to offer *betel* leaf by way of politeness, chiefly among the great men, who, when anyone pays them a visit, offer *betel* at the time or leaving as a mark of goodwill, and of the estimation in which they hold the person who is visiting them. It would be a great piece of rudeness to refuse it.

In Surat there is a class of men called Parsis, worshippers of fire, who in former days were inhabitants of Persia. But when first the Mahomedan religion got into Persia, the king tried to force them to become Mahomedans, for this reason they sent an embassy to the Hindu prince of Surat, asking him to grant them permission to emigrate into that country with their families, where they would become his permanent subjects. The Hindu prince received the embassy and allowed them to come, on condition that they should neither slaughter cows nor eat cows' flesh. He promised them the same rights as his other subjects. They came to Surat, where unto this day there are numbers of them, as also in different villages, and in the Portuguese territory adjacent to Daman.

Their religious belief is such that, if through misadventure anyone's house takes fire, on no account will he allow the fire to be interfered with or extinguished, it being, according to them, the greatest good luck and cause or rejoicing that he could have, he believing that his gods have conferred on him an especial gift and favour, in return for the adorations he has paid to them. And if ever, through negligence, the fire goes out in any of their houses, a fire that all of them maintain with especial care, there is great lamentation, much more than they would make if their nearest relation had died. After such a mishap the owner has recourse to his priest, begging his pardon for the crime he has committed in allowing the extinguishment of his household fire. The usual penance imposed is that the culprit must invite a number of families of the highest position among them. When these have all collected, well-washed and well-clad, they go off to the priest's house, and he, in their presence, makes a speech to the house-holder, and at the end of it delivers fire from his own house. This they carry, with a grand array of trumpets and drums, and arriving at the sinner's house, he is obliged to give them all a feast. These people have made a vow never to go upon the sea, in order not to defile it, since the sea unfailingly induces vomiting; and in gratitude for the benefits it has done to them they hold it in this great respect.

It happened at the time when I was in Surat that Shah Jahan, King of the Great *Mogul*, sent a severe reprimand to the governor because he had not acquired a lovely pearl of great value and forwarded it to the court. The reader should know that the governors sent by the king to Surat are persons of rank, men highly thought of and favoured by the king. These men have orders to buy all things that are most beautiful, precious, and rare, and send them to the king. Yet, this pearl passed through without the knowledge of the governor, and reached the king, who bought it at a fair price. Then he issued the aforesaid reprimand once more, enjoining on the governor to take special care to buy all the best things that came to that port, more especially pearls and horses, which come from Arabia and Persia. For all these things are used by the king as gifts to the princes and the court officials. Therefore he searches with great exactness through all merchandise to find out if there is anything rare or valuable.

We remained for seventy-five days in that port [Surat] the revenues of which had been given by Shah Jahan to his daughter, Begom Saeb, to meet her expenditure on *betel.* During this time we were making our preparations for going on to the court of the Great *Mogul.* I was much gratified at seeing such plenty in this place, for I had never had such a satisfaction since my Venice, and felt proud at staying some days in this port, especially after the arrival of the French. During the time we remained the English never ceased to offer a thousand civilities to milord, the ambassador. But his true friends told him not to trust them, for all they did was in order to get hold of him and carry him off to England. They did their very best once to persuade the ambassador to go on board of an English vessel, then about to depart for England, under the pretext of offering him a banquet with all the state befitting his dignity. But the truth was that they wanted to confine him in the ship, and he most politely made excuses. Then we began to get together our baggage, for which purpose the ambassador was in want of funds. Master Young secretly offered to supply all that was required, whether in money or in different sorts of goods, among the latter some fine broadcloth, a handsome clock, an Arab horse for a present to the king, with swords, pistols, matchlocks, and numerous European playthings. We started from Surat, bearing a passport given us by the governor, and in fifteen days we reached the town of [Burhanpur], where was the court of the prince Aurangzeb, with whom we had much to discuss. We did not meet with him, by reason of his being at that time in Aurangabad.

We found Burhanpur a town of medium size, and without a wall. [Two decades later,] Aurangzeb, in the year one thousand six hundred and seventy-six, being then absolute king, caused it to be enclosed by a bulwark and wall along the bank of the river which flows beneath it. This river is not very large, but its waters are very clear and good. The town is much frequented by Persian and Armenian traders, on account of the many kinds of excellent cloth manufactured there, chiefly various sorts of women's headdresses and cloth for veils, scarlet and white, of exceeding fineness; also for the quantity of iron to be procured there.

In this town there is plenty of fruit, such as *amb* or *mangos*—the best fruit to be found in India—oranges, limes, citrons, and grapes in abundance. There is also in this town, as throughout the kingdom of the *Mogul,* a large supply of vegetables of various sorts. On the road to this town we found every day different streams and brooks with good water, also villages, shady and pleasant woods, peopled with many varieties of animals of the chase, such as harts, stags, gazelles, wild oxen, peacocks, cooing doves, partridges, quail, blackbirds, geese, ducks, widgeon, and many sorts of birds. I would warn the reader never to stray far from his companions, because he might come across robbers in these woods. When they find any person apart from his company, they rob him. I was very near falling into their hands, for, having gone some distance from the rest of the caravan, I had got off my horse. I was about to shoot at a peacock with my matchlock, when all of a sudden there came out towards me two men with bows and arrows, who with signs and calls invited me to approach them. But I, apprehending what they wanted, went on my way in the direction the rest of the company had gone, never ceasing to have an eye upon those men. These, seeing me choose a different direction, placed arrows in their bows, and, hastening their pace, came after me, trying to overtake me. Seeing that otherwise I could never escape them, I stopped and put my matchlock to my cheek as if I meant to fire. Frightened at my firmness, they placed their hands on their heads as a sign of politeness, and, turning their backs, fled with even more agility than they had followed me. I continued on my way in dread of a similar encounter, and thus I learnt never more to leave the rest of the travellers, and I put off my longing to go out shooting until we should reach some place or village. Then I went out to shoot, and without hindrance, killed whatever I wished, there being no scarcity of things to kill.

We delayed eight days in Burhanpur, then, resuming our journey, we came in six days to a river called the Narmada, where there was a town called [Handia]; there was also on the bank of the above-named river a little fort situated at the crossing-place. This river is of great breadth, and full of large stones. Its waters divide the lands of the *Deccan* from those of Industan, which word means '*Gentile*dom'.

We crossed the river, and after going eight days through jungle, we arrived at a large town called [Sironj] which in old days was founded by a Hindu prince, but at present the overlord thereof is the Grand *Mogul*. This town lies in the midst of the territories of several Hindu princes of the *Rajput* tribe. Of these the nearest and the most powerful is the Rajah Champet Bondela, whose country extends to twenty leagues from Agra, and he has command over fifteen thousand horsemen and three hundred thousand infantry.

In this town is made much cloth, both white and printed; Armenian traders dwell there, who buy the cloth and send it to various parts. Sometimes European traders come there to do business in this cloth.

It happened that more than once the said Champet Bondela came to plunder this town, on account of certain dissensions between him and the *Mogul* king. For this reason it was always garrisoned by a considerable force of *Mogul* cavalry under a general. In spite of this, the fighting was not put an end to; there were many battles, in which on many occasions the *Moguls* had the worst of it. By reason of these Hindu princes, these routes are very dangerous for travellers. For the use of wayfarers there are throughout the realms of the *Mogul* on every route many '*saraes*'. They are like fortified places with their bastions and strong gates; most of them are built of stone or of brick. In every one is an official whose duty it is to close the gates at the going down of the sun. After he has shut the gates, he calls out that everyone must look after his belongings, picket his horses by their fore and hind legs; above all, that he must look out for dogs, for the dogs of Hindustan are very cunning and great thieves...

At six o'clock in the morning, before opening the gates, the watchman gives three warnings to the travellers, crying in a loud voice that everyone must look after his own things. After these warnings, if anyone suspects that any of his property is missing, the doors are not opened until the lost thing is found. By this means they make sure of having the thief, and he is strung up opposite the *sarae*. Thus the thieves, when they hear a complaint made, drop the goods somewhere, so as not to be discovered.

These *saraes* are only intended for travellers. Each one of them might hold, more or less, from 800 to 1,000 persons, with their horses, camels, carriages; and some of them are even larger. They contain different rooms, halls, and verandas, with trees inside the courtyard, and many provision shops; also separate abodes for the women and men who arrange the rooms and the beds for travelers...

We halted four days in Sironj, and then went on our way across inaccessible mountains, with numerous beautiful trees, and traversed by crystal streams whose waters are most wholesome, doing no harm to those who drink them fasting; rather are they beneficial and most palatable. In six days we reached the town of Narwar, which lies at the foot of a great range of hills six leagues in circumference. On the very highest point of these hills is a fortress, which occupies all the level ground on the summit, with a circumference of two miles—a little more or less—with many houses and rooms, a work made long ago by the Hindus. But in the course of years, and by the inclemency of the weather, the walls are crumbling away, through the negligence of the *Mogul* king [Aurangzeb]. His object is to destroy all the strong places of the Hindus of which he can get possession, so that their conquered princes may not rebel against him. His only anxiety is to fortify and supply the forts that are on the frontiers of his kingdom.

We did not halt at this place, but pressed onwards. In five days we arrived at the well-known fortress of [Gwalior], where it is usual for the *Mogul* to keep as prisoners princes and men of rank. This fortress is on the top of a great mountain having a circuit of three leagues. It is in the middle of a fertile plain, and thus there is no other high ground from which it could be attacked. There is only a single road to ascend it, walled in on both sides, and having many gates to bar the way, each having its guard and sentinels. The rest of the hill is of rock, perpendicular as a wall, though made by Nature. All around this mountain are to be seen many balconies, lanterns, rooms, and verandas, in different styles of architecture, with Hindu sculptures, all of this making the view most agreeable and pleasant to the visitor.

On the crest of the mountain is a great plain, on which are sumptuous palaces with many balconies and windows of various kinds of stone, and delightful gardens irrigated from many crystal springs, where cypress and other lovely trees raise their heads aloft, so as to be visible from a distance. Within this fortress is manufactured much oil of jasmine, the best to be found in the kingdom, the whole of the level ground on the summit being covered with that shrub. There are also in this district many iron-mines, of which numerous articles are made and sent to the principal cities in the *Mogul* country.

In the town, which lies at the foot of the hill, there dwell many musicians, who gain a livelihood with their instruments; and many persons maintain that it was on this mountain that the god Apollo first started Hindu music.

Continuing our route, we came in three days to the river called the Chambal, at which is the town named Dholpur, where Aurangzeb gave battle against his brother Dara, in [1658], at which I was present... Thence, in four days, we arrived at the city of Agra, having ended by doing four hundred and sixty leagues, for such is the number reckoned from Surat as far as Agra. At this place the governor assigned to us a handsome house to stay in.

...a few days after our arrival, the Englishmen who at that time were present at their factory came to visit the ambassador, showing themselves desirous of being useful to him, making him frequent and handsome offers. But these the ambassador would in no way accept. After several visits they invited him to their house, where they gave him a splendid feast, with dressed meats and beverages after their style. The ambassador complained very much of the great heat that has to be endured in that country, and the English offered him a powder, declaring that if he mixed it and drank it he would experience great relief and coolness.

When a few days had passed we resumed our route for [Delhi], where at that moment the king, Shah Jahan, was living. Then, after three days from our leaving Agra, towards the evening, when in sight of the place where we meant to halt for that night, the ambassador called out to me in great pain, asking me for water. Then he expired without allowing me time to give it to him, those being the last words that he uttered. He died on the twentieth of June [1656], at five o'clock in the evening. We carried the body at once to a *sarae* called Hodal, between Agra and Delhi, and, it being already late, we did not bury him that night. The official at the *sarae* sent notice to the local judicial officer, who hastened to the spot, and, putting his seal on all the baggage, laid all embargo upon it. I asked him why he seized and sealed up those goods. He answered me that it was the custom of that realm, and that he could not release the things until an order came from court, they being the property of an ambassador.

After seven hours of the night had passed, we removed the body of the defunct from the *palanquin* in order to enshroud it, and, as day began to dawn, we proceeded to lay him in the grave. Taking him by the arms, I tried to lift him, but, while in my hands, a blister burst from which exhaled such a fetid odour that all those standing by nearly fainted and fell down. We were forced to cease to lift him, and await the day. When day arose we somehow or other put him into a coffin, with all the haste that the odour compelled, and interred him on the bank of a reservoir which adjoined the town, marking the spot so that his bones might be transported elsewhere, as accorded with the rank of such a person. And as a fact they removed the remains after fifteen months to the city of Agra.

Having interred the ambassador, the servants all disappeared, and I was left alone, sad and anxious, having nothing to console me, nor anywhere to turn in order to recover my things, which had been sealed up by the official along with the ambassador's, although all the keys were in my possession.

After we had buried the ambassador I wrote to the English factory at Agra informing them of his death and the embargo imposed by the local official on his property as well as mine, wherefore I prayed them to send me the necessary recommendatory letters. I received no answer; but eight days afterwards two Englishmen appeared, one called Thomas Roch [? Roach] and the other Raben Simitt [? Reuben Smith], dressed after the fashion and in the costume of the country, men in the service of the king Shah Jahan, and captains of the bombardiers in the royal artillery.

They came to visit me, and when I saw them I asked what they had come about, they informed me that they had come under the king's orders to carry away the property of the ambassador, which lapsed to the crown. To that I retorted by asking if they bore any order, whereupon they laughed, and asked who I might be, I told them I was the servant of the ambassador, that the property in question had been made over to me, that I did not mean to let it go without their delivering to me my belongings—that is, two muskets, four pistols, clothes, and other trinkets, which had been set apart. Their answer was that the whole belonged to the king; and without another word they went to find those who had put on the seals, and obtaining their consent, made themselves masters of everything, arranging to remove the whole to the city of Delhi.

I did not mean to abandon the property, and resolved to set out in their company. On the road they showed me not the least little sign of civility, such as Europeans, even of different nations, are accustomed to display in all parts of Asia when they come across each other. Many a time did I entreat them for God's sake to make over to me what was mine; but as they saw I was only a youth, they scoffed at me, and said: 'Shut your mouth; if you say a word we will take your horse and your arms away.' Seeing there was no other way out of it, I dissembled for the time being, but never despaired of getting back what belonged to me.

After three days' journey we arrived at Delhi, where the Englishmen deposited the property in a *sarae*, put seals on the room doors, and told me to go about my business. Then I began to make request that they would be so good as to separate my property from that of the ambassador and make it over to me, for it did not belong to the king. They burst out laughing and mocked at me, giving me the customary answer. As I took my leave I prayed them to do me the favour of telling me their names, so that if anyone called me to account about that property I should be able to defend myself by pointing out the persons who had taken possession of it. I expressed my astonishment that they should lock up in a *sarae* room property that they said belonged to the king. I asked them angrily whether the king had no other place in which to store the goods that he owned; but they knew quite well that the property did not belong to them, and that they were taking the king's name in vain, solely in order that they might get hold of other people's goods. They replied that there was no need to know their names. As for my second remark, they only set to laughing, and thus went away in apparent triumph, not foreseeing what was to happen to them.

I retired to a room in the same *sarae*, not far from the one where the property was. Then I found out the names of those two Englishmen, so as to be able to take my own measures. Being anxious to know what was going on, there turned up on a visit to me a Frenchman called Clodio Malier, a founder employed in the artillery of Dara, first-born son of Shah Jahan. With him I talked over what had happened to me with those two Englishmen; and said again that it did not seem to me possible that so great a monarch as the *Mogul* king should possess no other place to store the goods that belonged to him than a mere *sarae*, where travellers took up their quarters. The Frenchman assured me that the Englishmen had not seized the goods by order of the king, but that Thomas Roch, learning of the ambassador's death, had sent in a petition to the prince Dara, by whom he was favoured, in the following terms: 'A man of my country, a relation of mine, came from Europe, his purpose being to obtain the honour of serving under your highness, but his good fortune was of such little duration and so scanty that he was unable to attain his desire, being overtaken by death on reaching the *sarae* of Hodal, whereupon those who govern in that place laid an embargo upon his goods. Therefore I pray as a favour that your highness be pleased to issue orders for their delivery to me.'

The prince dealt with this petition as Thomas Roch hoped; but Raben Simitt, getting word of what Thomas Roch was about, held it not to be right that he should acquire the whole of the ambassador's property, that it must be divided between the two of them. Thus he accompanied him as far as Hodal. Should he not consent to a division, he [Simitt] threatened to tell the whole story to the king. Thomas Roch accepted the situation, so as not to lose the whole. This was the story told me by Clodio Malier, who bade me adieu with much civility and many offers of service. Being thus informed of what was going on, and confiding in my knowledge of the Turkish, but more especially of the Persian language, which is that chiefly used and the most current at the court of the *Mogul*, I resolved to go to the secretary of the king, whose name was Vizir-can [Wazir Khan] to lodge a complaint. For this purpose I went to his house, and obtaining permission to enter, I reported to him what was going on. He directed me to sit down opposite to him, alongside one of his sons, who was of my age.

The secretary asked me whether I knew the accustomed mode of making obeisance before the king by those who enter his presence. I answered that I did. As he displayed a desire to see me do this, I arose, stood quite erect, and bending my body very low until my head was quite close to the ground, I placed my right hand with its back to the ground, then raising it, put it on my head, and stood up straight. This ceremonial I repeated three times, and this is done to the king only. The secretary was delighted to see a foreigner, young in years and newly arrived in the city, make his obeisances so confidently. I was dressed like a Turk, with a turban of red velvet bound with a blue ribbon, and dressed in satin of the same colour, also a waist-cloth of a gold-flowered pattern with a red ground. He was amused to see me got up like this, and asked the reason for adopting such a costume, and why I did not adopt the *Mogul* fashions, whereupon I acquainted him of the journey that I had made and the countries through which I had passed.

During this time a notice reached him that the king had decided to hold an audience that morning. Then, rising at once, he took me with him to the palace, telling me that it was requisite for me to go with him before the king. He warned me that, when I came into the king's presence, I must perform the same obeisances that I had practised before him. When we got to the palace the king had already taken his seat on the throne. The secretary directed two men to present me to the king, while he should be talking to him. Accordingly they did present me, ordering me to appear in front of the king at a distance of fifty paces, waiting until he should take notice of me before I made my obeisances.

I had noticed that when the secretary reached the place where is the railing, he made one bow, such as I had done in his house, then, when close to the throne, he made three bows, and approaching still nearer, he began to speak to the king. After a few words he raised his hand towards where I was, as if pointing me out. The king raised his eyes towards me, then the courtiers with me told me to make my obeisances, which I did. The secretary went on with his conversation, which I could not overhear by reason of the distance at which I was. All those who were present before the king were standing; only one man was seated at the side of the throne, but his seat was lower, and this was the prince Dara, the king's son.

I noted that the throne on which the king, Shah Jahan, was seated stood in front of and near to the palace of the women, so that as soon as he came out of its door he reached the throne. It is like a table, adorned with all sorts of precious stones and flowers in enamel and gold. There are three cushions, a large one, five spans in diameter, and circular, which serves as a support to the back, and two other square ones, one on each side, also a most lovely mattress. For in Turkey, and throughout the whole of Hindustan, they do not sit upon chairs, but upon carpets or mattresses, with their legs crossed. Around the throne, at the distance of one pace, are railings of gold of the height of one cubit, within which no one enters except the king's sons. Before they enter they come and, facing the king, go through their obeisance, then enter the palace and come out by the same door from which the king issued. Arriving there, they again make obeisance, and upon a sign from the king they take their seat in the same enclosure, but at the foot of and on one side of the throne. Thereupon the pages appear with the umbrella, parasol, *betel*, spittoon, sword, and fly-brusher.

Below the throne, several feet lower than it, a space is left, sufficient for the secretary and the greatest officials of the court. This space is surrounded by a silver railing. Near it stand *grusberdares*—that is to say, the bearers of golden maces, whose duty it is to carry orders from the court to princes of the blood royal. After a descent of a few more steps there is another space of greater size, where are the captains and other officials, also the *grusberdares* with silver maces, who convey the orders of the court to the governors, generals, and other princes. These are placed with their backs to a railing of wood painted vermilion, which surrounds the space.

The hall in which stood the royal seat is adorned with twenty highly-decorated pillars, which support the roof. This roof stretches far enough to cover the spaces enclosed within the silver railing, and is hidden half-way by an awning of brocade. Further, a canopy over the king's throne is upheld by four golden pillars.

Outside the wooden railing is a great square, where, close to the railing, stand nine horses on one side and nine on the other, all saddled and equipped. Near to the pillars are brought certain elephants on every day that the king gives audience, and there they make their obeisance... Behind the horses already spoken of were four handsomely-adorned elephants, and in the square a considerable number of soldiers stand on guard. At the end was a great hall, where were stationed the players on instruments, and these, upon the king's appearing to give audience, played very loudly, to give notice that the king was already in the audience hall.

The silence preserved was astonishing, and the order devoid of confusion. For this purpose there are officials, whose business it is to see that the people are placed in proper order. Some of these officials held gold sticks in their hand, and these came within the silver railing. The others carried silver sticks, and they took great heed that throughout the court nothing was done which could displease the king. After I had received my permission to go, I left in the company of the two courtiers, and returned to the *sarae*. There I showed them where I had put up, and the room in which was the property. Thereupon they broke the seals and brought out all the things and carried them away. The next day, about nine o'clock in the morning, there came two servants of the secretary to fetch me. They took me to his palace, where I found him seated in the same hall where I had spoken to him the day before. As I came in I observed that the ambassador's property was lying there. I made the usual obeisances to the secretary. Then, with a pleasant look on his face, he asked me if I identified the two thieves, pointing with his hand to one corner of the hall. Noticing this, I turned my face that way and saw the two English impostors, loaded with iron, fetters on their feet and shackles on their necks, and very much ashamed, being afraid they would be decapitated.

Turning again to the secretary, I craved leave to speak to them, and going near to them, I said: 'It would have been more honest to let me have the little that was mine, but then you wanted to acquire more than was yours; you suffer through your excess of greed, and in your desire to embrace all, you are left with nothing. You laughed, you scoffed, and had no tenderness for me, and now I sorrow for love of you, and feel compassion for the miserable condition in which I see you. You may make certain that I shall not fail to deal towards you with more charity and consideration than you showed to me on the road from Hodal.'

Returning to the secretary, he told me to look at the things and inform him whether any article was missing, for the prisoners would have to pay for anything deficient. I examined the property in his presence, and ascertained that it was complete. Since my things had been separated and were kept apart, I prayed him as a favour to issue orders that they should be returned to me. In addition, most of the ambassador's goods belonged to an English trader, named Master Young, dwelling in Surat, from whom the ambassador had obtained them, promising to repay him afterwards.

The secretary told me to sit down beside his son who was in front of him; he said he would give me many things, and making me great promises, said to me, that if I consented to remain in his house he would treat me like a son. In case I did not agree, he did not mean to give me anything. My answer was that I could not live in his house, that I cared very little about the loss of my own things, but should grieve a very great deal if he did not give to Master Young those that were his.

Upon this the secretary asked me minutely which were the ambassador's and which Master Young's things. I pointed them all out in detail, one of the secretary's clerks taking the whole down in writing. I told him that besides these goods Master Young had lent the ambassador the sum of four thousand *patacas* and an Arab horse (already in the secretary's possession). Finally, I begged leave to return to my abode, and he, in sending me off, directed me to return in two days to speak to him in the same place.

Accordingly this I did, and he said to me then that he had spoken to the king, who ordered that the property should be sent to the Governor of Surat for the purpose of being made over to Master Young, with the exception of the Arab horse, which the king kept for himself, giving an order to pay to the said Jonh one thousand *patacas*, the price at which it had been valued. He took nothing else but the litter which was destined for him.

After this I made a fresh application to the secretary that he would order my property to be given to me; but his answer was that the whole must go to Surat and be made over to Master Young, who, if he liked, might give them to me. Thus he was unable to dispose in any way of this property. But if I consented to live with him, he would give me a great deal more, and repeated that he would cherish me as his son, and many other promises. For all these words and the kindness he had displayed I gave him thanks over and over again; but as for living with him, that could never be. It was not right for me to do so, being a Christian. The secretary cut short my speech, and, losing his temper, said angrily: 'You do not know that you are the king's slave.'

Hearing these words, I rose to my feet, and answered that Europeans were not, and never would be, slaves of anyone; and in great haste I left the hall, resolved to give my life rather than live in his house. Coming out at the door, I vaulted lightly on to my horse, and took my way somewhat hurriedly, dreading lest the secretary might send some one after me to attack me. Then my groom warned me that two foot soldiers were hurrying after us, trying to overtake us. Then I turned my horse round, and, putting my hand on my cutlass, set off to face them. I asked what they wanted. They made me a bow, and answered that the secretary sent me ten gold rupees for the purchase of *betel*. I took them and went on my way. I was determined to return to Surat that I might find myself among Europeans.

At this time I met Clodio Malier, who carried me off to his house, and there I told him of my resolve. He did not approve. Then by his arguments he succeeded in persuading me. Having got as far as the court, what was the good of leaving it again without first seeing what there was there, so that I might report on the riches and greatness of the kings of the *Mogul*, exceeding the riches of other kings, as may be seen in the course of this my book?

As I was a youth, carried away by curiosity, but still more by the friendship shown to me by Clodio, and reflecting that I had already in him one friend who could do me some good in this kingdom, and be of help to me in some affair, I determined to remain where I was.

After three days had elapsed, Clodio Malier was sent for to the palace of Prince Dara, who inquired if he knew of the arrival of a European youth who had come with the ambassador of England, and a few days before had appeared in the king's presence to make a complaint of injuries done by a captain of artillery and other Englishmen. Clodio answered that he knew me well, that, seeing me unprotected, he had taken me into his house, adding that I was a youth of quality. He wished that, before allowing me to leave the *Mogul* kingdom, I should see something of the king's and the princes' riches, so that on my return to Europe I might declare the wealth and grandeur of the *Moguls*.

Thereupon the prince said to him that he wanted to speak to me, and thus he must not fail to find a way to bring me to his presence. When Clodio Malier came home, he said to me at once, with a joyous countenance, that I had already captured good fortune, for the eldest prince, a generous man and friendly to Europeans, had shown himself interested about me and wanted to speak to me. I rejoiced at this good news, knowing that the Europeans who served this prince had a good life of it, and received adequate pay. Thus I, too, was desirous of obtaining some employment at his court. I made up my mind, for that reason, not to put off my visit, and I asked Clodio if we should have to wait long before complying with the prince's desire. My friendly shelterer replied to me, that it was not wise to delay, otherwise we might lose the favourable opportunity. For the resolves of the great were like birds: if the bird-lime stuck to them, they were easily caught; but if they once flew away, it was very hard to lay hold of them a second time.

For these reasons we started the very same day, and repaired to the court of the above-named prince. As soon as he was informed of our arrival, he gave the order to allow us to enter. When I reached his presence, and had made the usual obeisances, he asked me if I could speak Persian, and put some other questions with a pleased and friendly expression on his face. He was delighted at seeing a youth of not more than eighteen years and a foreigner, with such quick-wittedness that he had learned to make the proper obeisance without any shyness. Then I answered the questions, showing myself acquainted with Turkey and Persia and other important matters. The whole of my replies were in Persian, by which I proved to the prince that I could speak sufficiently well the language about which he had asked me.

At the conclusion of the above talk he directed that the ambassador's letter be given to me. It had already been opened; and I was directed to translate it into Persian. The letter was in Latin, written in letters of gold, and it differed but little from the letter presented to the King of Persia. Being thus already acquainted with the business, I had little difficulty in translating it. Next the prince asked what the letter was written on, for it seemed to him like a skin, and not paper. I answered that it was of vellum skin, and it was the usage for European kings, when forwarding letters to far-off kingdoms, to have the more important matters written on vellum skin, in order that they might be better protected against the inclemencies of the weather and of the journey than they would be if they were on paper.

At the end of this conversation Dara asked me if I wished to remain for a time in the *Mogul* country, to which I replied affirmatively. He said to me, with a smile on his face: 'Would you like to enter my service?' As this was the very question, and none other, that I was hoping for, I replied that I should have put to very good use the wearinesses and fatigues of my journey if I had the good fortune to serve under so famous a prince.

He then directed that every month they should give me eighty rupees of pay, a sum equal to forty *patacas*. He ordered them to deliver to me at once, in his presence, a *serpao* and thirty rupees and a good horse. He put me in the charge of one of his trusted eunuchs called Coja Mosquis [Khwaja Miskin], with instructions to look after the little European and see that he was well trained and educated. I returned thanks to the prince, and seeing how well Dara was inclined towards me, I prayed for leave to entreat another favour—that is to say, the liberty of the two English prisoners; and through the mediation of the prince, they were released in a few days by order of the king.

I came out from the prince's presence. Although Dara desired that Khwaja Miskin should teach me the court ceremonial in order to turn me into a courtier, I took means to prevent my being made into a Mahomedan. So I did not go to seek out the said Khwaja Miskin, but kept in the company of the Europeans. Some of these were surgeons, but the greater number artillerymen in the *Mogul* service, an honourable employment. For European artillerymen who took service in that branch had only to take aim; as for all the rest—the fatigue of raising, lowering, loading, and firing—this was the business of artificers or labourers kept for the purpose. However, when Aurangzeb came to the throne, he, seeing the insolent behaviour and the drunkenness of such-like men, deprived them of all their privileges, except that of distilling spirits, and forced them to do sentry duty like other soldiers, thus leaving them with no estimation or reputation in the army. But the old plan continued in force up to the...beheadal of Prince Dara...

For some time I dwelt in the house of Clodio, and when I had acquired the means, I hired a separate house. Then came a man to me and said that he would put me in the way of gaining money. I inquired from him what it was he wanted. He told me that he wanted nothing beyond permission to distill spirits under my protection and close to my house. He would give me ten rupees every day; thus I should be put to no expense: all I had to do was to assert that he was my servant. I agreed to the bargain, and out of regard for me no one said a word to him, for the Europeans in the service of Dara had this privilege of distilling spirits and selling, them without hindrance. Finding myself with sufficient pay, and in good condition, I wrote to Master John at Surat, giving him notice of the king's orders—how he had ordered all the ambassador's property to be placed in the hands of the governor of Surat with directions to make it over to him. After some months he replied that he had then received delivery of everything.

When I left Venice I already knew sufficiently how to speak the Italian language, and in addition a little French. During this journey I learnt the Turkish and Persian languages. Finding myself established in India, I now set to work to learn the Indian tongue...

Manucci remained in India for the rest of his life. In Delhi in 1657, he married a fellow Italian, eighteen year-old Maria Veronea. During his six decades in India, he served various other Mughal officials as well as Raja Jai Singh of Rajasthan. Manucci's greatest prominence came from his self-taught profession as a physician. Late in life he moved to Goa,

then to Madras (under the patronage of the East India Company) and apparently died a wealthy man in Pondicherry in 1717.

Manucci composed his multi-volume work, *Storia do Mogor*, in French, Portuguese and Italian, depending on the amanuensis available at the time. This selection comes from William Irvine's translation, published as *Mogul India, 1653-1708*, 4 volumes (London: J. Murray, 1907-08).

Chapter Eight

François Bernier

F rench physician and natural philosopher François Bernier (1620-88) had a prosperous childhood, travelling through Europe while completing his studies. He published his first book, *Anatomis Rediculi Muris* in support of inductive reasoning and empirical scientific research, even before completing his doctorate in medicine in 1652 at the University of Montpellier. After living briefly as a physician in Paris, he resumed his travels, visiting Syria in 1654, then Egypt, before reaching India late in 1658. In Spring 1659, the defeated and fleeing Prince Dara Shukoh (who already had in his entourage Niccolao Manucci, Chapter 7) drafted Bernier as his personal physician. Within months, Prince Aurangzeb (who had imprisoned their ill father, Emperor Shah Jahan) consolidated his power by capturing and executing his elder brother, Dara. Bernier eventually found service in the entourage of courtier Danishmand Khan, as physician, tutor and conversation-partner. The following are a series of letters to a friend in France, Monsieur de Merveilles, that Bernier wrote while travelling across northern India, the Punjab and Kashmir during the cool and then hot seasons of 1664-65.

❦

First Letter, written at [Delhi], 14 December 1664
Monsieur,

Since the time of Aureng-Zebe's recovery it had been constantly rumoured that he intended to visit [Lahore] and [Kashmir], in order to benefit his health by change of air and avoid the approaching summer heat, from which a relapse might be apprehended. Many intelligent persons, it is true, could scarcely persuade themselves that the King would venture upon so long a journey while his father remained a prisoner in the citadel of Agra. Considerations of policy, however, have yielded to those of health; if indeed this excursion may not rather be attributed to the arts and influence of Rauckenara-Begum [Princess Rachanara Begum], who has been long anxious to inhale a purer air than that of the Seraglio, and to appear in her turn amid a pompous and magnificent army, as her sister Begum-Saheb had done during the reign of Shah-Jahan.

The King left this city on the sixth of December, at three o'clock in the afternoon; a day and hour which, according to the astrologers of Delhi, cannot

134

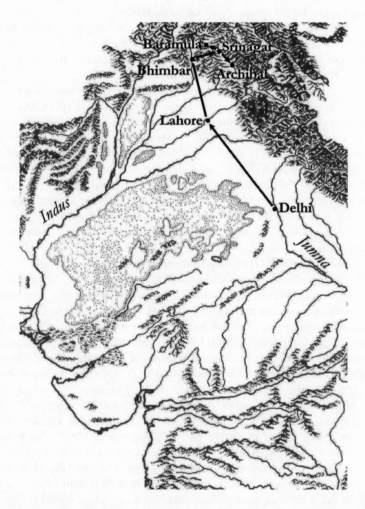

François Bernier's travels by land in north India, Punjab and Kashmir, 1664

fail to prove propitious to long journeys. Having reached [Shalimar], his country villa, which is about two leagues distant from the capital, he remained there six whole days in order to afford time for the preparations required by an expedition which was to last eighteen months. We hear to-day that he has set out with the intention of encamping on the Lahore road, and that after two days he will pursue his journey without further delay.

He is attended not only by the thirty-five thousand cavalry which at all times compose his body-guard, and by infantry exceeding ten thousand in number, but likewise by the heavy artillery and the light or stirrup-artillery, so called because it is inseparable from the King's person...

So large a retinue has given rise to a suspicion that instead of visiting Kashmir, we are destined to lay siege to the important city of Kandahar, which is situated equally on the frontiers of Persia, Hindustan and Usbec. It is the capital of a fine and productive country, yielding a very considerable revenue; and the possession of it has consequently been at all times warmly contested between the Monarchs of Persia and India.

Whatever may be the destination of this formidable force, every person connected therewith must hasten to quit Delhi, however the urgency of his affairs may require his stay; and were I to delay my own departure I should find it difficult to overtake the army. Besides, my *Navaab*, or *Agah*, Danech-mend-kan [Danishmand Khan], expects my arrival with much impatience. He can no more dispense with his philosophical studies in the afternoon than avoid devoting the morning to his weighty duties as Secretary of State for Foreign Affairs and Grand Master of the Horse. Astronomy, geography, and anatomy are his favourite pursuits, and he reads with avidity the works of Gassendy and Descartes. I shall commence my journey this very night, after having finally arranged all my affairs, and supplied myself with much the same necessaries as if I were a cavalry officer of rank. As my pay is one hundred and fifty *crowns* per month, I am expected to keep two good Turkoman horses, and I also take with me a powerful Persian camel and driver, a groom for my horses, a cook and a servant to go before my horse with a flagon of water in his hand, according to the custom of the country. I am also provided with every useful article, such as a tent of moderate size, a carpet, a portable bed made of four very strong but light canes, a pillow, a couple of coverlets, one of which, twice doubled, serves for a mattress, a solifra, or round leathern table-cloth used at meals, some few napkins of dyed cloth, three small bags with culinary utensils which are all placed in a large bag, and this bag is again carried in a very capacious and strong double sack or net made of leathern thongs. This double sack likewise contains the provisions, linen and wearing apparel, both of master and servants. I have taken care to lay in a stock of excellent rice for five or six days' consumption, of sweet biscuits flavoured with anise, of limes and sugar. Nor have I forgotten a linen bag with its small iron hook for the purpose of suspending and draining days, or curds; nothing being considered so refreshing in this country as lemonade and days. All these things, as I said before are packed in one large sack, which becomes so unwieldy that three or four men can with difficulty place it on the camel, although the animal kneels down close to it, and all that is required is to turn one of the sides of the sack over its back.

Not a single article which I have mentioned could conveniently be spared during so extended an excursion as the one in prospect. Here we cannot expect the comfortable lodgings and accommodations of our own country; a tent will be our only inn, and we must make up our minds to encamp and live after the fashion of Arabs and Tartars. Nor can we hope to supply our wants by pillage: in Hindustan every acre of land is considered the property of the King, and the spoliation of a peasant would be a robbery committed upon the King's domain. In undertaking this long march it is consoling to reflect that we shall move in a northern direction, that it is the commencement of winter, and that the periodical rains have fallen. This is, indeed, the proper season for travelling in the Indies, the rains having ceased, and the heat and dust being no longer intolerable. I am also happy at the idea of not being any longer exposed to the danger of eating the *bazar* bread of Delhi, which is often badly baked and full of sand and dust. I may hope, too, for better water than that of the capital, the impurities of which exceed my power of description; as it is accessible to all persons and animals, and the receptacle of every kind of filth. Fevers most difficult to cure are engendered by it, and worms are bred in the legs which produce violent inflammation, attended with much danger. If the patient leave Delhi, the worm is generally soon expelled, although there have been instances where it has continued in the system for a year or more. They are commonly of the size and length of the treble string of a violin, and might be easily mistaken for a sinew. In extracting them great caution should be used lest they break; the best way is to draw them out little by little, from day to day, gently winding them round a small twig of the size of a pin.

It is a matter of considerable satisfaction to me to think that I shall not be exposed to any of these inconveniences and dangers, as my *Navaab* has with marked kindness ordered that a new loaf of his own household bread, and a sourai of Ganges water (with which, like every person attached to the court, he has laden several camels) should be presented to me every morning. A sourai is that tin flagon of water, covered with red cloth, which a servant carries before his master's horse. It commonly holds a quart, but mine is purposely made to contain two, a device which I hope may succeed. This flagon keeps the water very cool, provided the cloth which covers it be always moist. The servant who bears it in his hand should also continue in motion and agitate the air; or it should be exposed to the wind, which is usually done by putting the flagon on three neat little sticks arranged so that it may not touch the ground. The moisture of the cloth, the agitation of the air, or exposure to the wind, is absolutely necessary to keep the water fresh, as if this moisture, or rather the water which has been imbibed by the cloth, arrested the little bodies, or fiery particles, existing in the air at the same time that it affords a passage to the nitrous or other particles which impede motion in the water and produce cold, in the same manner as glass arrests water, and allows light to pass through it, in consequence of the contexture and particular disposition of the particles of glass, and the difference which exists between the minute particles of water and those of light. It is only in the field that this tin flagon is used. When at home, we put the water into jars made of a certain porous earth, which are covered with a wet cloth; and, if exposed to the wind, these jars keep the water much cooler than the flagon. The higher sort of people make use of saltpetre, whether in town or with the army. They pour the water, or any other liquid they may wish to cool, into a tin flagon, round and long-necked, as I have seen English glass bottles. The flagon is then stirred, for the space of seven or eight minutes, in water into which three or four handfuls of saltpetre have been thrown. The liquid thus becomes very cold and is by no means unwholesome, as I apprehended, though at first it sometimes affects the bowels.

But to what purpose am I indulging in scientific disquisitions when on the eve of departure, when my thoughts should be occupied with the burning sun to which I am about to be exposed, and which in the Indies it is sufficiently painful to endure at any season; with the daily packing, loading and unloading; with the never-ceasing instructions to servants; with the pitching and striking of my tent; with marches by day, and marches by night; in short, with the precarious and wandering life which for the ensuing eighteen months I am doomed to experience? Adieu, my Friend; I shall not fail to perform my promise, and to impart to you from time to time all our adventures. The army on this occasion will advance by easy marches: it will not be disquieted with the apprehension of an enemy, but move with the gorgeous magnificence peculiar to the Kings of Hindustan. I shall therefore endeavour to note every interesting occurrence in order that I may communicate it as soon as we arrive at Lahore.

Second Letter, written at Lahore, 25 February 1665
Monsieur,

This is indeed slow and solemn marching, what here call *a la Mongole*. Lahore is little more than hundred and twenty leagues or about fifteen days' journey from Delhi, and we have been nearly two months on road. The King, it is true, together with the part of the army, diverged from the highway, in search of better ground for the sports of the field, and for the convenience of obtaining the water of the [Jumna], which we had gone in search of to the right; and we leisurely skirted its bank, hunting and shooting amid grass so high as almost to conceal our horsemen, but abounding in every kind of game. We are now in a good town, enjoying repose; and I cannot better employ my time than in committing to paper the various particulars which have engaged my mind since I quitted Delhi. Soon I hope to conduct you to Kashmir, and to show you one of the most beautiful countries in the world.

Whenever the King travels in military pomp he has always two private camps; that is to say, two separate bodies of tents. One or these camps being constantly a day in advance of the other, the King is sure to find at the end of every journey a camp fully prepared for his reception. It is for this reason that these separate bodies of tents are called *Peiche-kanes* or 'houses which precede'. The two *Peiche-kanes* are nearly equal, and to transport one of them the aid of more than sixty elephants, two hundred camels, one hundred mules, and one hundred men-porters is required. The most bulky things are carried by the elephants, such as the large tents, with their heavy poles, which on account of their great length and weight are made so as to be taken down into three pieces. The smaller tents are borne by the camels, and the luggage and kitchen utensils by the mules. To the porters are confided the lighter and more valuable articles, as the porcelain used at the King's table, the painted and gilt beds, and those rich *karguais* of which I shall speak hereafter

One of the *Peiche-kanes* has no sooner reached the place intended for the new encampment than the Grand Quarter-Master selects some fine situation for the King's tents, paying, however, as much attention as possible to the exact symmetry of the whole camp. He then marks out a square, each side of which measures more than three hundred ordinary paces. A hundred pioneers presently clear and level this space, raising square platforms of earth on which they pitch the tents. The whole of this extensive square is then encompassed with *kanates*, or 'screens', seven or eight feet in height, secured by cords attached to pegs, and by poles fixed two by two in the ground, at every ten paces, one pole within and the other without, and each leaning upon the other. The *kanates* are made of strong cloth, lined with printed Indian calico, representing large vases of flowers. The royal entrance, which is spacious and magnificent, is in the centre of one of the sides of the square, and the flowered calico of which it is composed, as well as that which lines the whole exterior face of this side of the square, is of much finer texture and richer than the rest.

The first and largest tent erected in the royal camp is named *Am-kas*, being the place where the King and all the nobility keep the *mokam*, that is, where they assemble at nine o'clock in the morning for the purpose of deliberating on affairs of state and of administering justice. The Kings of Hindustan seldom fail, even when in the field, to hold this assembly twice during the twenty-four hours, the same as when in the capital. The custom regarded as a matter of law and duty, and the observance of it is rarely neglected.

The second tent, little inferior in size and further within the enclosure, is called the gosle-kane, or the 'place for bathing'. It is here that all the nobility meet every evening to pay their obeisance to the King, in the same manner as when the court is at Delhi. This evening assembly subjects the *Omrahs* to much inconvenience; but it is a grand and imposing spectacle in a dark night to behold, when standing at some distance, long rows of torches lighting these Nobles, through extended lanes of tents, to the gosle-kane, and attending them back again to their own quarters. These flambeaux, although not made of wax, like ours in France, burn a long time. They merely consist of a piece of iron hafted in a stick, and surrounded at the extremity with linen rags steeped in oil, which are renewed, as occasion requires, by the masalchis, or 'link boys', who carry the oil in long narrow-necked vessels of iron or brass.

Still deeper in the square is the third tent, smaller than those I have spoken of, called Kaluet-kane, the 'retired spot', or the place of the privy council. To this tent none but the principal ministers of state have access, and it is here that all the important concerns of the kingdom are transacted.

Advancing beyond the Kaluet-kane, you come to the King's private tents, which are surrounded by small *kanates*, of the height of a man, some lined with Maslipatam chintz, painted over with flowers of a hundred different kinds, and others with figured satin, decorated with deep silken fringes.

Adjoining the royal tents are those of the Begums, or Princesses, and of the great ladies and principal female attendants of the Seraglio. These tents are also enclosed on every side by rich *kanates*; and in the midst of them are the tents of the inferior female domestics and other women connected with the Seraglio, placed generally in much the same order, according to the offices of the respective occupants.

The *Am-kas*, and the five or six other principal tents, are elevated above the rest, as well for the sake of keeping off the heat as that they may be distinguished at a distance. The outside is covered with a strong and coarse red cloth, ornamented with large and variegated stripes; but the inside is lined with beautiful hand-painted chintz, manufactured for the purpose at Maslipatam, the ornamentation of which is set off by rich figured satin of various colours, or embroideries of silk, silver, and gold, with deep and elegant fringes. Cotton mats, three or four inches in thickness, are spread over the whole floor, and these again are covered with a splendid carpet, on which are placed large square brocade cushions to lean upon. The tents are supported by painted and gilt pillars.

In each of the two tents wherein the King and nobility meet for deliberation is erected a stage, which is most sumptuously adorned, and the King gives audience under a spacious canopy of velvet or flowered silk. The other tents have similar canopies, and they also contain what are called *karguais* or 'cabinets', the little doors of which are secured with silver padlocks. You may form some idea of them by picturing to yourself two small squares of our folding screens, the one placed on the other, and both tied round with a silken cord in such a manner that the extremities of the sides of the upper square incline towards each other so as to form a kind of dome. There is this difference, however, between the *karguais* and our screens, that all their sides are composed of very thin and light deal boards painted and gilt on the outside, and embellished around with gold and silk fringe. The inside is lined with scarlet, flowered satin, or brocade. I believe that I have omitted nothing of consequence contained within the great square.

In describing what is to be seen without, I shall first notice two handsome tents on either side of the grand entrance, or royal gate. Here is to be seen a small number of the choicest horses, saddled and superbly caparisoned, ready to be mounted upon any emergency, but intended rather for ceremony and parade.

On both sides of the same royal gate are ranged the fifty or sixty small field-pieces of which the stirrup-artillery is composed, and which fire a salute when the King enters his tent, by which the army is apprised of his arrival.

A free space, as extensive as may be convenient or practicable, is always kept in front of the royal entrance, and at its extremity there is a large tent called *nagar-kane*, because it contains the trumpets and the cymbals.

Close to this tent is another of a large size, called *tchauky-kane*, where the *Omrahs* in rotation mount guard for twenty-four hours, once every week. Most of them, however, order one of their own tents to be pitched in its immediate vicinity, where they find themselves more comfortable and are in greater privacy.

Within a short distance of the three other sides of the great square are the tents of officers and others appropriated to particular purposes, which, unless there be local impediments, are always placed in the same relative situation. Every one of these tents has its particular appellation, but the names are difficult of pronunciation, and as it is not within my scope to teach you the language of the country, it may suffice to state that in one of them are deposited the arms of the King; in a second the rich harnesses; and in a third the vests of brocade, which are the presents generally made by the King. The fruits, the sweetmeats, the Ganges water; the saltpetre with which it is cooled, and the *betle* are kept in four other tents. *Betle* is the leaf...which, after it has undergone a certain preparation, is given as a mark of royal favour (like coffee in Turkey), and which when masticated sweetens the breath and reddens the lips. There are fifteen or sixteen other tents which serve for kitchens and their appurtenances; and in the midst of all these are the tents of a great number of officers and eunuchs. There are, lastly, six others, of considerable length, for led horses; and other tents for choice elephants and for the animals employed in hunting; for the birds of prey that invariably accompany the court, and are intended both for show, and for field sports; for the dogs; the leopards for catching antelopes; the *nil-ghaux*, or grey oxen, which I believe to be a species of elk; the lions and the rhinoceroses, brought merely for parade; the large Bengale buffaloes, which attack the lion, the tamed antelopes, frequently made to fight in the presence of the King.

The quarters of the Monarch are understood to comprehend not only the great square, but the numerous tents situated without the square, to which I have just drawn your attention. Their position is always in the centre of the army, or as much so as the nature of the ground will admit. You will easily conceive that there is something very striking and magnificent in these royal quarters, and that this vast assemblage of red tents, placed in the centre of a numerous army, produces a brilliant effect when seen from some neighbouring eminence; especially if the country be open, and offer no obstruction to the usual and regular distribution of the troops.

The first care of the Grand Quarter-master is, as before remarked, to choose a suitable situation for the royal tents. The *Am-kas* is elevated above every other tent, because it is the landmark by which the order and disposition of the whole army is regulated. He then marks out the royal *bazars*, from which all the troops are supplied. The principal *bazar* is laid out in the form of a wide street, running through the whole extent of the army, now on the right, then on the left of the *Am-kas*, and always as much as possible in the direction of the next day's encampment. The other royal *bazars*, which are neither so long nor so spacious, generally cross this one, some on one side and some on another side of the King's quarters. All of them are distinguished by extremely long poles stuck in the ground at the distance of three hundred paces from each other, bearing red standards, and surmounted with the tails of the Great Tibet cows, which have the appearance of so many periwigs.

The quarter-master then proceeds to plan the quarters for the *Omrahs*, that there may always be the same observance of regularity, and that each nobleman may be placed at his usual distance from the royal square, whether on the right or on the left, so that no individual may be permitted to change the place allotted to him, or which he expressed a wish to occupy before the commencement of the expedition.

The description I have given of the great square is, in many particulars, applicable to the quarters of the *Omrahs* and Rajas. In general they also have two *peiche-kanes*, with a square of *kanates* enclosing their principal tents and those of their wives. Outside this square are likewise pitched the tents of their officers and troopers, and there is a *bazar* in the form of a street, consisting of small tents belonging to the followers of the army, who supply it with forage, rice, butter, and other necessary articles of life. The *Omrahs* need not, therefore, always have recourse to the royal *bazars*, where indeed everything may be procured, almost the same as in the capital. A long pole is planted at both ends of each *bazar*, and distinguished by a particular standard, floating in the air, as high as those of the royal *bazars*, in order that the different quarters may be readily discerned from a distance.

The chief *Omrahs* and great Rajas pride themselves on the loftiness of their tents, which must not, however, be too conspicuous, lest the King perceive it and command that the tents be thrown down, as he did on our late march. For the same reason, the outside must not be entirely red, there being none but the royal tents that can be of that colour; and as a mark of proper respect every tent has also to front the *Am-kas*, or quarters of the King.

The remainder of the ground, between the quarters of the Monarch, those of the *Omrahs*, and the bazars, is filled with the tents of *Mansebdars*, or inferior *Omrahs*, of tradespeople of every description, of civil officers and other persons, who for various reasons follow the army; and, last of all, the tents of those who serve in the light and heavy artillery. The tents are therefore very numerous, and cover a large extent of ground; though with respect both to their number and the space occupied by them very extravagant notions are formed. When the army halts in a fine and favourable country, which leaves it at liberty to adopt the well-understood rules and order of a circular encampment, I do not believe that this space measures more than two leagues, or perhaps two leagues and a half in circumference, including here and there several spots of unoccupied ground. It should be mentioned, however, that the heavy artillery, which requires a great deal of room, is commonly a day or two in advance of the army.

What is said of the strange confusion that prevails in the camp, and of the alarm thereby occasioned to a newcomer, is also much exaggerated. A slight acquaintance with the method observed in the quartering of the troops will enable you to go, without much difficulty, from place to place as your business may require; the King's quarters, the tents and standards peculiar to every *Omrah*, and the ensigns and 'periwigs' of the royal *bazars*, which are all seen from a great distance, serving, after a little experience, for unerring guides.

Sometimes, indeed, notwithstanding all these precautions, there will be uncertainty and disorder, particularly on the arrival of the army at the place of encampment in the morning, when everyone is actively employed in finding and establishing his own quarters. The dust that arises often obscures the marks I have mentioned, and it becomes impossible to distinguish the King's quarter, the different *bazars*, or the tents of the several *Omrahs*. Your progress is besides liable to be impeded by the tents then pitching, and by the cords extended by inferior *Omrahs*, who have no *peiche-kanes*, and by *Mansebdars* to mark their respective boundaries, and to prevent not only the public path from passing through, but the fixing of any strange tent near their own, where their wives, if accompanying them, reside. A horde of their lusty varlets, with cudgels in their hands, will not suffer these cords to be removed or lowered; you then naturally retrace your steps, and find that while you have been employed in unavailing efforts to pass at one end, your retreat has been cut off at the other. There is now no means of extricating your laden camels but by menace and entreaty; outrageous passion, and calm remonstrance; seeming as if you would proceed to blows, yet carefully abstaining from touching anyone; promoting a violent quarrel between the servants of both parties, and afterward reconciling them for fear of the consequences, and in this way taking advantage of a favourable moment to pass your camels. But the greatest annoyance is perhaps in the evening when business calls you to any distance. This is the time when the common people cook their victuals with a fire made of cow and camel dung and green wood. The smoke of so many fires of this kind, when there is little wind, is highly offensive, and involves the atmosphere in total darkness. It was my fate to be overtaken three or four times by this wide-spreading vapour. I inquired, but could not find my way: I turned and roamed about, ignorant whither I went. Once I was obliged to stop until the smoke dispersed, and the moon arose; and at another time I with difficulty reached the *aguacy-die*, at the foot of which I passed the night with my horse and servant. The *aguacy-die* resembles a lofty mast of a ship, but is very slender, and takes down in three pieces. It is fixed toward the King's quarters, near the tent called *nagar-kane*, and during the night has a lighted lantern suspended from the top. This light is very useful, for it may be seen when every object is enveloped in impenetrable darkness. To this spot persons who lose their way resort, either to pass the night secure from all danger of robbers, or to resume their search after their own lodgings. The name *aguacy-die* may be translated 'Light of Heaven', the lantern when at a distance appearing like a star.

To prevent robberies every *Omrah* provides watchmen, who continually perambulate his particular quarters during the night, crying out Kaber-dar! or, 'Have a care!' and there are guards posted round the whole army at every five hundred paces, who kindle fires, and also cry out Kaber-dar! Besides these precautions, the Cotoual, or 'Grand Provost', sends soldiers in every direction, who especially pervade the *bazars*, crying out and sounding a trumpet. Notwithstanding all these measures, robberies are often committed, and it is prudent to be always on the alert; not to rely too much on the vigilance of servants; and to repose at an early hour, so as to watch during the remainder of the night.

I will now proceed to describe the different modes of travelling adopted by the Great *Mogol* on these occasions. Most commonly he is carried on men's shoulders in a *tact-ravan*, or 'field throne', wherein he sits. This *tact* is a species of magnificent tabernacle, with painted and gilt pillars and glass windows, that are kept shut when the weather is bad. The four poles of this litter are covered either with scarlet or brocade, and decorated with deep fringes of silk and gold. At the end of each pole are stationed two strong and handsomely dressed men, who are relieved by eight other men constantly in attendance. Sometimes the King rides on horseback, especially when the weather is favourable for hunting; and at other times he is carried by an elephant in a *mikdember*, or in a *hauze*, which is by far the most striking and splendid style of travelling, as nothing can surpass the richness and magnificence of the harness and trappings. The *mikdember* is a small house, or square wooden tower, gilt and painted; and the *hauze*, an oval chair with a canopy on pillars, also superbly decorated with colours and gold.

In every march the King is accompanied by a great number of *Omrahs* and Rajas, who follow him closely on horseback, placing themselves promiscuously in a body, without much method or regularity. On the morning of a journey, they assemble at break of day in the *Am-kas*, with the exception of those who may be exempted by age or the nature of their office. They find these marches very fatiguing, especially on hunting-days, being exposed like a private soldier to the sun and dust, frequently until three o'clock in the afternoon.

These luxurious lords move along very differently when not in the train of the King: neither dust nor sun then annoys them, but they are stretched, as on a bed, in a *paleky*, closed and covered or not as may be found more agreeable; sleeping at ease until they reach their tent, where they are sure to find an excellent dinner, the kitchen and every necessary article having been sent forward the preceding night, immediately after supper. The *Omrahs* are always surrounded by a number of well-mounted cavaliers, called *gourze-berdars*, because they carry a kind of club, or silver mace. The King is also attended by many of them, who go before him, both on the right and on the left, together with a multitude of footmen. The *gourze-berdars* are picked, good-looking men, of fine figures, and are employed to convey orders and despatches. With great sticks in their hands they drive everybody before them, and keep the way clear for the King.

The *Cours* follow the Rajahs surrounded by a large number of players on cymbals and trumpets. The *Cours*...consists of figures in silver, representing strange animals, hands, balances, fishes and other mystical objects, borne at the end of large silver poles.

A numerous body of *Mansebdars* or inferior *Omrahs* comes next, well mounted, and equipped with sword, quiver, and arrows. This body is much more numerous than that of *Omrahs*, which follows the King; because not only the *Mansebdars* who are on duty are obliged to assemble at break of day near the royal tent, for the purpose of accompanying the King, but there are many who join the train in the hope of attracting notice and obtaining preferment.

The Princesses and great ladies of the Seraglio have also different modes of travelling. Some prefer *tchaudoules*, which are borne on men's shoulders, and are not unlike the *tact-ravans*. They are gilt and painted and covered with magnificent silk nets of many colours, enriched with embroidery, fringes, and beautiful tassels. Others travel in a stately and close *paleky*, gilt and covered, over which are also expanded similar silk nets. Some again use capacious litters, suspended between two powerful camels, or between two small elephants. It is in this style I have sometimes seen Rachanara-Begum pursuing her journey, and have observed more than once in front of the litter, which was open, a young, well-dressed female slave, with a peacock's tail in her hand, brushing away the dust, and keeping off the flies from the Princess. The ladies are not unfrequently carried on the backs of elephants, which upon these occasions wear massive bells of silver, and are decked with costly trappings, curiously embroidered. These lovely and distinguished females, seated in *Mikdembers*, are thus elevated above the earth, like so many superior beings borne along through the middle region of the air. Each *Mikdember* contains eight women, four on a side: it is latticed and covered with a silken net, and yields not in richness and splendour to the *chaudoule* or the *tact-ravan*.

I cannot avoid dwelling on this pompous procession of the Seraglio. It strongly arrested my attention during the late march, and I feel delight in recalling it to my memory. Stretch imagination to its utmost limits, and you can conceive no exhibition more grand and imposing than when Rachanara-Begum, mounted on a stupendous Pegu elephant, and seated in a *Mikdember*, blazing with gold and azure, is followed by five or six other elephants with *Mikdembers* nearly as resplendent as her own, and filled with ladies attached to her household. Close to the Princess are the chief eunuchs, richly adorned and finely mounted, each with a wand of office in his hand; and surrounding her elephant, a troop of female servants, Tartars and Kashmerys, fantastically attired and riding handsome pad-horses. Besides these attendants are several eunuchs on horseback, accompanied by a multitude of Pagys, or 'lackeys on foot', with large canes, who advance a great way before the Princess, both to the right and to the left, for the purpose of clearing the road and driving before them every intruder. Immediately behind Rachanara-Begum's retinue appears a principal lady of the court, mounted and attended much in the same manner as the Princess. This lady is followed by a third, she by a fourth, and so on, until fifteen or sixteen females of quality pass with a grandeur of appearance, equipage, and retinue more or less proportionate to their rank, pay, and office. There is something very impressive of state and royalty in the march of these sixty or more elephants; in their solemn and, as it were, measured steps; in the splendour of the *Mikdembers*, and the brilliant and innumerable followers in attendance: and if I had not regarded this display of magnificence with a sort of philosophical indifference, I should have been apt to be carried away by such flights of imagination as inspire most of the Indian poets, when they represent the elephants as conveying so many goddesses concealed from the vulgar gaze.

Truly, it is with difficulty that these ladies can be approached, and they are almost inaccessible to the sight of man. Woe to any unlucky cavalier, however exalted in rank, who, meeting the procession, is found too near. Nothing can exceed the insolence of the tribes of eunuchs and footmen which he has to encounter, and they eagerly avail themselves of any such opportunity to beat a man in the most unmerciful manner. I shall not easily forget being once surprised in a similar situation, and how narrowly I escaped the cruel treatment that many cavaliers have experienced: but determined not to suffer myself to be beaten and perhaps maimed without a struggle, I drew my sword, and having fortunately a strong and spirited horse, I was enabled to open a passage, sword in hand, through a host of assailants, and to dash across the rapid stream which was before me. It is indeed a proverbial observation in these armies that three things are to be carefully avoided: the first, getting among the choice and led horses where kicking abounds; the second, intruding on the hunting ground; and the third, a too near approach to the ladies of the Seraglio. It is much worse, however, in Persia. I understand that in that country life itself is forfeited if a man be within sight even of the eunuchs, although he should be half a league distant from the women; and all the male inhabitants of the towns and villages through which the Seraglio is to pass must abandon their homes and fly to a considerable distance...

I observed that the great rivers are commonly without bridges. The army crossed them by means of two bridges of boats, constructed with tolerable skill, and placed between two or three hundred paces apart. Earth and straw mingled together are thrown upon the planking forming the footway, to prevent the cattle from slipping. The greatest confusion and danger occur at the extremities; for not only does the crowd and pressure occur most there, but when the approaches to the bridge are composed of soft moving earth, they become so broken up and so full of pits, that horses and laden oxen tumble upon one another into them, and the people pass over the struggling animals in the utmost disorder. The evil would be much increased if the army were under the necessity of crossing in one day; but the King generally fixes his camp about half a league from the bridges of boats, and suffers a day or two to elapse ere he passes to the opposite side of the river; when, pitching his tents within half a league from the bank, he again delays his departure so as to allow the army three days and nights at least to effect the passage.

As to the number of people, whether soldiers or others, which the camp contains, it is not easy to determine this accurately; so various are the opinions on this point. I may venture, however, to state generally that in this march there are at least one hundred thousand horsemen, and more than one hundred and fifty thousand animals, comprising horses, mules, and elephants; that besides these, there cannot be much less than fifty thousand camels, and nearly as many oxen or horses employed to carry the wives and children, the grain and other provisions belonging to the poor people connected with the *bazars*, who when they travel take with them, like our gypsies, the whole of their families, goods, and chattels. The servants in the army must be indeed numerous, since nothing is done without their assistance. I rank only with a two-horse cavalier, and yet I cannot possibly contrive with less than three men. Many are of opinion that the camp contains between three and four hundred thousand persons; some believe this estimate to be too small, while others consider it rather exaggerated. Accurately to determine the question, the people should be numbered. All I can confidently assert is that the multitude is prodigious and almost incredible. The whole population of Delhi, the capital city, is in fact collected in the camp, because deriving its employment and maintenance from the court and army, it has no alternative but to follow them in their march or to perish from want during their absence.

You are no doubt at a loss to conceive how so vast a number both of men and animals can be maintained in the field. The best solution of the difficulty will be found in the temperance of the Indians and simple nature of their diet. Of the five-score thousand troopers not a tenth, no not a twentieth part, eat animal food; they are satisfied with their *kichery*, a mess of rice and other vegetables, over which, when cooked, they pour boiled butter. It should be considered too that camels endure fatigue, hunger, and thirst in a surprising degree, live upon little, and eat any kind of food. At the end of every march, they are left to browse in the fields, where everything serves for fodder. It is important likewise to observe that the same tradesmen who supply the *bazars* in Delhi are compelled to furnish them in the camp; the shops of which they are composed being kept by the same persons whether in the capital or in the field.

These poor people are at great pains to procure forage: they rove about from village to village, and what they succeed in purchasing, they endeavour to sell in the army at an advanced price. It is a common practice with them to clear, with a sort of trowel, whole fields of a peculiar kind of grass, which having beaten and washed, they dispose of in the camp at a price sometimes very high and sometimes inadequately low...

I shall say nothing of the towns and villages between Delhi and Lahore: I have in fact scarcely seen any of them. My *Agah's* station not being in the centre of the army, which often kept to the highroad, but in the front of the right wing, it was our custom to traverse fields and bye-paths during the night, guided by the stars; frequently mistaking our way, and marching five or six leagues, instead of three or four, the usual distance between two encampments, till daylight again set us right.

Third Letter, written at Lahore

It is not without reason that the kingdom of which Lahore is the capital is named the Penje-ab, or the 'Region of the Five Waters'; because five rivers do really descend from the great mountains which enclose the kingdom of Kashmir, and, taking their course through this country, fall into the Indus, which empties itself into the ocean at [Sind], near the mouth of the Persian Gulf. Whether Lahore be the ancient *Bucefalos*, I do not pretend to determine. Alexander is here well known by the name of Sekander Filifous, or Alexander the son of Philip: concerning his horse, however, they know nothing. The river on which the city was built, one of the five, is as considerable as our Loire, and is much in want of a similar embankment as that on which the road is carried on the banks of the French river; for it is subject to inundations, which cause great injury and frequently change its bed: indeed within a few years the river has receded a full quarter of a league from Lahore, to the great inconvenience of the inhabitants. Unlike the buildings of Delhi and Agra, the houses here are very lofty; but, the court having resided during the last twenty years or more in one of those two cities, most of the houses in Lahore are in a ruinous state. Indeed, many have been totally destroyed and have buried many of the inhabitants under their ruins, in consequence of the heavy rains which have prevailed of late years. There are still five or six considerable streets, two or three of which exceed a league in length; but not a few of the houses in them are tumbling to the ground. The river having changed its bed, the King's palace is no longer seated on its banks. This is a high and noble edifice, though very inferior to the palaces of Delhi or Agra. It is more than two months since we arrived in this city: we have waited for the melting of the snow on the mountains of Kashmir in order to obtain an easier passage into that country; our departure is finally fixed, however, for to-morrow, as the King quitted Lahore two days ago. I have provided myself with a nice small Kashmir tent, which I purchased yesterday, as I was advised to do the same as others, and to proceed no further with my old tent, which is rather large and heavy. It will be difficult, they tell me, to find room for all our tents among the mountains of

Kashmir, which besides are impassable to camels; so that requiring porters for our baggage, the carriage of my old tent would be too expensive. Farewell!

Fourth Letter, written from the army camp, fourth day of the march.
Monsieur,

I hoped that, as I had survived the heat of Meka near the Straits of Bab-el-mandel, I should have nothing to fear from the burning rays of the sun in any part of the earth; but that hope has abandoned me since the army left Lahore four days ago. I am indeed no longer surprised that even the Indians themselves expressed much apprehension of the misery which awaited them during the eleven or twelve days' march of the army from Lahore to [Bhimbar], which is situated at the entrance of the Kashmir mountains. I declare, without the least exaggeration, that I have been reduced by the intenseness of the heat to the last extremity; scarcely believing when I rose in the morning that I should outlive the day. This extraordinary heat is occasioned by the high mountains of Kashmir; for being to the north of our road, they intercept the cool breezes which would refresh us from that quarter, at the same time that they reflect the scorching sunbeams, and leave the whole country arid and suffocating. But why should I attempt to account philosophically for that which may kill me to-morrow?

Fifth Letter, written from the army camp, sixth day of the march

I yesterday crossed one of the great rivers of India, called the [Chenab]. Its excellent water, with which the principal *Omrahs* are providing themselves, instead of the Ganges water that has hitherto supplied their wants, induces me to hope that the ascent of this river does not lead to the infernal regions, but that it may really conduct us to the kingdom of Kashmir, where they would make me believe we should be gladdened with the sight of ice and snow. Every day is found more insupportable than the preceding, and the further we advance the more does the heat increase. It is true that I crossed the bridge of boats at broad noonday, but I am not sure that my sufferings would have been less if I had remained stifling in my tent. My object was at least attained: I passed over this bridge quietly, while everybody else was resting and waiting to cross toward the close of the day, when the heat is less oppressive. Perhaps I owe my escape from some fatal accident to my prudence and foresight, for no passage of a river, since the army quitted Delhi, has been attended with such dreadful confusion. The entrance at one extremity of the bridge into the first boat, and the going out from the last boat at the other extremity were rendered extremely difficult and dangerous on account of the loose moving sand which it was necessary to pass, and which, giving way under the feet of such crowds of animals, was carried off by the current, and left considerable cavities, into which numbers of camels, oxen, and horses were thrown down, and trodden underfoot, while blows were dealt about without intermission. There are generally upon these occasions officers and troopers attached to *Omrahs*, who to clear the way for their masters and their baggage make an active use of their canes. My *Navaab* has lost one of his camels, with the iron oven it carried so that I fear I shall be reduced to the necessity of eating the *bazar* bread. Farewell!

Sixth Letter, eight day of the march
Monsieur,

Alas, my dear Sir! what can induce an European to expose himself to such terrible heat, and to these harassing and perilous marches? It is too much curiosity; or rather it is gross folly and inconsiderate rashness. My life is placed in continual jeopardy. Out of evil, however, may arise some good. When at Lahore I was seized with a flux, accompanied by acute pains in my limbs, in consequence of having passed whole nights on a terrace in the open air, as is commonly done in Delhi without danger. My health was suffering; but since we have been on the march the violent perspirations, continued for eight or nine days, have dissipated my bad humours, and my parched and withered body is become a mere sieve, the quart of water, which I swallow at a draught, passing at the same moment through every one of my pores, even to my fingers' ends. I am sure that to-day I have drunk more than ten pints. Amid all our sufferings, it is a great consolation to be able to drink as much water as we please with impunity, provided it be of a good quality.

Seventh Letter, tenth day of the march
Monsieur,

The sun is just but rising, yet the heat is insupportable. There is not a cloud to be seen nor a breath of air to be felt. My horses are exhausted; they have not seen a blade of green grass since we quitted Lahore. My Indian servants, notwithstanding their black, dry, and hard skin, are incapable of further exertion. The whole of my face, my feet, and my hands are flayed. My body too is entirely covered with small red blisters, which prick like needles. Yesterday one of our poor troopers, who was without a tent, was found dead at the foot of a tree, whither he had crept for shelter. I feel as if I should myself expire before night. All my hopes are in four or five limes still remaining for lemonade, and in a little dry curd which I am about to drink diluted with water and with sugar. Heaven bless you! the ink dries at the end of my pen, and the pen itself drops from my hand.

Eighth letter, at Bhimbar
Monsieur,

At length we have reached Bhimbar, situated at the foot of a steep, black, and scorched mountain. We are encamped in the dry bed of a considerable torrent, upon pebbles and burning sands,—a very furnace; and if a heavy shower had not fallen opportunely this morning, and I had not received from the mountains a seasonable supply of curdled milk, limes, and a fowl, I know not what would have become of your poor correspondent. But God be praised! the atmosphere is evidently cooler, my appetite is restored, my strength improved; and the first use I make of returning health is to resume my pen. You must now be made acquainted with new marches and fresh troubles.

Yesterday, at night, the King left these suffocating quarters. He was accompanied by Rachanara-Begum and the other women of the Seraglio, the Raja Ragnat, who acts as Vizier, and Fazel-kan, the High Steward, and last night the grand master of the hunt also left the camp, with some principal officers of the royal household, and several ladies of distinction. To-night it will be our turn to depart: besides my *Navaab* Danishmand Khan's family, the party will consist of Mahmet-Emir-kan, son of the celebrated Emir Jemla…, of my excellent friend Dianet-kan and his two sons, and of several other *Omrahs*, Rajas, and *Mansebdars*. The other Nobles who are to visit Kashmir will depart each in his turn, to lessen the inconvenience and confusion that must attend the five days' journey between this place and Kashmir, through difficult and mountainous paths…

That a scarcity of provisions may not be produced in the small kingdom of Kashmir, the King will be followed by a very limited number of individuals. Of females he takes only ladies of the first rank, the intimate friends of Rachanara-Begum, and those women whose services cannot easily be dispensed with. The *Omrahs* and military will also be as few as possible; and those Lords who have permission to attend the Monarch will be accompanied by no more than twenty-five troopers out of every hundred; not, however, to the exclusion of the immediate officers of their household. These regulations cannot be evaded, an *Omrah* being stationed at the pass of the mountains, who reckons every person one by one, and effectually prevents the ingress of that multitude of *Mansebdars* and other cavaliers who are eager to inhale the pure and refreshing air of Kashmir, as well as of all those petty tradesmen and inmates of the *bazars*, whose only object is to gain a livelihood.

The King has a few of the choicest elephants for his baggage and the women of the Seraglio. Though heavy and unwieldy, these animals are yet very sure-footed, feeling their way when the road is difficult and dangerous, and assuring themselves of the firm hold of one foot before they move another. The King has also a few mules; but his camels, which would be more useful, are all left behind, the mountains being too steep and craggy for their long stiff legs. Porters supply the place of camels; and you may judge of the immense number that will be employed if what they tell me be true, that the King alone has no fewer than six thousand. I must myself have three, although I left my large tent and a considerable quantity of luggage at Lahore, every person did the same, not excepting the *Omrahs* and the King himself, and yet it is calculated that there are at least fifteen thousand porters already collected in Bhimbar; some sent by the Governor of Kashmir and by the neighbouring Rajas, and others who are come voluntarily in the expectation of earning a little money. A royal ordinance fixes their pay at ten *crowns* for every hundred pounds weight. It is computed that thirty thousand will be employed; an enormous number, when it is considered that the King and *Omrahs* have been sending forward baggage, and the tradespeople articles of every sort, for the last month.

Ninth Letter, in Kashmir, the Terrestrial Paradise of the Indies, after three months.

Monsieur,

The histories of the ancient Kings of Kashmir maintain that the whole of this country was in former times one vast lake, and that an outlet for the water was opened by a certain pire, or aged 'saint', named Kacheb, who miraculously cut the mountain of [Baramula]. This account is to be met with in the abridgment of the above-mentioned histories, made by order of Jehan-Guyre [Emperor Jahangir], which I am now translating from the Persian. I am certainly not disposed to deny that this region was once covered with water: the same thing is reported of Thessaly and of other countries; but I cannot easily persuade myself that the opening in question was the work of man, for the mountain is very extensive and very lofty. I rather imagine that the mountain sank into some subterraneous cavern, which was disclosed by a violent earthquake, not uncommon in these countries. If we are to believe the Arabs of those parts, the opening of Bab-el-mandel was effected in the same manner; and it is thus that entire towns and mountains have been engulphed in great lakes.

Kashmir, however, is no longer a lake, but a beautiful country, diversified with a great many low hills: about thirty leagues in length, and from ten to twelve in breadth. It is situated at the extremity of Hindustan, to the north of Lahore; enclosed by the mountains at the foot of Caucasus, those of the Kings of Great Tibet and Little Tibet, and of the Raja Gamon, who are its most immediate neighbours.

The first mountains which surround it, I mean those nearest to the plains, are of moderate height, of the freshest verdure, decked with trees and covered with pasture land, on which cows, sheeps, goats, horses, and every kind of cattle is seen to graze. Game of various species is in great plenty,—partridges, hares, antelopes, and those animals which yield musk. Bees are also in vast abundance; and what may be considered very extraordinary in the Indies, there are, with few or no exceptions, neither serpents, tigers, bears, nor lions. These mountains may indeed be characterised not only as innocuous, but as flowing in rich exuberance with milk and honey.

Beyond the mountains just described arise others of very considerable altitude, whose summits, at all times covered with snow, soar above the clouds and ordinary mist, and, like Mount Olympus, are constantly bright and serene.

From the sides of all these mountains gush forth innumerable springs and streams of water, which are conducted by means of embanked earthen channels even to the top of the numerous hillocks in the valley; thereby enabling the inhabitants to irrigate their fields of rice. These waters, after separating into a thousand rivulets and producing a thousand cascades through this charming country, at length collect and form a beautiful river, navigable for vessels as large as are borne on our Seine. It winds gently around the kingdom, and passing through the capital, bends its peaceful course toward Baramula, where it finds an outlet between two steep rocks, being then joined by several smaller rivers from the mountains, and dashing over precipices it flows in the direction of [Attock,] and joins the Indus.

The numberless streams which issue from the mountains maintain the valley and the hillocks in the most delightful verdure. The whole kingdom wears the appearance of a fertile and highly cultivated garden. Villages and hamlets are frequently seen through the luxuriant foliage. Meadows and vineyards, fields of rice, wheat, hemp, saffron, and many sorts of vegetables, among which are intermingled trenches filled with water, rivulets, canals, and several small lakes, vary the enchanting scene. The whole ground is enamelled with our European flowers and plants, and covered with our apple, pear, plum, apricot, and walnut trees, all bearing fruit in great abundance. The private gardens are full of melons, pateques or 'water melons', water parsnips, red beet, radishes, most of our potherbs, and others with which we are unacquainted.

The fruit is certainly inferior to our own, nor is it in such variety; but this I am satisfied is not attributable to the soil, but merely to the comparative ignorance of the gardeners, for they do not understand the culture and the grafting of trees as we do in France. I have eaten, however, a great deal of very excellent fruit during my residence in Kashmir, and should entertain no doubt of its arriving at the same degree of perfection as that of Europe if the people were more attentive to the planting and soil of the trees and introduced grafts from foreign countries.

The capital of Kashmir bears the same name as the kingdom. It is without walls and is not less than three quarters of a league in length, and half a league in breadth. It is situated in a plain, distant about two leagues from the mountains, which seem to describe a semicircle, and is built on the banks of a fresh-water lake; whose circumference is from four to five leagues. This lake is formed of live springs and of streams descending from the mountains, and communicates with the river, which runs through the town, by means of a canal sufficiently large to admit boats. In the town there are two wooden bridges thrown over the river; and the houses, although for the most part of wood, are well built and consist of two or three stories. There is, however, plenty of very fine freestone in the country; some old buildings, and a great number of ancient idol-temples in ruins, are of stone; but wood is preferred on account of its cheapness, and the facility with which it is brought from the mountain, by means of so many small rivers. Most of the houses along the banks of the river have little gardens which produce a very pretty effect, especially in the spring and summer, when many parties of pleasure take place on the water. Indeed most houses in the city have also their gardens; and many have a canal, on which the owner keeps a pleasure-boat, thus communicating with the lake.

At one end of the town appears an isolated hill, with handsome houses on its declivity, each having a garden. Toward the summit are a Mosque and Hermitage, both good buildings; and the hill is crowned with a large quantity of fine trees. It forms altogether an agreeable object, and from its trees and gardens it is called, in the language of the country, Haryperbet or the 'Verdant Mountain'.

Opposite to this hill is seen another, on which is also erected a small Mosque with a garden and an extremely ancient building, which bears evident marks of having been a temple for idols, although named Tact-Souliman, the 'Throne of Solomon'. The Mahometans pretend it was raised by that celebrated King when he visited Kashmir; but I doubt whether they could prove that this county was ever honoured with his presence.

The lake is full of islands, which are so many pleasure-grounds. They look beautiful and green in the midst of the water, being covered with fruit trees, and laid out with regular trellised walks. In general they are surrounded by the large-leafed aspen, planted at intervals of two feet. The largest of these trees may be clasped in a man's arms, but they are as high as the mast of a ship, and have only a tuft of branches at the top, like the palm-trees.

The declivities of the mountains beyond the lake are crowded with houses and flower-gardens. The air is healthful, and the situation considered most desirable: they abound with springs and streams of water, and command a delightful view of the lake, the islands, and the town.

The most beautiful of all these gardens is one belonging to the King, called Shalimar. The entrance from the lake is through a spacious canal, bordered with green turf, and running between two rows of poplars. Its length is about five hundred paces, and it leads to a large summer-house placed in the middle of the garden. A second canal, still finer than the first, then conducts you to another summer-house, at the end of the garden. This canal is paved with large blocks of freestone, and its sloping sides are covered with the same. In the middle is a long row of fountains, fifteen paces asunder; besides which there are here and there large circular basins, or reservoirs, out of which arise other fountains, formed into a variety of shapes and figures.

The summer-houses are placed in the midst of the canal, consequently surrounded by water, and between the two rows of large poplars planted on either side. They are built in the form of a dome, and encircled by a gallery, into which four doors open; two looking up, or down, the canal, and two leading to bridges that connect the buildings with both banks. The houses consist of a large room in the centre, and of four smaller apartments, one at each corner. The whole of the interior is painted and gilt, and on the walls of all the chambers are inscribed certain sentences, written in large and beautiful Persian characters. The four doors are extremely valuable; being composed of large stones, and supported by two beautiful pillars. The doors and pillars were found in some of the idol temples demolished by Shah-Jahan, and it is impossible to estimate their value. I cannot describe the nature of the stone, but it is far superior to porphyry, or any species of marble.

You have no doubt discovered before this time that I am charmed with Kashmir. In truth, the kingdom surpasses in beauty all that my warm imagination had anticipated. It is probably unequalled by any country of the same extent, and should be, as in former ages, the seat of sovereign authority, extending its dominion over all the circumjacent mountains, even as far as Tartary and over the whole of Hindustan, to the island of Ceylon. It is not indeed without reason that the *Mogols* call Kashmir the terrestrial paradise of the Indies, or that Akbar was so unremitting in his efforts to wrest the sceptre from the hand of its native Princes. His son Jahangir became so enamoured of this little kingdom as to make it the place of his favourite abode, and he often declared that he would rather be deprived of every other province of his mighty empire than lose Kashmir…

The [Kashmiris] are celebrated for wit, and considered much more intelligent and ingenious than the Indians. In poetry and the sciences they are not inferior to the Persians. They are also very active and industrious. The workmanship and beauty of their *palekys*, bedsteads, trunks, inkstands, boxes, spoons, and various other things are quite remarkable, and articles of their manufacture are in use in every part of the Indies. They perfectly understand the art of varnishing, and are eminently skilful in closely imitating the beautiful veins of a certain wood, by inlaying with gold threads so delicately wrought that I never saw anything more elegant or perfect. But what may be considered peculiar to Kashmir, and the staple commodity, that which particularly promotes the trade of the country and fills it with wealth, is the prodigious quantity of shawls which they manufacture, and which gives occupation even to the little children. These shawls are about an ell and a half long, and an ell broad, ornamented at both ends with a sort of embroidery, made in the loom, a foot in width. The *Mogols* and Indians, women as well as men, wear them in winter round their heads, passing them over the left shoulder as a mantle. There are two sorts manufactured: one kind with the wool of the country, finer and more delicate than that of Spain; the other kind with the wool, or rather hair (called touz) found on the breast of a species of wild goat which inhabits Great Tibet. The touz shawls are much more esteemed than those made with the native wool. I have seen some, made purposely for the *Omrahs*, which cost one hundred and fifty roupies; but I cannot learn that the others have ever sold for more than fifty. They are very apt, however, to be worm-eaten, unless frequently unfolded and aired. The fur of the beaver is not so soft and fine as the hair from these goats.

Great pains have been taken to manufacture similar shawls in Patna, Agra, and Lahore; but notwithstanding every possible care, they never have the delicate texture and softness of the Kashmir shawls, whose unrivalled excellence may be owing to certain properties in the water of that country. The superior colours of the Maslipatam chittes or 'cloths, painted by the hand', whose freshness seems to improve by washing, are also ascribed to the water peculiar to that town.

The people of Kashmir are proverbial for their clear complexions and fine forms. They are as well made as Europeans, and their faces have neither the Tartar flat nose nor the small pig-eyes that distinguish the natives of Kacheguer, and which generally mark those of Great Tibet. The women especially are very handsome; and it is from this country that nearly every individual, when first admitted to the court of the Great *Mogol*, selects wives or concubines, that his children may be whiter than the Indians and pass for genuine *Mogols*. Unquestionably there must be beautiful women among the higher classes, if we may judge by those of the lower orders seen in the streets and in the shops. When at Lahore I had recourse to a little artifice, often practised by the *Mogols* to obtain a sight of these hidden treasures; the women of that town being the finest brunettes in all the Indies, and justly renowned for their fine and slender shapes. I followed the steps of some elephants, particularly one richly harnessed, and was sure to be gratified with the sight I was in search of, because the ladies no sooner hear the tinkling of the silver bells suspended from both sides of the elephant than they all put their heads to the windows. This is a stratagem with which I often amused myself in Kashmir, until a more satisfactory method of seeing the fair sex was devised by an old pedagogue, well known in the town, with whom I read the Persian poets. I purchased a large quantity of sweetmeats, and accompanied him to more than fifteen houses, to which he had freedom of access. He pretended I was his kinsman lately arrived from Persia, rich and eager to marry. As soon as we entered a house, he distributed my sweetmeats among the children, and then everybody was sure to flock around us, the married women and the single girls, young and old, with the twofold object of being seen and receiving a share of the present. The indulgence of my curiosity drew many roupies out of my purse; but it left no doubt on my mind that there are as handsome faces in Kashmir as in any part of Europe.

It remains only to speak of my journey through the mountains, from Bhimbar to this place... I was surprised to find myself on the very first night transported on a sudden from a torrid to a temperate zone: for we had no sooner scaled that frightful wall of the world, I mean the lofty, steep, black, and bare mountain of Bhimbar, and begun the descent on the other side, than we breathed a pure, mild, and refreshing air. What surprised me still more was to find myself, as it were, transferred from the Indies to Europe; the mountains we were traversing being covered with every one of our plants and shrubs, save the hyssop, thyme, marjoram, and rosemary. I almost imagined myself in the mountains of Auvergne, in a forest of fir, oak, elm, and plane trees, and could not avoid feeling strongly the contrast between this scene and the burning fields of Hindustan, which I had just quitted and where nothing of the kind is seen.

My attention was particularly arrested by a mountain, distant between one and two days from Bhimbar, covered on both sides with plants. The side facing the south, that is, looking toward Hindustan, is full of Indian and European plants, mingled together; but the side exposed to the north is crowded exclusively with the vegetable productions of Europe. It would seem that one side participates equally of the air and temperature of India and Europe, and that the other feels only the milder climate of the latter quarter of the globe.

I could not avoid admiring, in the course of our march, the successive generation and decay of trees. I saw hundreds plunged and plunging into abysses, down which man never ventured, piled dead one upon another and mouldering with time; while others were shooting out of the ground, and supplying the places of those that were no more. I observed also trees consumed by fire; but I am unable to say whether they were struck by lightning, or ignited by friction, when hot and impetuous winds agitate the trees against each other, or whether, as the natives pretend, trees when grown old and dry may ignite spontaneously.

The magnificent cascades between the rocks increase the beauty of the scene. There is one especially which I conceive has not its parallel. I observed it at a distance from the side of a high mountain. A torrent of water rolling impetuously through a long and gloomy channel, covered with trees, precipitates itself suddenly down a perpendicular rock of prodigious height, and the ear is stunned with the noise occasioned by the falling of these mighty waters. Jahangir erected on an adjacent rock, which was smoothed for the purpose, a large building from which the court might leisurely contemplate this stupendous work of Nature, which, as well as the trees before mentioned, bears marks of the highest antiquity, and is perhaps coeval with the creation of the world.

A strange accident cast a gloom over these scenes and damped all our pleasure. The King was ascending the [Pir-panjal] mountains, the highest of all the mountains, and from which a distant view of the kingdom of Kashmir is first obtained. He was followed by a long line of elephants, upon which sat the ladies in their *mikdembers* and *embarys*. The foremost, appalled, as is supposed, by the great length and acclivity of the path before him, stepped back upon the elephant that was moving on his track, who again pushed against the third elephant, the third against the fourth, and so on until fifteen of them, incapable of turning round or extricating themselves in a road so steep and narrow fell down the precipice. Happily for the women, the place where they fell was of no great height; only three or four were killed; but there were no means of saving any of the elephants. Whenever these animals fall under the tremendous burden usually placed upon their backs, they never rise again even on a good road. Two days afterward we passed that way, and I observed that some of the poor elephants still moved their trunks. The army, which had been marching four days in single file through the mountains, was subjected to serious inconvenience by this disaster. The remainder of the day and the following night, were employed in rescuing the women and in saving other matters, and the troops were under the necessity of halting during the whole of that time. Nearly every man continued pent up in the same spot, for it was impossible, in many places, to advance or recede, and the thieving varlets of porters with the tents and provisions were not within reach. My usual good fortune, however, attended me; I contrived to clamber out of the line of march and find a spot whereon I and my horse slept pretty comfortably. The servant who followed me had a small quantity of bread, which we shared. It was here, I recollect, that in stirring some stones, we found a large black scorpion, which a young *Mogol* of my acquaintance took up and squeezed in his hand, then in the hand of my servant, and lastly in mine, without any of us being stung. This young cavalier pretended that he had charmed the scorpion, as he had charmed many others, with a passage from the Koran; 'but I will not', added he, 'teach you that passage, because the occult power would then depart from me and rest with you, in the same manner as it left my teacher the moment he imparted the secret.'

While traversing this same mountain of Pir-panjal, where the elephants tumbled down, three things recalled my old philosophical speculations. The first was that we experienced the opposite seasons of summer and winter within the same hour. In ascending we were exposed to the intense heat of the sun, and perspired most profusely; but when we reached the summit, we found ourselves in the midst of frozen snow, through which a passage for the army had been recently cut; a small and congealed rain was falling, and the wind blew piercingly cold. The poor Indians, most of whom had never felt the severity of winter, and saw for the first time ice and snow, were in a state of great suffering and astonishment and fled with precipitation.

The second circumstance was, that within two hundred paces the wind blew from two opposite quarters. While climbing toward the summit it blew in my face, that is, from the north; but I no sooner began to descend on the other side than it blew on my back, that is, from the south; as if the vapours escaping from all sides, and rising to the summit of the mountain, had there condensed, and caused the wind; which, equally attracted by the warm exhausted air below, descended into the two opposite valleys.

The third extraordinary appearance was an aged hermit, who had resided on the top of this mountain ever since the time of Jahangir. Of his religion everybody was ignorant; but it was said that he wrought miracles, caused strange thunders, and raised storms of wind, hail, snow, and rain. His white and uncombed beard was extremely long and bushy; he had somewhat of the savage in his aspect, and was haughty in his manner of asking alms. He permitted the people to drink water out of some earthen cups placed in rows on a large stone, making signs with his hand that they should not stop, but hastily leave the summit of the mountain. The old man was also very angry with those who made a noise. After I had entered his cave, and softened his countenance by means of half a roupie, which I humbly put in his hand, he informed me that noise made there stirred up the most furious tempests imaginable. It was wise in Aurangzeb, he added, to be guided by his advice, and to order the army to pass with stillness and expedition. His father, Shah-Jahan, always acted with the same prudence; but Jahangir having upon one occasion derided his counsel, and, notwithstanding his earnest remonstrance, having ordered the cymbals to be beaten and the trumpets to be sounded; narrowly escaped destruction.

In regard to my excursions in different parts of this kingdom, I shall begin by informing you that we no sooner arrived in the city of Kashmir than my *Navaab*, Danishmand Khan, sent me to the further end of the country, three short journeys from the capital, that I might witness the 'wonders', as they are called, of a certain fountain. I was accompanied by a native, and escorted by one of my *Navaab's* troopers. The wonders consist in this: in the month of May, when the melting of the snows has just taken place, this fountain, during the space of fifteen days, regularly flows and ebbs three times a day,—when the morning dawns, at noon, and at night. Its flow generally continues three quarters of an hour, and is sufficiently abundant to fill a square reservoir ten or twelve feet deep, and as many in length and breadth. After a lapse of fifteen days, the supply of water becomes less copious and regular, and at the expiration of a month the spring ceases to run, unless in the time of heavy and incessant rains, when it runs with the ebb and flow of other fountains. The *Gentiles* have a small temple on the side of the reservoir dedicated to Brare, one of their deities; and hence this spring is called Send-brary, or 'water of Brare'. Pilgrims flock from all parts to this temple, for the purpose of bathing and purifying themselves in the sacred and miraculous water. Numberless fables are founded on the origin of this fountain, which, not having a shadow of truth, would be little entertaining in the recital. The five or six days that I remained in the vicinity of Send-brary were employed in endeavours to trace the cause of the wonder: I paid considerable attention to the situation of the mountain, at whose foot is found this supernatural spring. With much labour and difficulty I reached the top, leaving no part unexplored, searching and prying at every step. I remarked that its length extends from north to south, and that though very near to other mountains, yet it is completely detached from any. Its form resembles an ass's back; the summit is of extreme length, but the greatest breadth is scarcely one hundred paces. One side of the mountain, which is covered with nothing but green grass, has an eastern aspect; but the sun, being intercepted by the opposite mountains, does not shine upon it before eight o'clock in the morning. The western side is coveted with trees and bushes.

Having made these observations, it occurred to me that this pretended wonder might be accounted for by the heat of the sun, combined with the peculiar situation and internal disposition of the mountain. I supposed that the frozen waters, which during the winter, when the whole ground is covered with snow, had penetrated into the inner parts of that portion of the mountain exposed to the morning sun, became partially melted, that these waters running down, little by little, into certain beds of live rock, and being thence conveyed toward the spring, produced the flow at noon; that the sun quitting this part of the mountain (which then becomes cool) darts its vertical beams upon the summit, melting the congealed waters, which descend also by slow degrees, but through different channels, into the same beds of live rock, and are the cause of the flow at night; and finally, that the sun heating the western side of the mountain, similar effects are occasioned, and the morning flow is the consequence. That this last is slower than the others may be accounted for by the remoteness of the western side from the spring, by its being covered with wood, and therefore more sheltered from the sun, or simply by the coldness of the night. My reasoning may derive support from the fact of the water flowing most copiously during the first days, and that having gradually diminished in quantity it ceases to run altogether: as if the waters which had remained frozen in the earth were in greater plenty at the commencement than afterwards. It may be observed too, that even at the beginning the supply of water as to the quantity is very uncertain, and that the flow is sometimes greater at noon than at night or in the morning, or in the morning greater than at noon; because, as I conceive, some days are hotter than others, and because clouds, sometimes rendering the heat unequal, thus become the cause of inequality in the flow of water.

Returning from Send-brary, I turned a little from the high road for the sake of visiting [Achibal], a country house formerly of the Kings of Kashmir and now of the Great *Mogol*. What principally constitutes the beauty of this place is a fountain, whose waters disperse themselves into a hundred canals round the house, which is no means unseemly, and throughout the gardens. The spring gushes out of the earth with violence, as if it issued from the bottom of some well, and the water is so abundant that it ought rather to be called a river than a fountain. It is excellent water, and cold as ice. The garden is very handsome, laid out in regular walks, and full of fruit-trees, apple, pear , plum, apricot, and cherry. Jets-d'eau in various forms and fish-ponds are in great number, and there is a lofty cascade which in its fall takes the form and colour of a large sheet, thirty or forty paces in length, producing the finest effect imaginable; especially at night, when innumerable lamps, fixed in parts of the wall adapted for that purpose, are lighted under this sheet of water.

From Achibal I proceeded to another royal garden, embellished much in the same manner. One of its ponds contains fish so tame that they approach upon being called, or when pieces of bread are thrown into the water. The largest have gold rings, with inscriptions, through the gills, placed there, it is said, by the celebrated Nour-Mehulle [Nur Mahal], the wife of Jahangir, grandfather to Aurangzeb.

Danishmand Khan seemed well satisfied with the account I brought of Send-brary, and wished me to undertake another journey, that I might bear my testimony to what he called a real miracle, such a miracle as would induce me to renounce my religion and become a Musulman. 'Hasten to Baramula', said he; 'the distance is not greater than to Send-brary: there you will see a Mosque which contains the tomb of a celebrated Pire, or Holy Dervish, who though dead yet miraculously cures the sick and infirm. Perhaps you may deny the reality either of the disease or of the cure; but another miracle is wrought by the power of this holy man, which no person can see without acknowledging. There is a large round stone that the strongest man can scarcely raise from the ground, but which eleven men, after a prayer made to the saint, lift up with the tips of their eleven fingers with the same ease as they would move a piece of straw.' I was not sorry for another little excursion, and set out with both my former companions, the trooper and the native of the country. I found Baramula a rather pleasant place; the Mosque is a tolerable building and the Saint's tomb is richly adorned. It was surrounded with a great number of people, engaged in acts of devotion, who said they were ill. Adjoining the Mosque is a kitchen, wherein I observed large boilers filled with meat and rice, which I conceived at once to be the magnet that draws the sick, and the miracle that cures them. On the other side of the mosque are the apartments and garden of the *Mullahs*, who pursue the even tenor of their way under the shadow of the Pire's miraculous sanctity. They are sufficiently zealous in celebrating his praises, but as I am always unhappy on similar occasions, he performed no miracle upon the sick while I remained there. As to the round and heavy stone that was to convert me, I noticed that eleven *Mullahs* formed themselves into a circle round it, but what with their long cabayes, or 'vests', and the studied compactness of the circle, I had great difficulty to see the mode in which they held the stone. I watched narrowly, however, the whole of this cheating process, and although the *Mullahs* stoutly maintained that each person used only the tip of one finger, and that the stone felt as light as a feather, yet I could clearly discover that it was not raised from the ground without a great effort, and it seemed to me that the *Mullahs* made use of the thumb as well as of the forefinger. Still I mixed my voice with the cries of these impostors and bystanders, exclaiming Karamet! Karamet!—'a miracle! a miracle!' I then presented them with a roupie, and assuming a look of the deepest devotion, entreated that I might have for once the distinguished honour of being among the eleven who lifted the stone. The *Mullahs* were reluctant to comply with my request, but having presented them with a second roupie, and expressed my belief in the truth of the miracle, one of them gave up his place to me. No doubt they hoped that ten would be able, by an extraordinary effort, to lift the stone, although I contributed no other aid than the tip of my finger, and they expected to manage so adroitly that I should not discover the imposture. But they were much mortified to find that the stone, to which I persevered in applying the end of my finger only, was constantly inclining and falling towards me. I considered it prudent at last to hold it firmly with both my finger and thumb, when we succeeded, but with great difficulty, in raising it to the usual height. Observing that every person looked at me with an evil eye, not knowing what to think of me, and that I incurred the danger of being stoned, I continued to join in the cry of Karamet! and throwing down a third roupie, stole away from the crowd. Though I had taken no refreshment since my arrival, I did not hesitate to mount my horse directly, and to quit for ever the Dervish and his miracles. I availed myself of this opportunity to visit those celebrated rocks that form the outlet of all the waters of the kingdom...

I was induced to quit the high road for the sake of approaching a large lake that I saw at some distance. It is well stocked with fish, particularly eels, and covered with ducks, wild geese, and many other water-birds. The Governor comes hither in the winter, when these birds are in greatest plenty, to enjoy the sport of fowling. In the centre of the lake is an hermitage, with its little garden, which it is pretended floats miraculously upon the water. The hermit passes the whole of his life there; he never leaves the place. I shall not fill up this letter by recounting the thousand absurd tales reported of this hermitage, except it be the tradition that one of the ancient Kings of Kashmir, out of mere fancy, built it upon a number of thick beams fastened together. The river which runs toward Baramula passes through the middle of this lake.

Leaving this lake, I went in search of a spring, considered an object of curiosity. It bubbles gently and rises with some force, bringing with it a certain quantity of very fine sand, which returns the way it came; after which the water becomes still a moment or two without ebullition and without bringing up sand, and then bubbles as before, and with the same effect: thus continuing its motion at irregular intervals. But the wonder, they say, consists in this, that the least noise made, either by speaking or knocking the feet against the ground; agitates the water and causes it to run and bubble in the manner described. I discovered, however, that its movements are influenced neither by speaking nor knocking, and that its action is the same whether you make a noise or are silent. As to the real cause of the water rising in this manner, I have not reflected sufficiently upon the subject to give you a satisfactory solution; unless it be that the sand by returning continues to obstruct the narrow channel of this small and weak spring, until the water thus opposed and closed in makes an effort to raise the sand and open a passage; or it may rather be, that the wind pent in the channel of the spring rises at intervals, as is the case in artificial springs.

When we had sufficiently examined this fountain, we ascended the mountains, for the purpose of seeing an extensive lake, in which there is ice, even in summer, which the winds heap up and disperse, as in a frozen sea. We then passed through a place called Sengsafed, that is to say, 'Whitestone', remarkable for producing in summer every kind of flower, the same as in a well-stored garden; and for a circumstance said to have been observed from time immemorial, that when many persons visit this spot and make much noise and agitate the air, a heavy shower of rain invariably descends. Whether this be generally the case or not, there can be no doubt that a few years ago, when

Sengsafed was visited by Shah-Jahan, the whole party was in danger of perishing in consequence of the violent and extraordinary rains which fell, although he had issued orders that no unnecessary noise should be made. This fact will remind you of the aged hermit's conversation with me on the summit of Pir-panjal.

I was pursuing my journey to a grotto full of wonderful congelations, two days' journey from Sengsafed, when I received intelligence that my *Navaab* felt very impatient and uneasy on account of my long absence...

Bernier soon left the Mughal imperial entourage and travelled down the Ganges to Bengal (occasionally in the company of Jean-Baptiste Tavernier, Chapter Nine) then south and west to Surat. During his travels, he wrote other sets of letters about Mughal India to influential Frenchmen, including Jean-Baptiste Colbert, finance minister to King Louis XIV. Bernier left India in 1667, journeying through Persia before reaching France in 1669. He then published extensively in French about his experiences, including a four-volume autobiographical travel narrative and other works on his explorations and discoveries, before his death in 1688. This selection comes from a translation by Irving Brock published as *Travels in the Mogul Empire* (London: W. Pickering, 1826).

Chapter Nine

Jean-Baptiste Tavernier

Jean-Baptiste Tavernier (1605-89), came from a Huguenot Protestant family originally of Antwerp but settled in France, his father being a skilled engraver and cartographer. Tavernier himself loved travel, as a military officer and then successful merchant-broker. In all, he made six voyages to Asia (1637-68), importing and exporting uncut gems, jewellery and other preciosities. As a dealer in luxuries but also as informal ambassador from King Louis XIV to the Mughals he grew wealthy.

In this selection, Tavernier retrospectively describes his journey from Agra to Bengal during the cool season of 1665-66, nearly 30 years after he first began travelling in India. Always striving to comprehend local customs, he depicted in rich detail but differing degrees of accuracy: banjaras (transporting castes, also mentioned by Peter Mundy, Chapter Five), the holy city of Benares/Varanasi and the burgeoning trade between Europeans and Indians (profitable, but also tension-filled).

I started from Agra for Bengal on the 25th of November 1665 and halted the same day at a poor *caravansarai* distant 3 *coss* from Agra. The 26th I reached Beruzabad, 9 *coss*. It is a small town, where, on my return, I received 8,000 rupees of the balance of the money which Ja'far Khan owed me for the goods which he had brought from me at Jahanabad. The 27th to Serail Morlides, 9 *coss*; 28th to Estanja, 14 *coss*; 29th to Haii-Mal, 12 *coss*; 30th to Sekandera, 13 *coss*; 1st of December to Sanqual, 14 *coss*.

On this day I met 110 wagons, each drawn by 6 oxen, and there was upon each wagon 50,000 rupees. It was the [Emperor's] revenue of the Province of Bengal, which, all charges being paid and the purse of the Governor well filled, amounted to 5,500,000 rupees.

…it is appropriate to speak of the conveyances and of the manner of travelling in India, which, in my opinion, is not less convenient than all the arrangements for marching in comfort either in France or in Italy. Differing from the custom in Persia, you do not employ in India in caravans or journeys either asses, mules, or horses, everything being carried here on oxen or by waggon, as the country is sufficiently level. If any merchant takes a horse from

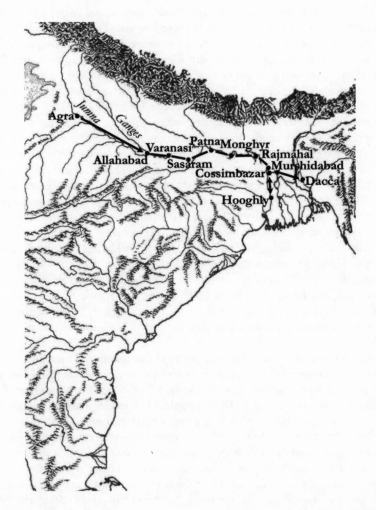

Jean-Baptiste Tavernier's travels by land in north and east India, 1665-66

Persia he does it only for show, and to have him led by hand, or in order to sell him advantageously to some noble.

They give an ox a load weighing 300 or 350 *livres*, and it is an astonishing sight to behold caravans numbering 10,000 or 12,000 oxen together, for the transport of rice, corn, and salt—to the places where they exchange these commodities—carrying rice to where only corn grows, and corn to where only rice grows, and salt to the places where there is none. They use camels also for caravans, but rarely, and they are specially reserved to carry the baggage of the nobles. When the season presses, and they wish to get the goods quickly to Surat, in order to ship them, they load them on oxen, and not on carts. As all the territories of the Great *Mogul* are well cultivated, the fields are enclosed by good ditches, and each has its tank or reservoir for irrigation. This makes it so inconvenient for travellers, because, when they meet caravans of this description in narrow roads, they are sometimes obliged to wait two or three days till all have passed. Those who drive these oxen follow no other trade all their lives; they never dwell in houses, and they take with them their women and children. Some of them possess 100 oxen, others have more or less, and they all have a Chief, who acts as a prince, and who always has a chain of pearls hanging from his neck. When the caravan which carries corn and that which carries rice meet, rather than give way one to the other, they often engage in very sanguinary encounters. The Great *Mogul*, considering that these quarrels were prejudicial to commerce and to the transport of food in his kingdom, arranged that the Chiefs of the two caravans should come to see him. When they arrived, the King, after he had advised them for their mutual benefit to live for the future in harmony with each other, and not to fight again when they met, presented each of them with a *lakh*, or 100,000 rupees, and a chain of pearls.

In order to enable the reader to understand this manner of carrying in India, it should be remarked that among [such transporting] idolaters of this country there are four tribes, whom they call 'Manaris', of which each numbers about one hundred thousand souls. These people dwell in tents, as I have said, and have no other trade but to transport provisions from one country to another. The first of these tribes has to do with corn only, the second with rice, the third with pulse, and the fourth with salt, which it obtains from Surat, and even from as far as Cape Comorin. You can also distinguish these tribes in this manner—their priests…mark those of the first with a red gum, of the size of a *crown*, on the middle of the forehead, and make a streak along the nose, attaching to it above some grains of corn, sometimes nine, sometimes twelve, in the form of a rose. Those of the second are marked with a yellow gum, in the same places, but with grains of rice; those of the third with a grey gum, with grains of millet, and also on the shoulders, but without placing grains there. As for those of the fourth, they carry a lump of salt, suspended from the neck in a bag, which weighs sometimes from 8 to 10 *livres* (for the heavier it is the more honour they have in carrying it), with which, by way of penance before praying, they beat their stomachs every morning. Generally all have a string, or tress, round the shoulders, from which hangs a small box of silver in the form of a reliquary, of the size of a good hazel nut, in which they keep a superstitious writing which their priests have enclosed in it. They place them also on their oxen, and on the other animals born in their herds, for which they entertain a special affection, loving them as dearly as they would do their children, especially when they happen to be childless.

The dress of the women is but a simple cloth, white or coloured, which is bound five or six times like a petticoat from the waist downwards, as if they had three or four, one above the other. From the waist upwards they tattoo their skin with flowers, as when one applies cupping glasses, and they paint these flowers divers colours with the juice of roots, in such a manner that it seems as though their skin was a flowered fabric.

While the men load their animals in the morning and the women fold up their tents, the priests who follow them set up in the most beautiful parts of the plain where they are encamped, an idol in the form of a serpent, entwined about a staff of six or seven feet in height, and each one in order goes to make reverence to it, the girls turning round it three times. After all have passed, the priests take care to remove the idol and to load it on an ox assigned for that purpose.

The caravans of waggons do not ordinarily consist of more than one hundred or two hundred at the most. Each waggon is drawn by ten or twelve oxen, and accompanied by four soldiers, whom the owner of the merchandise is obliged to pay. Two of them walk on each side of the waggon, over which two ropes are passed, and the four ends are held by the soldiers, so that if the waggon threatens to upset in a bad place, the two soldiers who are on the opposite side hold the ropes tight, and prevent it turning over...

But you should take care when you buy or hire an ox for riding that he has not horns longer than a foot, because, if they are longer, when the flies sting him, he chafes and tosses back the head, and may plant a horn in your stomach, as has happened several times. These oxen allow themselves to be driven like our horses, and have for a bridle only a cord, which passes through the tendon of the muzzle or the nostrils. In level tracts, where there are no stones, they do not shoe these oxen, but they always do so in rough places, both on account of the pebbles and because of the heat, which may injure the hoof. Whereas in Europe we attach our oxen by the horns, those of India have a large hump on the neck, which keeps in position a leather collar about four fingers wide, which they have only to throw over the head when they harness them.

They have also, for travelling, small, very light carriages, which can carry two persons; but usually you travel alone, in order to be more comfortable, being then able to have your clothes with you; the canteen of wine and some small requisites for the journey having their place under the carriage, to which they harness only a pair of oxen. These carriages, which are provided, like ours, with curtains and cushions, are not slung; but, on the occasion of my last journey, I had one made after our manner, and the two oxen by which it was drawn cost me very nearly 600 rupees. The reader need not be astonished at this price, for there are some of them which are strong, and make journeys lasting 60 days, at 12 or 15 leagues a day, and always at the trot. When they have accomplished half the journey, they give to each two or three balls of the size of our penny rolls, made of wheaten flour, kneaded with butter and black sugar, and in the evening they have a meal of chick-peas, crushed and steeped in water for half an hour. The hire of a carriage amounts to about a rupee a day...

Those who can afford to take their ease make use of a *palankeen*, in which they travel very comfortably. It is a kind of bed, 6 or 7 feet long and 3 feet wide, with a small rail all round. A sort of cane, called bamboo, which they bend when young, in order to cause it to take the form of a bow in the middle, supports the cover of the *palankeen*, which is of satin or brocade; and when the sun shines on one side, an attendant, who walks near the *palankeen*, takes care to lower the covering. There is another, who carries at the end of a stick a kind of basket-work shield, covered with some kind of beautiful stuff, in order that he may be able promptly to shelter the occupant of the *palankeen* from the heat of the sun when it turns and strikes him on the face. The ends of the bamboo are attached on both sides to the body of the *palankeen* between two poles, joined together in a saltier, or St. Andrew's Cross, and each of these poles is 5 or 6 feet long. Some of these bamboos cost as much as 200 *écus*, and I have paid 125 for one. Three men, at most, place themselves at each of these ends, and carry the *palankeen* on their shoulders, one on the right and the other on the left, and they travel in this way faster than our chairmen in Paris, and with an easier pace, being trained to the trade from an early age. When you wish to make haste, and travel as much as 13 or 14 leagues a day, you take 12 men to carry the *palankeen*, so that they may relieve one another from time to time. You pay each of them only 4 rupees a month inclusive, but you pay up to 5 rupees when the journey is long, and when they are required to travel for more than sixty days.

He who desires to travel with honour in India, whether by carriage or *palankeen*, ought to take with him 20 or 30 armed men, some with bows and arrows and others with muskets, and you pay them as much per month as those who carry the *palankeen*. Sometimes, for greater show, you carry a flag. This is always done by the English and Dutch, for the honour of their Companies. These attendants not only conduce to your honour, but they watch also for your protection, and act as sentinels at night, relieving one another, and striving to give you no cause of complaint against them. For it should be mentioned that in the towns where you hire them they have a head man who answers for their honesty, and when you employ them, each one gives him a rupee.

In the large villages there is generally a *Musalman* governor, and there you find sheep, fowl, and pigeons for sale; but in the places where there are only *Banians*, you find only flour, rice, vegetables, and milk.

The great heat of India compels travellers who are not accustomed to it to travel by night, in order to rest by day. When they enter towns which are closed they must leave by sunset, if they wish to take the road. For when night comes, and the gates are closed, the Governor of the place, who has to answer for thefts which occur within his jurisdiction, does not allow anyone to go out, and says that it is the Emperor's order, which he must obey. When I entered such places I took provisions, and left early, in order to camp outside under some tree in the shade, waiting till it was time to march...

At one league on this side of Sanqual you cross a river called Sengar, which flows into the Jumna, only at a distance of half a league. You cross this river Sengar by a stone bridge, and when you arrive from the Bengal side, to go to Sironj and Surat, if you wish to shorten the journey by ten days, when quitting the road to Agra you must come as far as this bridge, and cross the river Jumna by boat. Nevertheless the route by Agra is generally taken because by the other there are five or six days' stony marches, and because one must pass through the territories of Rajas where there is danger of being robbed.

The 2nd [December, 1665] I came to a *caravansarai* called Cherourabad, 12 *coss*. Half-way you pass Jahanabad, a small town near which, about a quarter of a league on this side, you pass a field of millet, where I saw a rhinoceros eating stalk of this millet, which a small boy nine or ten years old presented to him. On my approaching he gave me some stalks of millet, and immediately the rhinoceros came to me, opening his mouth four or five times; I placed some in it, and when he had eaten them he continued to open his mouth so that I might give him more.

The 3rd I came to Serrail Chageada, 10 *coss*; the 4th, to Serrail Atakan, 13 *coss*; the 5th, to Aurangabad, a large town, 9 *coss*. Formerly this town had another name, and it is the place where Aurangzeb, who reigns at present, gave battle to his brother Sultan Shuja, who held the government of the whole of Bengal. Aurangzeb having been victorious gave his name to the town, and he built there a handsome house with a garden and a small mosque.

The 6th to Alinchan, 9 *coss*. About two leagues on this side of Alinchan you meet the Ganges. Monsieur Bernier, Physician to the King, and a man named Rachepot, who was with me, were surprised to see that this river, so much talked about, is not larger than the Seine in front of the Louvre, it being supposed that it equalled in width, at the least, the Danube below Belgrade. There is actually so little water between the months of March and June or July, when the rains commence, that boats are not able to ascend it. On arrival at the Ganges, we each drank a glass of wine which we mixed with water—this caused us some internal disturbance; but our attendants who drank it alone were much more tormented than we were. The Dutch, who have a house on the banks of the Ganges, never drink the water of the river, except after it has been boiled; as for the native inhabitants, they have been accustomed to it from their youth; the Emperor even and all his court drink no other. You see every day a large number of camels which do nothing else but fetch water from the Ganges.

The 7th we came to Allahabad, 8 *coss*. Allahabad is a large town built on a point of land where the Ganges and the Jumna meet one another. It has a fine castle built of cut stone, with a double ditch, and it is the dwelling of the Governor. He is one of the greatest nobles in India, and as he is troubled with bad health he employs some Persian Physicians, and he then also had in his service M. Claude Maille of Bourges, who practised both surgery and medicine. It was he who advised us not to drink any of the Ganges water, which would produce disturbance of the stomach, but to drink rather the water from wells. The chief of these Persian Physicians, whom this Governor had in his pay, one day threw his wife down from the top of a terrace to the ground, impelled apparently to this cruel action by a freak of jealousy. He thought that she was killed, but she had only two or three ribs broken, and the relations of the woman threw themselves at the feet of the Governor to demand justice. The Governor summoned the Physician, and commanded him to withdraw, not wishing to keep him any longer in his service. He obeyed this order, and, having placed his disabled wife in a *palankeen*, he departed with all his family. He was not more than three or four marches from the town when the Governor, finding himself unusually ill, sent to recall him, upon which the Physician stabbed his wife, four of his children, and thirteen female slaves, after which he returned to the Governor, who said nothing to him about it, and took him again into his service.

On the 8th I crossed the Ganges in a large boat, having waited from the morning till midday on the bank of the river, till M. Maille brought a letter from the Governor giving us permission to cross. For on each side there is a *Darogha*, who allows no one to pass without an order; and he takes note also of the kind of merchandise carried, each wagon being charged four rupees, and a chariot paying but one, without counting the boat, for which it is necessary to pay separately. This day the halt was at Saudoul Serail, 16 *coss*.

The 9th at Yakedil-sera, 10 *coss*; 10th at Bouraky-sera, 10 *coss*; 11th at Banarou, 10 *coss*.

Benares is a large and very well-built town, the majority of the houses being of brick and cut stone, and more lofty than those of other towns of India; but it is very inconvenient that the streets are so narrow. It has several *caravanserai*, and, among others, one very large and well built. In the middle of the court there are two galleries where they sell cottons, silken stuffs, and other kinds of merchandise. The majority of those who vend the goods are the workers who have made the pieces, and in this manner foreigners obtain them at first hand. These workers, before exposing anything for sale, have to go to him who holds the contract, so as to get the imperial stamp impressed on the pieces of calico or silk, otherwise they are fined and flogged. The town is situated to the north of the Ganges, which runs the whole length of the walls, and two leagues farther down a large river joins it from the west.

The idolaters have one of their principal pagodas in Benares... The most remarkable thing about it is that from the door of the pagoda to the river there is a descent by stone steps, where there are at intervals platforms and small, rather dark, chambers, some of which serve as dwellings for the Brahmans, and others as kitchens where they prepare their food. For after the idolaters have bathed, and have gone to pray and make their offerings in the pagoda, they prepare their food without anyone but themselves touching it, through the fear they have lest anyone who approached it might be unclean. But above all things, they ardently desire to drink the water of the Ganges, because, as soon as they have drunk it, they believe...that they are cleansed from all their sins. Every day large numbers of these Brahmans are to be seen going to the clearest part of the river to fill round, small-mouthed, earthen pots, which hold about a bucketful, with this water. When they are full they are taken to the chief priest, who directs the mouth to be covered with a very fine cloth of fire-colour, in three or four folds, upon which he applies his seal. The Brahmans carry this water at the end of a stick, flat like a lath, from which hang six small cords, and to each of them one of these pots is attached. They rest themselves by changing the shoulder frequently, and they sometimes travel three or four hundred leagues of country with this load, and then sell it, or make a present of it, but only to the richest persons, from whom they expect a liberal reward. Some of these idolaters, when they celebrate any festival—especially when their children are married—drink this water at a cost of 400 or 500 *écus*. It is drunk only at the end of the repast, as we drink hypocras or muscat in Europe, each guest receiving a cup, or two, according to the liberality of the host. The principal reason why this water of the Ganges is so highly esteemed is that it never becomes bad, and engenders no vermin; but I do not know whether we should believe what is said about this, taking into consideration the number of bodies which are constantly being thrown into the Ganges.

Returning to the pagoda at Benares. The building, like all the other pagodas, is in the figure of a cross, having its four arms equal. In the middle a lofty dome rises like a kind of tower with many sides terminating in a point, and at the end of each arm of the cross another tower rises, which can be ascended from outside. Before reaching the top there are many niches and several balconies, which project to intercept the fresh air; and all over the tower there are rudely executed figures in relief of various kinds of animals. Under this great dome, and exactly in the middle of the pagoda, there is an altar like a table, of 7 to 8 feet in length, and 5 to 6 wide, with two steps in front, which serve as a footstool, and this footstool is covered with a beautiful tapestry, sometime of silk and sometimes of gold and silk, according to the solemnity of the rite which is being celebrated. The altar is covered with gold or silver brocade, or some beautiful painted cloth. From outside the pagoda this altar faces you with the idols upon it; for the women and girls must salute it from the outside, as, save only those of a certain tribe, they are not allowed to enter the pagoda. Among the idols on the great altar one stands 5 or 6 feet in height; neither the arms, legs, nor trunk are seen, only the head and neck being visible all the remainder of the body, down to the altar, is covered by a robe which increases in width below. Sometimes on its neck there is a rich chain of gold, rubies, pearls, or emeralds. This idol has been made in honour and after the likeness of Bainmadou, formerly a great and holy personage among them, whose name they often have on their lips. On the right side of the altar there is also the figure of an animal or rather of a chimera, seeing that it represents in part an elephant, in part a horse, and in part a mule. It is of massive gold, and is called Garou, no person being allowed to approach it but the Brahmans. It is said to be the resemblance the animal on which this holy personage rode upon when he was in the world, and that he made long journeys on it going about to see if the people were doing their duty and not injuring anyone. At the entrance of the pagoda, between the principal door and the great altar, there is to the left a small altar, upon which an idol made of black marble is seated, with the legs crossed, and about two feet high. When I was there, near it, on the left, sat a small boy, son of the chief priest, and all the people who came there threw him pieces of taffeta, or brocade like handkerchiefs, with which he wiped the idol and then returned them to the owners. Others threw him chains made of beads like small nuts, with a naturally sweet scent, which these idolaters wear on their necks and use to repeat their prayers over each bead. Others threw chains of coral or yellow amber, others fruits arid flowers. Finally, with everything which is thrown to the chief Brahman's child he wipes the idol and makes him kiss it, and afterwards, as I have just said, returns it to the people. This idol is called Morli Ram, that is to say, the God Morli, brother of the idol on the great altar.

Under the principal entrance of the pagoda one of the chief Brahmans is seated, and close to him is a large dish full of yellow pigment mixed with water. All the poor idolaters one after the other present themselves to him, and he anoints their foreheads with some of this colour, which is continued down between the eyes and on to the end of the nose, then on the arms and in front of the chest; and it is by these marks that those who have bathed in the Ganges are distinguished. Those who bathe only in their houses—for they are all obliged to bathe before eating, and even before cooking—those, I say, who have bathed only in well-water, or in that brought from the river, are not properly purified, and so they cannot be anointed with this colour. It may be remarked that the idolaters, according to their castes, are anointed with different colours; and in the Empire of the Great *Mogul*, those who are anointed with yellow belong to the most important tribe, and are the least impure. For, when attending to the ordinary necessities of nature, the others content themselves with carrying a pot of water to wash themselves, while these always use a handful of sand, with which they first rub themselves, and then bathe. So they can say their bodies are clean, that no impurity remains, and that they may then take their food without fear.

Adjoining this great pagoda, on the side which faces the setting sun at midsummer, there is a house which serves as a college, which the Raja Jai Singh, the most powerful of the idolatrous princes in the Empire of the Great *Mogul*, has founded for the education of the youth of good families. I saw the children of the Prince, who were being educated there by several Brahmans, who taught them to read and write in a language which is reserved to the priests of the idols, and is very different from that spoken by the people. Entering the court of this college, being curious to see it and throwing my eyes upwards, I perceived a double gallery which ran all round it, and in the lower the two Princes were seated, accompanied by many young nobles and numerous Brahmans, who were making different figures, like those of mathematics, on the ground with chalk. As soon as I entered the Princes sent to inquire who I was, and having learnt that I was a Frenchman they invited me to ascend, when they asked me many things about Europe, and especially about France. One of the Brahmans had two globes, which the Dutch had given him, and I pointed out the position of France upon them. After some conversation of this kind they presented me with *betel*; and before I took leave I asked the Brahmans at what hour I should be able to see the pagoda open. They told me to come on the following morning a little before sunrise, and I did not fail to be at the house by that time, where the Raja had built a pagoda on the left of the entrance. In front of the door there is, as it were, a gallery sustained by pillars, where many people were already assembled—men, women, and children—awaiting the opening of the door. When the gallery and a part of the court are full of people, eight Brahmans approach, four on each side of the door of the pagoda, each carrying a censer; and there are many other Brahmans who make a great noise with drums and other instruments. The two oldest of the Brahmans chant a canticle, and all the people, after they have intoned it, repeat it while singing and playing instruments, each one waving a peacock's tail, or other kind of fan, to drive away the flies; so that when the door of the pagoda is opened the idol may not be inconvenienced by them. All this fanning and music lasted a good half-hour, when the two principal Brahmans began to sound two large bells three times, and, with a kind of small mallet, they then knocked at the door. At the same moment it was opened by six Brahmans, who were inside the pagoda, and 7 or 8 paces from the door there was an altar with an idol upon it, which is called Ram-Kam, who is the sister of Morli Ram. She has on her right a child in the form of Cupid, who is known as the god Lakshmi, and on her left arm she carries a small girl called the goddess Sita. As soon as the door of the pagoda was opened, and after a large curtain had been drawn, and the people present had seen the idol, all threw themselves on the ground, placing their hands upon their heads and prostrating themselves three times; then rising they threw a quantity of bouquets and chains in form of chaplets, which the Brahmans placed on the idol, and then returned to the people. An old Brahman in front of the altar held in his hand a lamp with nine lighted wicks, upon which, from time to time, he threw a kind of incense when moving the lamp towards the idol. All these ceremonies lasted about an hour, after which the people retired, and the pagoda was closed. The people presented the idol with a quantity of rice, flour, butter, oil, and milk, of which the Brahmans let nothing be lost. As this idol has the form of a woman, all the women invoke her, and regard her as their patron; this is the reason why the temple is always crowded with women and children.

The Raja desiring to have this idol in the pagoda of his house and to remove it from the great pagoda, has expended in gifts to the Brahmans and in alms to the poor more than 500,000 rupees, which make 750,000 *livres* of our money.

On the other side of the street in which this college is situated, there is another pagoda called Richourdas, from the name of the idol on the altar inside, and lower down on another small altar is the idol whom they call Goupaldas brother of this Richourdas. Only the faces of these idols, which are made of stone or wood, are exposed to view. They are black as jet, with the exception of the image of Morli Ram, which is in the great pagoda and is uncovered. As for the idol Ram-Kam, which is in the pagoda of the Raja it has two diamonds in the eyes which the Prince has placed there, together with a large necklace of pearls, and a canopy sustained by four silver pillars over its head...

About 500 paces from the town, in a north-western direction, there is a mosque where you see several *Musalman* tombs, of which some are of a very beautiful design. The most beautiful are placed each in the middle of a garden enclosed by walls which have openings of half a foot square, through which the passers-by can see them. The most considerable of all is like a great square pedestal, each face of which is about forty paces long. In the middle of this platform you see a column of 32 to 35 feet in height, all of a piece, and which three men could with difficulty embrace. It is of sandstone, so hard that I could not scratch it with my knife. It terminates in a pyramid, and has a great ball on the point, and below the ball it is encircled by large beads. All the sides of this tomb are covered with figures of animals cut in relief in the stone, and it has been higher above the ground than it now appears; several of the old men who guard some of these tombs having assured me that since fifty years it has subsided more than 30 feet. They add that it is the tomb of one of the kings of Bhutan, who was interred there after he had left his country to conquer this kingdom, from which he was subsequently driven by the descendants of Tamerlane. It is from this kingdom of Bhutan that they bring musk...

I remained at Benares on the 12th and 13th [December], and during these two days there was continual rain; but it did not prevent me from resuming my journey, and on the evening of the 13th I crossed the Ganges with the passport of the Governor. They examine all travellers' baggage before embarking in the boat, personal property pays nothing, and it is only on merchandise that one must pay duty.

The 13th I halted at Baterpour, 2 *coss*; 14th at Satragy-sera, 8 *coss*; 15th at Moniarky-sera, 6 *coss*. During the morning of this day, after having travelled two *coss*, I crossed a river called Carnasar-sou, and at three *coss* from thence one crosses another named Saode-sou, and both are crossed by fords. The 16th at Gourmabad, 8 *coss*.

It is a town on a river called Goudera-sou, and you cross it by a stone bridge. The 17th at Sasaram, 4 *coss*.

Sasaram is a town at the foot of the mountains, near to which there is a large tank. You see a small island in the middle, where there is a very beautiful mosque, in which there is the tomb of a *Nawab* named Salim Khan [sic, Sher Shah Suri (r. 1540-45)], who had it built during the time he was Governor of the Province. There is a fine stone bridge to cross into the island, which is all flanked and paved with large cut stones. On one of the sides of the tank there is a large garden, in the middle of which is another beautiful tomb of the son of the same *Nawab*, Salim Khan, who succeeded his father in the government of the Province. When you wish to go to the mine of Soulmelpour…you leave the main road to Patna, and turn straight southwards by Akberbourg and the famous fort of Rhotas… The 18th I crossed, in a boat, the river Sonsou, which comes from the mountains of the south; and, after crossing it, those who have goods have to pay a certain duty. This day my halt was at Daoud-Nagar-Sera where there is a fine tomb, 9 *coss*. The 19th to Halva-sera, 10 *coss*; 20th to Aga-sera, 9 *coss*. In the morning I met 130 elephants, both large and small, which were being taken to Delhi to the Great *Mogul*. The 21st to Patna, 10 *coss*.

Patna is one of the largest towns in India and is situated on the margin of the Ganges, on its western side, and it is not less than two *coss* in length. The houses are not better than those in the majority of the other towns of India, and they are nearly all roofed with thatch or bamboo. The Dutch Company has an establishment there on account of the trade in saltpetre, which is refined at a large village called Chapra, situated on the right bank of the Ganges, 10 *coss* above Patna.

Arriving at Patna with M. Bernier, we encountered some Dutchmen in the street who were returning to Chapra, but who halted their carriages in order to salute us. We did not separate before we had emptied together two bottles of Shiraz wine in the open street, regarding which there is nothing to remark upon in this country, where one lives without ceremony, and with perfect liberty.

I remained eight days in Patna, during which time an occurrence happened which will show the reader that unnatural crime does not rest unpunished by the *Musalmans*. A *Mimbachi* who commanded 1,000 foot[soldiers] disgraced a young boy who was in his service; …the boy, overwhelmed with grief, chose his time to avenge himself, and being one day out hunting with his master, and removed from the attendants by about a quarter of a league, he came behind him and cut off his head with his sword. He then rode immediately to the town at full speed, crying aloud that he had slain his master for such a reason, and came at once to the house of the Governor, who placed him in prison. But he left it at the end of six months, and although all the relatives of the deceased did what they could to procure his execution, the Governor did not dare to condemn him, as he feared the people, who maintained that the young man had acted rightly.

I left Patna by boat to descend to Dacca on the 29th of January [sic, December], between 11 o'clock and noon. If the river had been strong, as it is after the rains, I should have embarked at Allahabad, or at the least at Benares. The same day I slept at Sera Beconcour, 15 *coss*.

Five *coss* on this side of Beconcour you meet a river called Pompon-sou, which comes from the south and flows into the Ganges. The 30th to Sera D'Eriia, 17 *coss*. On the 31st, after having gone 4 *coss* or thereabouts, you meet the river Kaoa, which comes from the south; 3 *coss* lower you see another called Chanon, which falls from the north; 4 *coss* farther you discover that called Erguga, which comes from the south; and again, 6 *coss* below, that of Aquera, which comes from the same quarter, and these four rivers lose their names in the Ganges. All that day I beheld lofty mountains on the south side and at a distance from the Ganges, some 10 *coss* and some 15 *coss*, and I came to a halt at [Monghyr] town, 18 *coss*.

The first day of January 1666, after having sailed two hours I saw the Gandak enter the Ganges from the north. It is a large navigable river. This evening the halt was at Zangira 8 *coss*. But as the Ganges twisted much during the day the distance is fully 22 *coss* by water. During the 2nd between 6 o'clock in the morning and about 11 o'clock, I saw three rivers enter the Ganges, and they all three come from the north side. The first is called Ronova, the second Tae, and the third Chanan. I slept at [Bhagalpur], 18 *coss*.

The 3rd, after four hours' travelling on the Ganges, I encountered the river Katare, which comes from the north, and slept this day at a village called Pongangel, at the end of the mountains which abut on the Ganges, 13 *coss*. On the 4th, one hour below Pongangel, I met a great river called Mart-nadi, which comes from the north, and I slept at [Rajmahal], 6 *coss*.

Rajmahal is a town on the right bank of the Ganges, and when you approach it by land you find that for one or two *coss* the roads are paved with brick up to the town. It was formerly the residence of the Governors of Bengal, because it is a splendid hunting country, and, moreover, the trade there was considerable. But the river having taken another course, and passing only at a distance of a full half league from the town, as much for this reason as for the purpose of restraining the King of Arakan, and many Portuguese bandits who have settled at the mouths of the Ganges, and by whom the inhabitants of Dacca, up to which they made incursions, were molested—the Governor and the merchants who dwelt at Rajmahal removed to Dacca, which is to-day a place of considerable trade.

On the 6th, having arrived at a great town called [Dunapur], at 6 *coss* from Rajmahal, I left M. Bernier, who went to [Cossimbazar], and from thence to [Hooghly] by land, because when the river is low one is unable to pass on account of a great bank of sand which is before a town called Soutiqui. I slept this evening at [Tardipur], distant from Rajmahal 12 *coss*. At sunrise I beheld a number of crocodiles asleep on the sand. The 7th I reached Acerat, 25 *coss*.

From Acerat to Dacca, by land, there are still 45 *coss*. During this day I beheld so large a number of crocodiles that, at length, I became desirous to shoot one in order to ascertain if what is commonly said is true, namely, that a shot from a gun does not affect them. The shot struck him in the jaw and the blood flowed, but he did not remain where he was, and escaped into the river. On the 8th I again saw a great number of these crocodiles lying on the bank of the river, and I fired at two with two shots, each charge having three balls. Immediately they were wounded they turned over on the back, opening the mouth and dying on the spot. This day I slept at Douloudia, 17 *coss*. The crows were the cause of our finding a fine fish which the fisherman had concealed on the bank of the river in the reeds. For when our boatmen observed that there were a great number of crows which cawed and entered the reeds, they concluded that they must contain something unusual, and they searched so well that they found sufficient to make a good meal.

On the 9th, at 2 P.M., we encountered a river called Chativor which comes from the north, and our halt was at Dampour, 16 *coss*. The 10th we slept on the margin of the river in a place far removed from houses, and made this day 15 *coss*. On the 11th, having arrived towards evening at the spot where the Ganges divides into three branches, one of which goes to Dacca, we slept at the entrance of this channel, at a large village called Jatrapour, 20 *coss*. Those who have no baggage can proceed by land from Jatrapour, to Dacca, and they shorten their journey very much, because the river winds about considerably. On the 12th, at noon, we passed before a large town called Bagamara, and slept at Kasiata, another large town, 11 *coss*.

On the 13th, at noon, we met a river at 2 *coss* from Dacca called Laquia, which comes from the north-east. Opposite the point where the two rivers join, there is a fortress with several guns on each side. Half a *coss* lower down you see another river called Pagalu, over which there is a fine brick bridge, which Mir Jumla ordered to be built. This river comes from the north-east, and half a *coss* below you find another called Cadamtali, which comes from the north, and which you also cross by a brick bridge; on both sides of the river you see several towers, where there are as it were enshrined many heads of men who have robbed on the high roads.

We arrived at Dacca towards evening, and accomplished this day 9 *coss*. Dacca is a large town, which is only of extent as regards length, each person being anxious to have his house close to the Ganges. Its length exceeds 2 *coss*; and from the last brick bridge, which I have mentioned above, up to Dacca, there is a succession of houses, separated one from the other, and inhabited for the most part by the carpenters who build galleys and other vessels. These houses are, properly speaking, only miserable huts made of bamboo, and mud which is spread over them. Those of Dacca are scarcely better built, and that which is the residence of the Governor is an enclosure of high walls, in the middle of which is a poor house merely built of wood. He ordinarily resides under tents, which he pitches in a large court in this enclosure. The Dutch, finding that their goods were not sufficiently safe in the common houses of Dacca, have built a very fine house, and the English have also got one which is fairly good. The church of the Rev. Augustin Fathers is all of brick, and the workmanship of it is rather beautiful.

On the occasion of my last visit to Dacca, the *Nawab* Shaista Khan, who was then Governor of Bengal, was at war with the King of Arakan, whose navy generally consists of 200 galleys besides several other small boats. These galleys traverse the Gulf of Bengal and enter the Ganges, the tide ascending even beyond Dacca.

Shaista Khan, uncle of the King Aurangzeb, who reigns at present, and the cleverest man in all his kingdom, found means for bribing many of the officers of the King of Arakan's navy, and forty galleys, which were commanded by Portuguese, promptly joined him. In order to secure these new allies firmly in his service, he gave large pay to each of the Portuguese officers and to the soldiers in proportion, but the natives received only double their ordinary pay. It is most surprising to see with what speed these galleys are propelled by oars. Some are so long that they have up to fifty oars on each side, but there are not more than two men to each oar. Some are much decorated, whereon the gold and blue paint have not been spared.

The Dutch keep some of them in their service in which they carry their merchandise, and they occasionally have to hire some from others, thus affording a means of livelihood to many people.

The day following my arrival in Dacca, which was the 14th of January, I went to salute the *Nawab*, and presented him with a mantle of gold brocade, with a grand golden lace of 'point d'Espagne' round it, and a fine scarf of gold and silver of the same 'point' and a jewel consisting of a very beautiful emerald. During the evening, after I had returned to the Dutch with whom I lodged, the *Nawab* sent me pomegranates, China oranges, two Persian melons, and three kinds of apples.

On the 15th I showed him my goods, and presented to the Prince, his son, a watch having an enamelled gold case, a pair of pistols inlaid with silver, and a telescope. All this which I presented, both to the father and to the young lord of about ten years of age, cost me more than 5,000 *livres*.

On the 16th I agreed with him as to the price of my goods, and afterwards I went to his *wazir* to receive my bill of exchange payable at Cossimbazar. Not that he was unwilling to pay me at Dacca, but the Dutch, who were more experienced than I, warned me that there was risk in carrying silver to Cossimbazar, where one cannot go except by re-ascending the Ganges, because the land route is very bad and full of jungle and swamps. The danger consists in this, that the small vessels which are employed are very subject to be upset by the least wind, and when the sailors discover that one carries money, it is not difficult for them to wreck the boat, to recover the silver afterwards, at the bottom of the river, and appropriate it.

On the 20th I took leave of the *Nawab*, who invited me to return to see him, and gave me a passport in which he described me as a gentleman of his household; this he had already previously done during the time that he was Governor of Ahmadabad, when I went to the army to meet him in the Province of *Deccan*, which the Raja Shivaji had entered... In virtue of these passports I was able to go and come throughout all the territories of the Great *Mogul* as one of his household...

On the 21st the Dutch gave a great banquet in my honour, to which they invited the English and some Portuguese, with an Augustin friar of the same nation. On the 22nd I went to visit the English, who had for Chief or President Mr. Prat, and after that the Reverend Portuguese Father, and some other Franks. Between the 23rd and the 29th I made some purchases for 11,000 rupees, and all being embarked I went to bid farewell. On the 29th, in the evening I left Dacca, and all the Dutch accompanied me for two leagues in their small armed boats, and the Spanish wine was not spared on this occasion. Having been on the river from the 29th of January to the 11th of February, I left my servants and goods in the boat at Hazrahat, where I hired another boat which carried me to a large village called Mirdapur.

On the 12th I hired a horse to carry myself, and not being able to hire another for my baggage, I was obliged to employ two women, who took charge of it. I arrived the same evening at Cossimbazar, where I was well received by M. Arnoul van Wachttendonk, Director of all the settlements of the Dutch in Bengal, who invited me to lodge with him. On the 13th I passed the day agreeably with the Dutch gentlemen, who desired to enjoy themselves in honour of my arrival. On the 14th M. Wachttendonk returned to Hooghly, where the principal settlement is, and on the same day one of my servants, who had preceded me, came to give me notice that the people whom I had left in the boat with my goods had been in great danger on account of the strong wind, which had lasted two days, and which became stronger during the night.

On the 15th the Dutch gave me a *pallankeen* to go to Murshidabad. It is a great town, 3 *coss* from Cossimbazar, where the Receiver-general of Shaista Khan resided, to whom I presented my bill of exchange. After having read it he told me that it was good, and that he would have paid me if he had not on the previous evening received an order from the *Nawab* not to pay me in case he had not already done so. He did not tell me the reason why Shaista Khan acted in this manner, and I returned to my lodging not a little surprised at this proceeding. On the 16th I wrote to the *Nawab* to know what reason he had for ordering his Receiver not to pay me. On the 17th, in the evening, I left for

Hooghly in a boat with fourteen oars, which the Dutch lent me, and that night and the following I slept on the river.

On the 19th, towards evening, I passed a large town called Nadia, and it is the farthest point to which the tide reaches. There arose so furious a wind, and the water was so high, that we were compelled to stop for three or four hours and draw our boat ashore.

On the 20th I arrived at Hooghly, where I remained till the 2nd of March, during which time the Dutch made me welcome, and sought to give me all the amusement which the country could afford. We made several excursions on the river, and we enjoyed all the delicacies found in our European gardens, salads of several kinds, cabbages, asparagus, peas, and principally beans, the seed of which comes from Japan, the Dutch desiring to have all kinds of herbs and pulses in their gardens, which they are most careful to cultivate, but they have been unable, however, to get artichokes to grow.

On the 2nd of March I left Hooghly and arrived on the 5th at Cossimbazar. The following day I went to Murshidabad to know if the Receiver who had refused to pay me had received another order from the *Nawab*. For as I have above said, I immediately wrote to Shaista Khan to complain of his action and to know for what reason he did not wish my bills of exchange to be paid. The Director of the Dutch factories added a letter to mine, and pointed out to the *Nawab* that I was too well known to him—having, formerly at Ahmadabad, at the army of the *Deccan*, and in other places, had many transactions with him—not to deserve favourable treatment; that he ought to remember that I, being the only person who often brought to India the choicest rarities of Europe, it was not the way to make me wish to return as he had invited me, if I should leave discontented; besides which, owing to the credit which I enjoyed, I should be easily able to dissuade those who intended to come to India with rare objects, by making them fear the treatment I had received. Neither my letter nor that of the Director produced the effect we had hoped, and I was in no wise satisfied with the new order which the *Nawab* had sent to the Receiver, by which he ordered him to pay me with a rebate of 20,000 rupees from the sum which I ought to receive, and was carried by my bill of exchange, according to the price upon which we had agreed. The *Nawab* added that if I was unwilling to content myself with this payment I might come to take back my goods... I was more than four months disputing in vain with this Governor...

Tavernier, despite his gifts to the Mughal Emperor and influential officials, finally agreed to rebate 10,000 rupees to the Nawab.

Over decades of astute trading in luxury goods between Europe and India, Tavernier made himself wealthy. Further, his publication of his autobiographical and descriptive travel narrative, *Six Voyages*, made

him famous throughout Europe. Ennobled by the French King in 1669, Tavernier purchased the estate and title of 'Baron of Aubonne' (in Switzerland). After he retired, however, his family squandered his fortune, forcing him to sell his estate. Further, the revocation of the Edict of Nantes in 1685 removed royal protection over Protestants like Tavernier, compelling him to flee France and move to the German Lutheran electorate of Brandenburg. He died there in 1689, while planning his seventh journey to Asia that would recoup his fortune and fame. This selection comes from three sections of Tavernier's narrative translated by Valentine Ball and published as *Travels in India* (London: Macmillan, 1889).

Chapter Ten

Friar Domingo Fernández de Navarrete

Spanish Friar Domingo Fernández de Navarrete (1618-86) joined the Dominican order at age sixteen. After ordination, he studied and taught at the College of San Gregorio (in northeast Spain) for a decade before volunteering for missionary work in the Philippines, which he reached via Mexico in 1648. He taught as Professor of Theology in the University of St Thomas in Manila and then travelled to China to convert Chinese people to Christianity. He opposed the Jesuits vehemently in the 'rites controversy' (the Jesuits tolerated Chinese Confucian rituals but Dominicans considered these rites antithetical to Christianity). To pursue this controversy, Navarrete sailed home via India in 1670, along with a Chinese servant and Chinese books but little money.

He brought to his observations on India a dozen years in East Asia but no experience of the local peoples and places he would encounter on his journey. This selection from his narrative, originally written in Spanish, picks up as he approaches India's southeast coast. He describes Madras, including the tomb of the Apostle St Thomas and various local political, cultural and theological conflicts. He then travelled inland to and from Golconda, the wealthy capital of the regionally powerful, semi-independent Qutb Shah Sultanate which was about to be conquered by the Mughals.

On the second of May [1670] we anchor'd before [Madras]. I had an extraordinary desire to be ashore. A Portuguese came aboard, and I got into the boat that brought him, so did others. Those are very odd boats, they have no nails or pins, but the boards are sew'd together with ropes made of Coco outward shells; and tho the infidels assur'd us they were safe, yet we could not but be in great fear. When they come towards the shore, they take the surges, which drive them up so that we stept out of the boat upon the dry sand. Thousands of souls waited there to know the ship, and who came aboard it. I went immediately to the church of the French capuchins, who resided there, to give God thanks for having deliver'd us from the Sea.

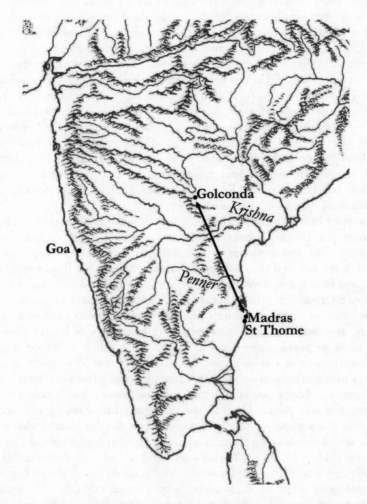

Friar Fernández de Navarrete's travels by land in south and central India,
1670-71

When we came to this place, we found it beseig'd by the king [Abdullah Qutb Shah, 1626-72] of Golconda's army, but without his orders; their design was to extort something from the English, but they were disappointed. It is on the coast of Coromandel, half a league short of the city of S. Thomas, otherwise called Meliapor. Here the English have a noble fort; they have also other walls but small, within which live all the Portugueses, who after the losing of Jafanapatan, Negapatan, and S. Thomas, went to seek places to dwell. The English receiv'd them, and they live under their protection and government. They stand the English in stead, for upon occasion they make use of them, as they did at this time, when all men took arms and guarded the walls. The enemy had stopp'd all the avenues, so that provisions grew scarce. There is neither port nor water, this last they get out of some small wells they have dig'd. Ships lie safe six months, then they go away till the fair weather comes again. The English allow a publick Church, kept by two French capuchins [Fathers Ephraim de Nevers and Zenon de Baugé]; and tho there are several clergy-men, they all have to say mass there, with no small subjection and dissatisfaction; but the English who are Masters there, favouring the religious men, they must have patience per force.

Two years before, there had been a great contest there betwixt two English governors [Sir Edward Winter and George Foxcroft], both of them would govern the place, and there was no reconciling of them. The Portugueses were divided, some favour'd the one, and others the other. One [Foxcroft] got the better, and banish'd many of the Portugueses that oppos'd him, together with the French Capuchins. Above a year after he gave them leave to return.

It is in about twelve or thirteen degrees of north latitude, and an excellent Climate, any nice man may live there; the conveniency of buying clothes is great, all those people living upon it. I took up in a little room the religious men gave me, there I study'd, and eat what an honest Portuguese sent me. Another maintain'd the religious men. There I found a Biscainer, whose name was Dominick Lopez, an honest man in good repute, had a wife and two children, but was poor. He told me very great hardships he had endur'd among the Portugueses. I advis'd him to send his sons to Manila; what he did I know not. I also found a German who was a mighty mathematician, ingineer and good soldier; he did the Portugueses good service, but they requited him ill. Knowing who he was, and how well look'd upon, I propos'd to him to go away to Manila, where he might come to preferment with ease. He agreed to it, I writ to the governor about it, and directed him how to send his answer.

I went with him to S. Thomas, we were first in a church of Franciscans, which they call our Lady of light, there was a religious man there even poorer than I; he gave us to eat, and his hat, because I had none. I spoke with the governor of the bishoprick, who told me he would go the next day to the mount. We spent that evening in a house of jesuits but there was never a one in it. There we saw the fountain the holy apostle made between two rocks, and drank of it with much satisfaction; we also saw two crosses cut in the hard rocks, the workmanship of the same saint. We went into the cave where we pray'd, it was very small, they afterwards cut the rock and enlarg'd it. On one side there is a breach in the rock, which made a small window. They recount for a certain truth, and receiv'd tradition, that when the infidels came to kill him, he [Saint Thomas] would transform himself into a peacock, and get out that way.

In the way hither it is that happen'd to me which I have often told: A pair of small curious Chinese wallets slip'd off the little horse I rode on, and in them my breviary and some other petty things; I did not observe it, but met two *Moors* with their spears, they saluted me, and went their way; soon after I heard loud calling out, which made me turn about to see what was the matter, and perceiv'd the *Moors* pointing with their spears to my wallets. I return'd, and made signs to them to reach them up to me; they would not touch it. I made signs again that they reach them me upon the point of their Spears. They understood me, and one of them taking them up with his spear gave it me. I thank'd them by signs, and went my way. What European would have done so much here, or there?

That evening we came to the mount, there are two little houses at the foot of it uninhabited, besides others gone to ruin. When the infidels took the city, they destroy'd all about it, but durst not meddle with the apostle's church, nor with that of our Lady of light I spoke of before. The ascent of the mountain is steep and difficult, but well provided with seats and resting-places at certain distances. On the top is a small flat or plain, kept in good order, wall'd about breast-high, with good seats, and large trees to make a shade. In the middle is a curious little church, with a house for a priest and two servants. The prospect all about the hill is incomparable, and extends as far as the sight can reach. To lie that night, we went down from the mountain, and took up under a tree upon the bare ground. Our rest lasted not long, for a violent shower came on, which oblig'd us to get into a little house, into which we felt our way, and feared to meet with some vermin. It secur'd us from the rain, but we had a troublesome night of it, for we were engag'd with the knats which never ceas'd tormenting of us.

Next day we went up the mount again. The governor came and we said mass, I uncover'd the holy cross and picture of our blessed Lady. The holy cross is exactly as historians describe it, part of it is bloody, they say it is the apostle's blood; I worship'd it and touch'd my beads, and other that were brought me to it. Our Lady's picture is painted upon board, very beautiful, but the colours somewhat decay'd. There they said, it had been found at the same time with the cross, which is a mighty evidence against antient and modern hereticks, who oppose pictures; we worship'd, and I touch'd the beads to it. The second mass being ended, the tabernacle in which those great relicks are kept, was cover'd and lock'd up. The good priest made much of us, we spent another night there upon the bricks. The bed not being very easy, we got a horseback betimes in the morning; I went to say mass at our Lady of light, there I stay'd till evening, being left with only my Chinese, and that holy religious man, for the German went home, carrying my horse with him. We went to see the city of S. Thomas; the *Moors* would not let us in; from the gate we saw some good buildings, the walls are very fine. A gentleman that was with me lamented that loss very much. The English are not so strong at Madras, yet they hold it and are like so to do. What signify walls and bulwarks, where there is no government? I saw some curious temples of the natives, and wonderful large, deep and wide ponds, with artificial islands in the middle curiously contriv'd. I walk'd gently home along those habitations of infidels, observing what was worthy of it. This was the twenty first of June, and on the twenty fourth I was to travel by land.

But before I set out it is requisite to observe some things, and to know them; not to follow, but in order to reject them: the Inhabitants of the city of S. Thomas came to be very rich and powerful and consequently grew very proud. It is generally reported of one woman [Justa Padrao], that she grew to that height of vanity, that when she went to church attended by many women-slaves, one went before with a censor perfuming her with burnt-sweets. Can any madness be greater? She had, say they, so many S. Thomas's (they are *Crown*-pieces with the Effigies of the apostle) that she measur'd them by the peck. What follows is worse; many told me, (would to God it were a lie, and I had not heard it) that catholick men were pimps to catholick women, with Mahometans and *Gentiles*. Friar de Anjelis will do well to note this; A beautiful and honest maid was forc'd out of her father's house, and deliver'd to a Mahometan. The king of Golconda has a concubine to this day, the daughter of a Portuguese. At a procession of the holy week in the city of S. Thomas [some Portuguese] drew their swords one against another; a special procession and good example! It was common to permit the infidels to make processions within the city walls, and so it was to be godfathers at christnings and weddings, in heretick churches along that coast. At Travancor one Portuguese kill'd another close by the altar, as mass was saying by F. Michael John, who had then consecrated, and whom I visited, saw and discours'd with at Madras.

These two [French] Capuchins are not belov'd by the Portugueses; one of them holds some odd opinions. One is that the apostle S. Thomas did not touch our Saviour's Wounds, and therefore [that Capuchin] does not paint him as we do, but with his hands joined. I had never heard of any such opinion before...

There was a great and scandalous contention about who should be governour of that diocese, two Competitors strove for it. Silva was one of them, and Diaz of Canara the other. The latter was at [Tranquebar] and the first near S. Thomas, and is the same that went with me to the mountain, when I visited that holy place. F. Pesoa favour'd him; and the Franciscan, Augustinian, and Dominican fathers having spoke for the other at Goa, Pesoa said, they were all ignorant fellows. Pesoa went away to Madras, and affirm'd that Silva was legally excommunicated by F. Diaz, who was the lawful governour. Notwithstanding all this, the next day he admitted him to say mass in his church. Pesoa's companion sided with Diaz. He writ a large paper in defence of Diaz, and his opinion, and challeng'd the French capuchins, who stood for Silva, to dispute that point with them, appointing the English preacher judge betwixt them. Was ever the like heard of among the barbarous blacks?

Diaz took the short cut, and had recourse to the Mahometan king of Golconda to use force; he sent his officers, who carry'd away with them F. Silva, two jesuits, and above forty Portugueses men and women prisoners. They were brought before the king, who bid them chuse one of the two in his presence, and obey him. They did not agree, were cast into prison, where one Portuguese kill'd another; they gave very ill example; one jesuit was expell'd the society, some men and women dy'd of the fatigue of the journey. F. Ephrem, a Capuchin, assur'd me that above fourscore had been foresworn upon the evangelists in that quarrel.

Diaz, afterwards betook himself to the English governor of Madras, and sought his protection. So he sollicited the assistance of a Mohametan and a Heretick. The dispute is still afoot. When I left there were two governors, I know not whether either of them is dead, this is the only way of adjusting that difference.

It is a sad thing to see the Portuguese nation, formerly so famous, and dreadful in those parts, now so oppress'd and trampl'd on by those people.

F. Silva, the day we were at S. Thomas his mount, told me some passages that had happen'd at Goa, concerning some wills made there; but many things are said, which are not prov'd, we must not believe all things.

At Madras I spoke with the Malabar master the Capuchins had at their church to instruct the natives. Inquiring into some particulars, I found that nation [believes in] five elements, fire, earth, water, air, and wind. They adore the sun, moon and stars (tho' Mahometanism is introduced there, yet most of the natives stick to their paganism). They have a great reverence for cows; they say, a certain god took flesh upon him in one of them, and that they are that god's horses. The greatest oath kings swear, is by a cow, and they never break it. They kill no creature, undervalue those that eat them, and despise those of their country that become Christians. The greatest reproach they cast upon a Christian, is to tell him, he eats beef. When they are near death, they endeavour to have a cow near at hand, and they clasp her fundament as near as they can to the dying person's mouth, that as he breaths out his soul at his mouth it may go in at the cow's back-door. They honour the lion, saying another god rides on him; and they pay a respect to deer, dogs, mice and kites. Many days they will not break their fast till they have seen a kite. When they yawn they call the dog, snapping their fingers, which is calling of the god that rides upon the dog, who has power to hinder the devil from entring the body when the mouth opens.

When we arriv'd at Madras, our Pilot said he would make a Voyage to [Tenasserim], or some other place [before sailing to Goa], to make amends for the great expence he had been at; his resolution was dislik'd. For this reason, and to avoid the sea which had quite tir'd me, I resolv'd to go to Goa by land: They gave me such a description of the road, that it would have put any man into the mind of seeing it, tho he had never so little mind to travel. I sold some rags at a poor rate, left some books and papers with my friends, borrow'd eight *pieces of eight* to be paid in Goa. I went to the English governor, rather to beg an alms, than to take my leave; told him my want and design, he immediately with much courtesy gave me five *pagodes* of gold, which amount to little less than ten *pieces of eight*. A native of Canara gave me two, so I thought I had enough for my journey. The day before I set out, I took more notice than I had done before of the practice of the European factors in those parts; they are all serv'd by the natives, who are most faithful, submissive, and punctual in doing what they are commanded. Some factors have above a hundred servants; they are very chargeable for everyone has a *piece of eight* and half, or two *pieces of eight* wages a month; all these come together in the evening to bid good night to the factor, governor, or commander, and take their leave to go to their own homes to bed. They rank themselves over against the fort; some have lighted torches in their hands, others beat kettle-drums, others sound trumpets, others play on fifes, the rest beat their spears and bucklers together for above a quarter of an hour. After this a great *lanthorn* was hung out on the top of the governor's palace; he appear'd at a balcony, they all made him a low bow, and there was an end of the ceremony, which indeed was pleasant enough to see. Those gentlemen take great state upon them; I thought it too much.

I bought a horse to carry me my journey for the eight *pieces of eight*, for four more I hir'd an ox to carry my Chinese and a *Gentile* who spoke a little Portuguese. A poor Portuguese went along with me to add to my charge. On Midsummer-day at three in the afternoon we set out of Madras. During this journey, which held me twenty four days, God be prais'd, nothing hap'ned amiss. The lodging houses, which they call 'chauril', were not all alike, but all open alike, without any door, free to all the world. Nevertheless we always lay quiet and safe, sometimes in great towns, without being molested by any body in the least, which would be rare among Christians. The Portugueses had a small leather-bottle for water; they are made at Golconda, they would be of no less value in our parts than in those hot regions for when the water had been an hour in it, tho the weather were never so hot, it become so cool, I daily admir'd it anew; in two or three hours it was very cold; thus we never wanted good drink all the way. I afterwards bought one, which lasted me a long time, and was well worth my money; at Surat I gave it to an Indian of Manila; they would save a great expence of ice in Europe. Our food was not good, for there was nothing but milk, whey, curds and onions; but abundance of these things, as well in towns as on the mountains, on which there is abundance of cattle. When we saw a cottage, at the least call out came the Shepherds with a pot of milk, and four of us would drink our belly-full for a halfpenny.

A very remarkable passage befel me with the *Gentile*, who was owner of the ox: He carry'd his pot to dress his meat (so they do all) wrap'd in cloths, and put into a sack: My man touch'd it over the sack, the heathen saw it, and came to me in a rage, complaining that his pot was defil'd, and there was no pacifying of him. At last he pull'd the pot out of the sack, and with wonderful rage dash'd it against the stones, I was forced to buy him another. I said enough to have convinc'd a stock, but these people are harder than bronze in the observation of their barbarous customs. There are three ranks or degrees of people in that country: the *banianes* are the nobility and gentry, they are great fasters, and abstain from flesh all their life-time; their ordinary food is rice, sour curds, herbs, and the like. Others are call'd *parianes*, these neither eat nor drink any thing that another has touch'd, nor out of a Vessel that another has touch'd, tho there be many clothes over it. My heathen ox-driver was one of these, he would never eat any thing from my hand, nor drink out of any vessel of mine; he broke the pot because it had been touch'd. Among these *parianes*, there is one sort who are look'd upon by the rest as base and vile people. These on the roads, when they see one of the others, step aside and give them the way: In towns they come not to anybody's door but their equals; in the streets so soon as ever they see a man that is not of their own rank, they run or hide themselves. They are despis'd and hated by all men, and look'd upon as leprous and contagious persons. I heard say, they had been formerly the noblest people in that country, and that for a piece of treachery they committed, they were so cast down; in so much that the others will not admit of them as servants or slaves; and if it were made out that one of them had been within the house of one of the others, he would immediately pull down the whole structure. They are the most miserable people in the world; the greatest affront is to call them *Parian*, which is worse than among us dog, and base slave.

It is wonderful what numbers of great and small cattle we met with in the fields; I saw two species of sheep and goats, some like those of Spain, others much bigger. There are also those sheep which are found in many other parts, and which we usually call five quarters. The goats are vastly taller than ours; the shes had at their throat two little dugs longer than their ears. As the Egyptians kept ewes and cows for their milk and wool; so do these people for the same reason. A Lapide, in 47 Gen[esis] v. 17.

There are infinite groves of wild palm-trees. At Manila they are not minded, and here they are the greatest riches of the earth: They draw from them a great deal of the [*toddy*] liquor I said was call'd 'Tuba' at Manila, which yields them good profit. They also produce a sort of fruit which I saw not in any other place, and is like snow, the coolest thing in the world. It is wonderful to see what woods there are of tamarine-trees, we often travel'd a considerable way under their shade. I gather'd the berries as I rode, and eat them with a gust.

Near them we often found stately ponds all of stone; when it rains they fill up to the top, and that water lasts all the dry season; there travellers stop, rest, drink, and water their beasts. They told me they were the work of great and rich heathens, who being mov'd to compassion, seeing there was no water for travellers in several places, had caus'd those ponds to be made to supply this defect and want.

The tamarine trees are planted very regularly; the natives make use of their shade to weave their webs in it, sheltered from the sun. Their houses are little and dark, they cannot see in them to weave, nor is there room for their looms, therefore they have provided that shade for this purpose. They make much use of the fruit in dressing their diet.

We also saw stately and ancient temples, and wonderful mosques of the Mohametans. The further we travel' d, the greater towns we met with; in some of them there was a mighty concourse of passengers, horses, elephants, and abundance of camels, which in that country carry all burdens. The Mahometans travel with great state; the governors of large towns went in royal state. They were always very civil to me, I had occasion to speak to one of them; I took off my hat, he would not hear word till I was cover'd and sat down by him. In some places I met Persians and Armenians, fine men, graceful, tall, well-shap'd, very courteous, and they have the best horses in the world.

About the middle of July, near a town, we found a little brook so clear and cool we were surpriz'd at it; I guess'd the spring was near and we drank unmercifully, and our diet being slender it did us harm, but me particularly so we were forc'd to stay a day there. Next day a scorpion stung the Portuguese, I really thought he would have dy'd, and this somewhat retarded our journey. We came to a river so wide and deep, that the horse, who was but small, could not carry me over; It was some hardship, for we waded with the water up to our breasts; the current was rapid, the Portuguese a poor heartless bit of a man began to cry out, the water carry'd him away; and it was so, we had all enough to do to bring him off. After this we pass'd another river but not so deep; for more safety I deliver'd the papers and letters I had to my man, charging him to be very careful. No sooner was he in the river, but he fell; and left all he carry'd in the water. I was much concern'd at this misfortune; to remedy it in some measure, I laid all the papers in the sun, and some Chinese books, which being of extraordinary fine paper suffer'd the more; in this place we spent some hours. To mend the delay we came afterwards to a lake, the *Gentile* was positive we must cross it to shorten the way; I was so unlucky that my horse fell, and I too, with my wallets that carry'd the papers; I gave all for lost, tho with some trouble and loss of time all was reasonably retriev'd.

By the way we met a Pagan youth of a good presence; the horse he rode on was very fine, his attendance numerous; he was going to court to be marry'd, and had with him for state a mighty elephant, well adorn'd with clothes and bells. This was the second I had seen till that time; whenever we stop'd, I would draw near to take a full view of him. This I did particularly one afternoon: as soon as I came near him, his governor spoke one word to him which I did not understand; but the consequence show'd what he had said, for he presently fac'd me, and made a profound reverence, bowing all his four-feet at once; I saw them give him meat and drink. It hap'ned a native, without reflecting on it, was going to pass before him; as he came up the elephant stretch'd out his trunk, and gently gave him a blow on the forehead, which sounded like a good cuff on the ear. The man's colour chang'd, and he stagger'd backward a good way as if he had been besides himself. Our laughing brought him to himself, and he passed by keeping well off from that mountain of flesh. I fancy'd the elephant thought it unmannerly to go by so near him, and therefore he friendly warn'd the man to look before he leap'd. I was much astonish'd at that action which I had seen.

After this we came to a mighty river, the boat was lost the day before, for they had swam an elephant over, ty'd to the boat; and he growing angry, carry'd the boat down the river; then he got to the shore, broke the rope, and ran about the fields; his driver went to catch him, but the elephant being still in a fury, took hold of him with his trunk, cast him up into the air, of which he died. There were two other ferries there, and the comicallest that can be imagin'd; they were round wicker baskets, cover'd without with cows' hides; we hired one and put in all our baggage, more people came up, and fourteen passengers of us went into it; the horse and ox swam, we holding the halters; we struck aslant over, and sail'd a quarter of a league whilst one might say the creed three or four times. The current was violent, we all quak'd for fear, and were cram'd together without the least motion. We landed, I paid our passage, the owner took his basket out of the water, and clapping it on his head, walk'd up the river to carryover to the town others that waited for him.

Four leagues short of the court we stop'd at a great town which they call the Queen's Palace. The mother or grand-mother of the king then reigning, had built that sumptuous palace, from which the town took its name. We could not go in, but the front and all we could see of it might vie with the best in Europe: Before it is a square which is not inferior to any in Spain. We went into a most beautiful and spacious court almost square; in the midst of which was a stone mosque well built, with a porch before it. The court is like a cloister, arch' d all round except where the gates interrupt it. At every six foot distance there are stone arches, and in the hollow of the six foot there is a fine cell within vaulted like the rest, and all white as snow. I counted a hundred and eighteen cells in all, well contriv'd, and curious and exact windows and doors. The floor was of very hard plaister; those rooms were for the king's followers, when they came thither to divert themselves. The square was in the same nature, but had a storey above, which the court had not.

In one corner there was a door which led to a large and deep pond cut out of the said rock, with stairs cut out of the same stone to go down for water; all we passengers drank that water; I don't doubt but what we saw cost many millions. I would have seen the mosque, but as I was going in a *Moor* came out, who would have thrown me down the stairs and [I] said nothing, but desisted. Before I came to this town, and from thence to court I took notice of another thing which the Portuguese had given me a hint, and was, that I saw several parcels of horses, mules and asses, loaded with the 'tuba' of the palm-trees I have mentioned, all running as fast as they could; and the drivers, who strain'd their hearts, took care with their lashes that the beasts should not stop a moment. This they do that the liquor may come sweet before it sours; abundance of it is consum'd at court, especially the Mahometan women drink much of it. The drink is extremely pleasant, it would take more money at Madrid than mead or sherbet. Those people say the king's greatest revenue comes out of it.

To save time and charges we did not go through a great gate of the court; all that come in through these gates wait for leave from some great men, have all they carry search'd and pay duties. I was not concern'd for the search, tho something must be always given. We went almost two leagues round-about, which was a great trouble; nevertheless we past three custom-houses, but they said not a word to us. Being come to the fourth, they talk'd big to us but were satisfy'd with a few pence. Half a league further we came to the place where they sold horses, there was a pleasant grove, divided by four large and spacious walks, in which were abundance of people, and very fine horses, which they rode about to shew them. Then we past a river, and saw a multitude of people on the bank; we drew near, and it prov'd to be the funeral of a young woman, who lay barefac'd on the bier, very well set out and adorn'd with flowers; next to the corps were musicians and dancers. There was one (perhaps the husband) whose body was dy'd of several colours, and he skip'd and made a thousand motions. Other ancients used to weep when a child was born, and rejoice at its death; so did those we saw. At last we came to a little church, where one Martinez, a Portuguese priest resided; he receiv'd me with all possible kindness, and great tokens of affection. There I rested a little, but not so much as I had need.

I was inform'd there was in those parts one D[on] Felix Enriquez, a native of Madrid, whom I had been acquainted with in the apothecaries shop in S. Paul in Valladolid, tho I could not call to mind his name. He was physician and surgeon to the king's army there. I presently sent him a note, his answer was very civil and next day I went to his house. It is a long league from the city to the forts, where the king is always close for fear of his subjects, as I was told. The road, besides its being very plain and broad, was so full of people, that there were scarce more in the cities of China, all of them clad as white as snow, most afoot, several in half coaches, half carts, drawn by oxen, and well cover'd, and many on mules; some Persians and *Moors* excellently mounted, and well attended. Some great men were carry'd in rich and sightly *palanquines*; instead of umbrelloes they use large shields gilt and painted of several colours, the servants carry them on their arms, and lifting them up defend their masters from the sun. They carry plumes of peacocks feathers with the quills stuck in silver, which they serve to drive the flies away, they are properly fans. All the European captains and factors in those countries make the same use of those feathers. It all look'd to me like court-grandeur. There were about that place abundance of great and lesser elephants, I was much diverted with the sight of them, and admir'd their motion; I rode upon a good horse, and had much ado to keep up with their walk.

I took notice that there was abundance of people on the one side of the way, and that more continually flock'd to them. I ask'd the black that went with me, what it meant? He answer'd, Father, the saints of this country are there. I drew near, and saw they were men quite naked, as if they had liv'd in the state of innocence; perhaps they were Adamites. Their habitations were on certain mountains, whence those men came down at certain times to beg alms. They walk'd among the people stark naked, like brute beasts. When I return'd to the church I saw them again, and women looking at them very devoutly. Presently I discover'd a sumptuous palace and beautiful towers and pinnacles all cover'd with lead. The palace of Segovia is not more beautiful, I admir'd nothing so much in that country, methought I was looking upon Madrid. I came up to the great fort where the king's apartment is; I went not in, but it had a fine outside, and look'd great, the walls were strong and stor'd with cannon, the situation high, the ditches wide and deep. They told me the king had nine hundred concubines within there, and among them the Portuguese woman of S. Thomas I mention'd above. Next I met some Portugueses who expected me, many of them serve in that king's army for bread. They carry'd me to D. Felix's house, which was very little, low and inconvenient, like the rest of the commonalty. He receiv'd me very lovingly and truly, I knew him again, tho I had not seen him in twenty four years, he had a good mark to be known by. He gave me an account of his life; he had been in Ceylon physician to the Dutch, marry'd there; left his wife at Columbo, and went over to Madras; was there physician to the English, and then went to Golconda, where he receiv'd the king's pay, twenty *pieces of eight* a month, besides what he made of his slaves. Hard by was a mighty army commanded by the great *Nababo* [Riza Kuli, d. 1672], (that is as much as the great duke of that kingdom) he was an eunuch and man of great parts, he govern'd all; the king kept in his Mahomet's paradise among women, musick, dancing and other sports, all unbecoming the duty of a king. It is a shameful thing, says S. Thomas de Erudit, <u>Princ. Lib</u> I., cap. 10, that he who is lord over others, should be a slave to his senses. And talking of musick, he tells how Antigonus, master or preceptor to Alexander the great, broke his lute, and said, He that is of age to reign, may be asham'd to be subject to these passions. The saint has much that is very good to this purpose. The king of Golconda lives in worldly pleasures and pastimes, without the least regard to the government, having committed the whole charge of it to the great *Nababo*. What can this king expect but what Job says, cap. xii. They take the timbrel and harp, and rejoice at the sound of the organ: They spend their days in wealth, and in a moment go down to Hell? The moment that puts an end to their pleasures, begins their eternal torments. What an unhappy and wretched case! The same will befall all that follow such a course. There cannot be a double glory, that of the life to come is not the consequence of the worldly. The words of Tertullian are common: After gall, the honey-comb. Christ tasted not the sweetness of honey till he had gone thro' the bitterness of his passion. What can be the consequences of dancing, musick, plays, feasting, and the pleasures of this life, but the neglect of one's duty, forgetfulness of ones soul; and in the future, calamities? The Chinese is much more vigilant and careful of the government, and if he forgets himself, they mind and reprove him... Two years before this, one of the *Nababo's* teeth dropt out, he sent it with six thousand *ducats* to Mecca an offering to Mahomet's rotten bones. At this time another dropt out, and it was reported he would send it with six thousand more. He order'd a temple to be built, which I saw, but it was not yet finish'd, because they said he had dream'd he should die when the building was finish'd, so he order'd the work to cease. He was then ninety years of age, paid the soldiers punctually, and gave the Persians great wages. In that country there is abundance of very fine silver, and they say abundance of rich diamonds, I was assur'd the Mahometans gave above fifty thousand *ducats* for some.

I discours'd D. Felix about my journey to Goa, he represented it very easy; others objected difficulties, and no doubt but there were enough, especially in going from one kingdom to another. Next day I said mass in a chappel the Portuguese soldiers and some mungrels and blacks had there. They gave me to understand it would please them I should stay there three months, till it were time to go away to Goa, and they offer'd to assist me according to their power, which was small. I had certainly stay'd there, had not what I shall write presently hapned, and I believe it had gone very ill with me. I went that afternoon to see the Dutch factor, for whom I had a letter. I went on D. Felix's horse, which was better than mine. I again observ'd what I had seen before, and again was astonish'd at the multitude and diversity of people. I cross'd all the capital city, which is very large, and in it at small distances excellent buildings, and innumerable multitudes of people. The great square was very beautiful; the royal palace, an admirable structure, fills one side of it. They show'd me a glaz'd balcony, and told me the king sometimes shew'd himself there to his subjects. It was a long time before I came to the Dutch factory. Those men had a fine palace there, and richly furnish'd. The factor [Willem Karel Hartsinck] was a mungrel begot on a Japonese woman, and show'd it in his carriage. We discours'd a while with a great deal of coldness on his side; the European Hollanders did not serve me so, and this appear'd presently, for within half an hour another Dutchman came out of a room who was infinitely obliging; he gave me *cha* of China to drink, and some of the wine they made there, he courteously shew'd me the orchards, gardens, and a stately bath. There I was inform'd of the great modesty and reserv'dness of the women of that country, not much inferior to that of China, as they told me. A great shame for European Christian women.

When I took my leave he ask'd me, Whether I had visited the French that were in that city? I answer'd I had not, nor thought of it because I knew none of them, nor had any business with them. He earnestly desir'd me to visit them. I did all I could to excuse my self, but still he urg'd it. I, to avoid that visit not knowing that therein my luck then consisted, said, Sir, I neither know their house, nor have I any body to conduct me to it. I'll send a servant of mine, said he, to wait upon the father, and show him the house. There was no withstanding it any longer, I went thither directly, they receiv'd me with singular kindness and affection; brought out fruits of Persia, dates, almonds, raisins, and other things of the country. They treated me well, I thank'd them, and took leave. They would not suffer me to be gone presently, so we held on our discourse. The director spoke good Spanish for he had been several times at Cadiz, and carry'd millions of *pieces of eight* from thence into France, and told me how he dealt with our ships and with the people ashore. It is a shame to see the way many of our officers manage the king's business. He freely offer'd me passage in his ship as far as Surat, and thence into Europe, with all the accommodation his people could afford me. I went back to lie at the church, and he sent me in his *palanquine* with twenty four servants to attend me. Perceiving how difficult a matter it was to go to Goa, and that the difficulty every day increas'd, because a rebel whose name was Subagi [Maharaja Shivaji, 1627-80] rang'd those countries with a powerful army, I made those gentlemen a second visit, and finding a fit opportunity accepted of the favour they offer'd me. They assur'd me they had orders from their king to be assisting to the missioners, and that they went to India for that purpose. There is no doubt but the end is very good and holy.

We left the royal city on the 28th of July, there went twenty two carts loaden with goods and necessaries for the journey, six officers of the company a-horseback, four stately Persian led horses with rich furniture. One of them dy'd by the way, that had cost five hundred *pieces of eight*: Four colours, four trumpets, four waits, two kettle-drums, sixty servants, and five *palanquines*, with five or six men to carry each of them; it was a train for a king. We cross'd a wide but shallow river, there were a great many elephants washing in it. We observ'd with how much ease those mountains of flesh tumbled in the water and started up again. All the carts were cover'd with oil'd cloths, so that not a drop of rain-water came through. The *palanquines* had the same covering. There is no such easy and restful way of travelling in the world. We past through the middle of the royal city with all that noise, attendance and musick, and went to lie at a stately orchard. Half a league of the way was among fine trees, the rest of the way very plain and easy. We came to a noble stone-palace, which had beautiful halls, rooms, and balconies, and much ornament in several curious riches, with several figures of plaister and stone. The orchard was vastly big, full of abundance of fruit-trees and innumerable oranges and lemons. The walks were wide and very clean, with ponds at distances, and water-works continually playing; it appear'd to me a place fit for any prince. Two days we stay'd there, and spent the time in observing with attention, what I have writ with brevity.

My company carry'd good provisions and plenty, which made the way easy to me, and made amends for the want I endur'd in my journey to the royal city, whence we now came. One morning we came to a place, where there was the liquor of palms I spoke of in the last chapter; we drank to our hearts content, it was as cold as ice, and sweeter than honey; it did us much good, for it purg'd us to excellent purpose. We past over a mighty river with some trouble, but on the further side found the best olaves [sic, mangoes?] in the world, for a penny a pound. It is incredible what quantities of delicate painted and plain calicoes there were in every town; they came out to the roads to offer and press us to buy.

In every town we found women that play'd on musick and danced. There are certain women there, who alone can follow this trade, for which they pay a duty to the king. When any guests of note come, they presently repair to their house, make their obeisance, and immediately some begin to dance, and others to play. They were well dress'd, and had gold and silver enough about them, spent two, or three hours in this exercise, were well paid, and went their ways. I was seldom present at these entertainments, but indeed they were worth seeing and hearing.

It was also very common to meet with many tumblers that show'd tricks of activity; they have no settled place of abode, but ramble up and down like gypsies. Sometimes we met them under the trees in the field, sometimes near towns in the barracks made of wicker which they always carry about with them. As soon as they see any likely people, they make to them, and offer to show their activity; then they set up their sticks and canes, and play wonderful tricks. Both the men and women would certainly be much admir'd in Europe. Two women, one old and the other young, did such things in a town, as amaz'd us all. One man besides many strange tricks, took a stone betwixt his teeth; his companions threw others up, which he catch'd in his mouth without ever missing a jot; afterwards he lay'd it upon one eye, and on it receiv'd the other that fell from above, and never miss'd in all the time. Another thing astonish'd us yet more, and we thought the devil had a hand in it. He ty'd a stone, of about a quarter of an hundred weight to a stick, which had another cross it; he alone, laying hold of the stick with one hand, held up the stone in the air, and kept it without the least motion; then he put together eight or ten men, and gave them the stick to hold as he had done, and they could never bear it up tho they put all their strength to it, but the stone bore them all down. We could never find out what art that black us'd to do that which we saw with our eyes.

There is another sort of men, who make a trade of carrying about snakes that dance; they are ridiculously dress'd, wear feathers on their heads, and little bells about their body, all naked but their privy-parts, and daub'd with several colours. They carry a little trumpet in their hand, and two baskets cover'd on their shoulders full of hideous snakes; they go where they are call'd, open their baskets, and as the trumpet sounds the snakes rise, using several motions with their bodies and heads; sometimes they cling to their master's arm or thigh, and set their teeth in it. I saw one of them whose body was all over as if it had been pink'd by the snakes. A strange way of getting their living! At first it was dreadful to me to see that dancing. They give them a half-penny or a penny, the snakes return to their baskets, and away they go. I observ'd several times, that as soon as they catch'd and laid them in the basket, they roll'd themselves up, and remain'd immovable; and tho they open'd the basket, they never stirr'd without the trumpet sounded. Some were thicker than a man's wrist, they said those that carry'd them were anointed with the juice of several herbs, so that tho' they bit they could do no harm. There are others who have dancing cows, and get their living by them.

One night we lay in an idol-temple, one of the beautifulest in the world; it had jasper-stone and marble, as curiously wrought as any in Italy, and three chappels dedicated to three gods. There were in it some cows cut in stone as black as jet, and as lively as possible. The priest came to us, and we discours'd him with the help of some servants of the French company, who spoke several languages. He gave a very bad account of the origin of those three gods, made them all men, and said they came thither upon the waters of the sea from very far countrys, and had produc'd the world. We objecting, how it could be made out that they had produced the world when there was before them a sea, and other countries from whence they came thither; He answer'd, 'It was so written in their books.' Speaking of the parents of his gods, he asserted they were of other countries; and we answering, 'Then there were men before those gods'; he laugh'd and said, 'I say nothing but what is in this book.' Two leagues short of Musulapatan we found a great many Frenchmen in a noble orchard, expecting their director and companions. There was musick, dancing, and a plentiful entertainment. That afternoon we went into the city, it was the eighth of August, past over a wooden-bridge, little less than half a league in length, a wonderful crowd of people came out to see us, English, Dutch, Persians, Armenians, Portugueses, Mungrels, Mahometans, *Gentiles*, Blacks and natives, were all spectators. The factory was a stately large house, the people many in number. There was a great confusion that night, however we had some rest.

After leaving Madras late in 1670, Navarrete sailed around the tip of India to Goa, (where his Chinese servant remained). He then continued homeward, reaching Lisbon in 1672 before proceeding to Rome to battle the Jesuits at the Papal court. After returning to his native Spain, he retired to priories in Penafiel (where he had first entered his order nearly

forty years earlier) and then in Madrid. Thus secluded, he composed in Spanish his *Tratados historicos, politicos, ethicos y religiosos de la monarchia de China*. After thorough examination by several levels of censors, Navarrete's original work began to emerge in print in 1676. It immediately generated heated global controversy for its critique of the rival Jesuits in China. Indeed, Jesuits published rejoinders, denounced Navarrete to the Inquisition and suppressed the second edition of his book. Nonetheless, his work soon appeared in partial and full translations in several European languages, including English in 1704. Our selection comes from an anonymous translation published by John and Awnsham Churchill, eds, *A Collection of Voyages and Travels*, 6 volumes, 3rd edition (London: John and Awnsham Churchill, 1744), vol. 1, pp. 276-85.

Undaunted by the growing antagonism to his writings, Navarrete completed in 1677 the even more critical and controversial *Controversias antiguas y modernas entre los missionarios de la gran China...* Even as this work came under the censors' scrutiny, he left for his new post as Archbishop of Santo Domingo and Primate of Spanish Indies. The Pope had appointed him, over his repeated demurrals, to this once distinguished but then decrepit post. Life in Santo Domingo, even for someone of the status of Archbishop, was pitiful, with few funds available and little support. Navarrete died there a broken man in 1686. His *Controversias* was suppressed even before the printer had finished setting the type.

Glossary

Adowyae/hundabhada contractor for transporting goods including payment of tolls.

Agah/aga 'Lord', title/honourific.

Altyn/altin small denomination Russian coin (see note below).

Am-kas/am-khas the 'ordinary' - 'special' audience halls or tents used by the emperor.

Amochi bodyguard of the king of Malabar in today's Kerala, sworn to fight unto death.

Amrawe/amirs/umara noblemen, high ranking among officials holding rank, s.v. *mansabdar*.

Areca nut wrapped in *betel*-leaf to form *pan*.

Armesine/Ormesine type of silk cloth, originally from Hormuz in Iran.

Babare 'Oh Grandfather!', formulaic appeal for protection

Bairam Muslim Id al-Azha animal sacrifice on the 10th day of month Zu al-Hijja; customarily seen as commemorating Abraham's willingness to sacrifice Ishmael.

Balloach/Baluch ethnicity of Muslims originally from today's southwest Pakistan.

Banian Hindu *jati*/caste of traders/merchants.

Banjara/Banjare Hindu *jati*/caste of transporters, customarily using pack-bullocks.

Beawly/baoli 'step-well'.

Betel/betle/bettell leaf wrapping areca-nut and other condiments to form *pan*.

Boot/bhut 'demon' but Nikitin uses it for a Hindu deity; Bootkhana 'temple'.

Brammen/Brahman/Brahmin highest *varna*/caste in orthodox Hindu social hierarchy.

Bucefalos Alexander of Macedon's horse and a city named after it.

Burres/bar banyan-tree, Indian Fig, *Ficus Indica*.

Cahare/kahar palanquin-bearer.

Cannatt/kanat canvas screen surrounding an enclosure or tent.

Caphila/kafila caravan.

Caramossora/caravanserai 'travellers rest-house', often built by kings or charitable donors.

Cha/chai Chinese/Indian term for 'tea'.

Chaboothare/chabutara raised platform, often covered in plaster.

Chacore/chakar servant

Chauril/chavati/choultry 'rest house', South Indian term for *caravanserai*.

Chitini/Chetti south Indian Hindu *jati*/caste of merchants.

Choqui-dar/chauki-dar customs-post official or guard.

Chowdree/chaudhari 'headman' of a village, *jati* or other group.

Chowtree/chautara raised square platform.

Coolee/Koli hillmen or labourers; Mundy's term for Mina *Rajput* villagers.

Coss/course/kos unit of distance varying locally between 1 and 8 km., often about 3 km.

Cour/kaukaba honorific objects/symbols carried on poles in processions.

Crown high denomination European gold coin (see note below).

Darogha an 'official', term used for police chief, mayor, governor or manager.

Debua small denomination European coin (see note below).

Deccan plateau region of central India; Deccani, an inhabitant of the Deccan

Dewra/deura Hindu temple.

Doay Padcha/dohai padshah appeal for imperial favour.

Doopata/dupatta shawl or head or shoulder mantle.

Ducat high denomination European gold coin (see note below).

Dulatqhan/daulat-khana throne room or royal palace.

Écu small denomination European coin (see note below).

Embary/ambari canopied enclosure carried on an elephant's back.

Ename/inam gratuity, customarily presented by a superior to an inferior in rank.

Falchine/fachini one of a team of men who carry a palanquin.

Fardle 'bundle' of variable weight depending on the commodity and region; in north India, for indigo often about 100 kg., for saltpetre often about 135 kg.

Fata Russian term for shawl or cloth for head, shoulder or waist.

Fontie small denomination Indian coin (see note below).

Footoon high denomination Indian coin (see note below).

Formon/farman official order, including a passport.

Fust/foist armed boat with both sails and oars, used by both Portuguese and south Indians.

Gentile European term for Hindu.

Gosle-kane/ghusul-khana 'bath-room', hence private audience room.

Gourze-berdar/grusberdare/gurz-bardar attendant carrying a mace of club of gold or silver.

Hagarene Lycurgus European term for the Prophet Muhammad; combining 'descendant of Hagar and her son Ishmael' and the name of a Spartan law giver.

Harquebush portable European-style firearm, ranging from a small cannon to a musket.

Hauze/howda decorated open enclosure carried on an elephant's back.

Holi Hindu spring festival.

Jaggatt/zakat customs-charges or octroi.

Jaggueere/jagir land revenue assigned to an official, s.v. *mansabdar*.

Jati social group/caste specified by 'birth' in Hindu social hierarchy;.

Jatt/Jat Hindu *jati*/caste of yeoman farmers and carters.

Kafir community of non-believers; non-Muslims.

Kaluet-kane/khalwat-khana 'private room' or the meeting place of the privy council

Kanate/kanat standing 'screen' of coloured cloth, blocking the view of outsiders.

Karguai cabinet for precocities.

Kentar/kantar variable Mediterranean unit of weight, often about 100 pounds.

Kheernee/khirni Mimusops kauki tree.

Kichery/khicari rice boiled with lentils and spices.

Kos unit of distance varying regionally between 2 and 10 km., often about 3 km.

Lack/lakh unit of measure meaning 100,000.

Lanthorn lantern with case having translucent windows of horn, glass or talc.

Laskarre/lashkar army or squadron or military troop or encampment.

Livre French unit of weight equal to .5 kg.; also a high value gold coin (see note below).

Magh ethnicity from the southern coast of today's Bangladesh and from Burma/Myanmar.

Mamadie/mahmudi low denomination silver coin especially circulating in western India (see note below)..

Mansebdar/mansab-dar 'office holder', with rank based on number of horsemen provided to the emperor, paid through a land revenue assignment, s.v. *jagir*.

Masadie/al-madiya type of log canoe.

Maund/man variable unit of weigh, often about 25 kg.; in Jahangir's time officially equivalent to 30 kg..

Mekshenie small denomination Indian coin (see note below).

Mikdember/ambari a large decorated and canopied enclosure carried on elephant-back.

Mossit/masjid Muslim mosque.

Mimbachi/mubashi commanding officer, superintendent.

Moccadame/muqaddam headman, leader.

Moccame/maqam daily stage on a journey or an assembly.

Mogol/Mogor/Mogul/Mongol a central Asian people, occasionally used for Mughal.

Moher/muhr high denomination Indian gold coin (see note below).

Mohol/mahall 'mansion', also title of a consort, mother of a prince.

Mokam/maqam assembly or daily stage on a journey.

Mongol central Asian people, led by Genghis Khan, occasionally used for Mughal.

Monsull/manzil stage of a journey.

Moor/Moore European term for Muslim.

Mossaffo the Quran

Mossit/masjid Muslim mosque.

Muana/mina port or river mouth

Muharram Muslim, especially Shi'ite, commemoration of Hasan's and Husain's martyrdom.

Mullah Muslim religious scholar.

Musalman/Mussellman/Mussulman variant spellings of an Indian term for Muslim.

Nababo/nawab 'deputy' of a ruler; provincial governor a province; title/honorific.

Nagar-kane/naqar-khana 'drum room' or porch of a palace where musicians play.

Nair matrilineal *jati*/caste of landholders and warriors in Kerala, south India.

Navaab/nawab 'deputy' of a ruler who governs a province; also a title/honorific.

Nilgaues/nil-ghau Indian 'blue bull', *Antilope picta*.

Nouroze/nau-roz Persian New Year's Day.

Omrah/umara collective plural for highest Mughal courtiers.

Pagie Indian coin (see note below).

Pagody/pagoda Hindu temple and the high denomination Indian coin (hun) with a temple on it, especially circulating in southern India (see note below).

Paique/paik oarsman or foot-soldier.

Palanchine/palankeen/palanqueene/palanquine/paleky/palki couch or chair carried by horizontal poles, often canopied.

Pall/pal small tent.

Pan areca-nut and other condiments wrapped in *betel*-leaf.

Parian/Pariah the name of an allegedly 'untouchable' *jati* in south India.

Pataca high denomination European coin (see note below).

Pathan ethnicity of Muslims originating in today's northwest Pakistan.

Peelooe/pilu *Careya arborea* or *Salvadora persica* tree from which tooth-brushes come.

Peiche-kanes/peshconna/pesh-khana 'advance-camp' sent one day's march ahead.

Piece of eight/peso Spanish coin (see note below).

Rashpoot/Rajput 'son of a raja/king/prince', name of a caste/*jati* of landholders and rulers.

Rotti/rati unit of weight for bullion or jewellery, roughly .9 carets.

Sarae/sarai 'traveller's rest-house', built by rulers or charitable donors; *caravanserai*.

Scied/sayyid people claiming descent from the Prophet Muhammad.

Sehebsooba/sahib-subah governor of a province.

Serpao/sar-a-pa honorific garments from 'head to toe'.

Sharaffe/sarraf money-changer or broker.

Shash turban-sash, originally from Turkistan.

Siguidar/shiq-dar governor of a city.

Stadia Latin unit of distance equalling 185 metres.

Suare/suwar cavalryman.

Tact-ravan/takht-i ravan travelling royal throne carried on a platform.

Tanka/tanga/tangkam high denomination Indian coin (see note below).

Tava/dabba/dhow a sailing vessel, usually with one mast and lateen-rig sail.

Tchaudoule/cau-dol decorated and covered sedan chair with two poles.

Tchauky-kane/chauky-kane/chauki-khana 'guard room'.

Toddy/tadi fermented sap from a species of wild palm-trees.

Tuturegan/tuwargan pulses.

Varna 'caste' or 'caste group'; one of four orders in Brahmanic social hierarchy.

Wazir 'chief minister' or advisor.

Xabandar/shah-bandar 'harbour-master'.

Zung/sang band of pilgrims travelling together.

Note on currency equivalences the bullion content (and thus value) of coins varied by region and year. Skilled money-changers made a profession of assessing each coin individually. Hence no exact equivalences are possible to reconstruct today.

Index